QUEEN MARGARET UNIVERSITY

100 305 278

Queen Margaret University Library
Withdrawn from

"To say this publication is timely would be a gross understatement. From theory to research to application, Dr. Pike reminds us—in her deft, clear and at times lyrical manner—how to overcome the struggles and limitations of our artificial experiences by looking outside, metaphorically and literally, to find the most natural space and mindful tools available. Eco-art therapy is more than a method or approach; it's a whole new paradigm that simultaneously simplifies and makes profound the journey towards wellness. Quite frankly, I didn't realize this was a book that I needed to read … until I read it."

—Dave Gussak, PhD, ATR-BC, professor, The Florida State University

"Eco-Art Therapy in Practice offers a unique, eco-friendly approach to merging the healing properties of nature with art therapy. Dr. Pike's easy to follow protocols teach us a simpler, more organic way of relating to life within the field of a psychotherapy."

—Ella Dufrene, MPS, ATR, founder of
Madre Tierra Creative Arts & Yoga Retreats

"Working in both a private practice and an agency setting requires me to be flexible and continue to adapt my interventions for a wide range of clients. Dr. Pike's expansive knowledge is evident, and this book is one I will return to repeatedly to help meet my client's diverse needs! Using nature in art making has a lot of therapeutic potential."

—Devon Schlegel, MA, ATR-BC, LPC, LMHC, co-founder of Indigo
Art Therapy Studio

"Eco-Art Therapy in Practice provides a rooted framework for holistically integrating the self-affirming benefits of art-making and engagement with the natural world. Dr. Pike's exhaustive aggregation of data supports some of our most deeply felt understandings regarding identity in relationship to our environment. It reminds us to check-in not only with our screen time, but more importantly with our time spent in natural light."

—Summer Bowie, managing editor, Autre Magazine

D1380735

Eco-Art Therapy in Practice

Eco-Art Therapy in Practice is uplifting, optimistic, and empowering while outlining cost-effective, time-efficient, and research-based steps on how to use nature in session to enhance client engagement and outcomes.

Dr. Pike employs her background and credentials as a certified educational leader and board-certified art therapist to walk readers through establishing ecologically based practices—such as growing art materials using hydroponics regardless of facility constraints. Each chapter is aligned with the continuing education requirements for art therapy board certification renewal to make its relevance clear and to orient the book for future training program integration. The appendices feature clinical directives in easy-to-follow, one-page protocols which encourage readers to consider client needs when applying methods, along with intake forms to bolster real-world application.

This text will help clinicians and educators to employ eco-art therapy in practice, in turn empowering their clients and conveying an inclusive message of respect—respect for self, others, community, and the world.

Amanda Alders Pike, PhD, ATR-BC, is a board-certified art therapist and past president of the Florida Art Therapy Association. She is currently Education Chair for the Palm Beach County Native Plant Society.

Queen Margaret University Library
Withdrawn from
QUEEN MARGARET UNIVERSITY LRC

Eco-Art Therapy in Practice

Amanda Alders Pike

Routledge
Taylor & Francis Group

NEW YORK AND LONDON

First published 2021
by Routledge
52 Vanderbilt Avenue, New York, NY 10017

and by Routledge
2 Park Square, Milton Park, Abingdon, Oxon OX14 4RN

*Routledge is an imprint of the Taylor & Francis Group, an informa
business*

© 2021 Amanda Alders Pike

The right of Amanda Alders Pike to be identified as author of this
work has been asserted by her in accordance with sections 77 and 78 of
the Copyright, Designs and Patents Act 1988.

All rights reserved. No part of this book may be reprinted or
reproduced or utilised in any form or by any electronic, mechanical, or
other means, now known or hereafter invented, including
photocopying and recording, or in any information storage or retrieval
system, without permission in writing from the publishers.

Trademark notice: Product or corporate names may be trademarks or
registered trademarks, and are used only for identification and
explanation without intent to infringe.

Library of Congress Cataloging-in-Publication Data
Names: Pike, Amanda Alders, author.
Title: Eco-art therapy in practice / Amanda Alders Pike.
Description: New York, NY : Routledge, 2021. | Includes
    bibliographical references and index. | Summary: "Eco-Art Therapy
    in Practice is uplifting, optimistic, and empowering while outlining
    cost-effective, time efficient, and research-based steps on how to use
    nature in session to enhance client engagement and outcomes. This
    text will help clinicians and educators to employ eco-art therapy in
    practice, in turn empowering their clients and conveying an inclusive
    message of respect- respect for self, others, community, and the
    world"– Provided by publisher.
Identifiers: LCCN 2020047703 (print) | LCCN 2020047704 (ebook) |
    ISBN 9780367548773 (hardback) | ISBN 9780367548766
    (paperback) | ISBN 9781003091004 (ebook)
Subjects: LCSH: Art therapy. | Ecology in art. | Nature–Therapeutic
    use.
Classification: LCC RC489.A7 P55 2021 (print) | LCC RC489.A7
    (ebook) | DDC 616.89/1656–dc23
LC record available at https://lccn.loc.gov/2020047703
LC ebook record available at https://lccn.loc.gov/2020047704

ISBN: 978-0-367-54877-3 (hbk)
ISBN: 978-0-367-54876-6 (pbk)
ISBN: 978-1-003-09100-4 (ebk)

Typeset in Times New Roman
by Taylor & Francis Books

MIX
Paper from
responsible sources
FSC
www.fsc.org   FSC™ C013985

Printed in the United Kingdom
by Henry Ling Limited

In many ways, this book is written for my family, but especially my son. Because of him, I strive to be a better person, live a better life, and leave the world a better place. Although eco-art therapy is a contractable professional service and one which I believe greatly benefits the community, it is also a lifestyle which I endeavor to share with and teach to my son. I wish nothing more than for my son to "inherit" his corner of earth and find it rich with meaning and fulfillment.

Contents

Illustrations

Author Biography

Amanda Pike, PhD, ATR-BC is a board-certified art therapist, professional educator, certified educational leader, and past president of the Florida Art Therapy Association. As a business owner, Dr. Pike established a private practice which grew into a tri-county staffing company. She hired, trained, placed, and supervised art therapists in locations such as assisted living facilities, homeless shelters, eating disorder clinics, and substance abuse recovery treatment centers. Dr. Pike has also served as a Curriculum Content Manager within higher education, providing quality assurance for online programs. She currently owns a two-acre permaculture farm in Jupiter, Florida where she grows fruit trees and flowers with her family and homeschools her son. At present, Dr. Pike serves as Education Chair for the Palm Beach County chapter of the Native Plant Society and provides on-going consultations for educational and community-based programs.

Preface

As I write this, people around the world are sheltering-in-place due to COVID-19/coronavirus. With city and commercial conveniences limited and connections to other people stifled, nature has been a sanctuary worldwide. Communities are remembering the role of nature in physical, mental, and emotional healthcare. I am no different: As a mom, educator, therapist, and farmer, I have seen the importance of remaining connected to nature for my own and my family's well-being. I have witnessed the benefits of mindfully engaging with nature for a sense of purpose, connection, belonging, and health.

Beyond literature reviews and scholastic research, the breadth of this book draws from both my professional and personal experiences. Culturally, I grew up as a military "brat," relocating frequently and so attachment to location was an intellectual interest but never an emotional experience. However, when I became a mom, I wanted to settle down for the sake of my future family. Ethnically, I'm a blend of Scottish, European, and American Indian (First Nation/Fraser River Basin in Canada). I wanted to recreate what I saw my grandparents do over my summer visits: cultivate a range of plants, carve trails through woods, farm, and garden, and use nature as artistic inspiration. Given these influences, after gaining years of professional experience in agency, academic, community, and private practice settings, I wanted to set my future trajectory in a direction which prioritized nature.

Using my professional and personal experiences, the objective of this book is to empower therapists and educators to enhance client engagement and outcomes by using nature as a setting, subject, and material in session. Within each chapter, I outline cost-effective, time-efficient, and research-based steps, and include clinical directives in easy-to-follow, one-page protocols. I employ my background and credentials as a certified educational leader and board-certified art therapist to enable a variety of helping professionals to establish ecologicallysound practices. That said, each chapter is aligned with the continuing education requirements for art therapy board certification renewal to specifically target professional development among my immediate peers. Although I am writing this book specifically for art therapists and educators, mental health counselors and psychologists may also benefit from the content.

Acknowledgements

I am beyond grateful to the many art therapists, community members, and educators for their influence and feedback throughout the preparation of this book. My garden and therefore my eco-art therapy toolbox would not exist without the endless seed exchanges, cuttings, and garden tours given by my permaculture community. In particular, the Jupiter Farms community has connected me with like-minded people, which has resulted in not only friendships but invaluable knowledge. I am appreciative of Alexander Farms LLC, El Sol, and the local farmer's market for introducing new plants and techniques into my garden. Special thanks to bee-keeper, Tucka "Bee," who provided me with books affording insights into eco-art therapy methods and materials and for beekeeping on my farm which ensures my flowers bloom, plants thrive, and therefore my art materials grow vividly throughout the seasons.

Along these lines, I must extend appreciation to permaculture consultants and experts including Connor Murphy with Incredible Edible Landscapes and Mel, "The Worm Queen," at Let It Rot. Plant donations have done a lot to foster my onsite selection of eco-art therapy materials and so I very much appreciate Bongard Nursery & Landscaping and Indian Trials Native Nursery. Similarly, without mulch, my plant selection and soil health would be much lower and so I have special gratitude towards Integrity Tree Service, Landscape Solutions LLC, Tree Works LLC, Stephen's Tree Trimming, and Only Trees.

Importantly, thank you to all my peers and mentors who have supported my efforts. Dr. Dave Gussak's inspiring dedication to the art therapy field and his encouragement to seek a publisher for this book were paramount. I also have gratitude towards Lourdes Figueroa for sharing many inspirational art therapy texts. Special thanks to Winnie Said, President of the Palm Beach County Native Plant Society (PBCC FNPS), whose familiarity with the needs and ideas of the local community was helpful during the early phase of this undertaking. Although I have never met you personally, thank you, Geoff Lawton for documenting your tireless efforts towards permaculture around the world.

Finally, my garden and therefore my eco-art therapy resources would not exist without the help of my husband who moved mountains of mulch with me, planted seedlings, co-parented in the garden, and trusted my on-going explorations.

From the bottom of my heart: Thank you, everyone.

1 Theories and Practice

Introduction to Eco-Art Therapy

As therapists and educators, we find ourselves at a pivotal time in human history; one marked by tremendous possibility and human need (Scheirich, 2020). More than 85% of a person's daily life is spent indoors and as blue and green spaces decrease in the U.S. and abroad, clients yearn to reconnect with nature for psychosocial and physical well-being (Lee, Lee, Park, & Miyazaki, 2015). For instance, with COVID-19 and related sheltering-in-place and quarantining came profound social isolation resulting in unprecedented mental health and education challenges for people across the world (Iyengar & Shin, 2020). Many found themselves indefinitely at home turning to natural environments for a sense of place, belonging, and community to keep mentally and physically healthy (Iyengar & Shin, 2020).

Now more than ever, helping professionals have an opportunity to employ holistic methods, like eco-art therapy, to empower communities and support those in greatest need (Horesh & Brown, 2020). The mission of any helping profession is to improve the quality of life, health, and well-being of those in need (Li, Louis Kruger, & Krishnan, 2016). To achieve this goal, helping professionals seek methods which empower their clients and equip them with life-long coping skills (Li, Louis Kruger, & Krishnan, 2016). Eco-art therapy is one such method as nature offers a sanctuary and can provide a sense of relief, peace, and wonder (Houghton & Worroll, 2016).

Within our current society, clients and helping professionals alike have a choice of perspective. We may focus on the stressors posing as obstacles to well-being or on elements which elevate our joy and health (Pritchard, 2020). Rather than focus on the negative, eco-art therapy processes take on positive psychology tenets to enable clients to lead lives with greater fulfillment. Optimism, gratitude, peace, meaning, purpose, and hope underlie research-based eco-art therapy directives and highlight client strengths. As a result, sessions which center on the question "What lifts you up?" help clients focus on rising above and moving beyond limitations and challenges (Pritchard, 2020).

Methodologically, "eco-art therapy" is based upon applying an eco-psychology theory to art therapy practices to invigorate the senses and facilitate clients in sharing emotions, memories, and wisdom (Sweeney, 2001–2002; Sweeney, 2013a; Sweeney, 2013b). Given this foundation of art therapy and its holistic form of treatment backed by research, eco-art therapy has a lower perceived stigma than typical psychotherapy; some even describe the process as a free-flowing, collaborative, and expressive effort between the client and therapist (Gwinner, 2016 as cited in Daughtry, 2018). Within eco-art therapy, clients create art and reflect on the art product and processes, thereby increasing awareness of themselves, others, and the world around them. This process enables clients to cope more effectively with symptoms to experience enhanced quality of life. Simply put, through eco-art therapy practices, clients can relish the beauty and health-providing benefits of nature because through art making, the therapeutic impact of nature is heightened. For instance, imagine yourself in a forest (adapted from O'Malley, 2020): *Feel the fresh breeze on your face and breathe in the fragrant oils released by the trees, melting stress away and strengthening your immune system. Take time to marvel at a spider's web glistening in a shaft of light or a flower in full bloom. In this moment—here and now—embrace the sensations of wellness and vitality.*

By creating art with or in nature, clients are able to prolong such sensory-based, wonder-infused moments, contemplating their connection to the world around them and cultivating synergy between environmental and personal well-being (McMaster, 2013; Chalquist, 2007, p. 35). This is because many clients find nature's vibrancy an inspiration for artistic expression (Whitaker, 2010, p. 120 as cited in di Maria Nankervis et al., 2013). Art making is a form of thinking and as such it aids in the exploration of sensory and perceptual experiences (Kapitan, 2010, p. 162 as cited in Gardner, 2016). For instance, touching nature during art making expands awareness and presence as clients center attention on their senses, promoting trust and empathy in themselves and, by extension, others (Berger & Tiry, 2012; Houghton & Worroll, 2016).

Art and nature have been linked since man's history began; research shows art making is a fundamental element of being human and helps us process the way we live and see life as an art in and of itself (Sweeney, 2001–2002). Take as an example research documenting art making as an effective stress reduction technique (Abbott, Shanahan, & Neufeld, 2013). When clients express why art making helped them therapeutically, they typically explain that the process is fun, thoughtful, and relaxing (Sheller, 2007). Pairing this process with nature allows therapists and educators to maximize therapeutic potential.

Natural materials, subjects, and settings can help clients to process significant and meaningful events, places, and relationships (Stace, 2016). Handmade paper, natural textures, branches, dried seaweed, berries, flowers, photography, and journaling are all used in eco-art therapy and can help orient clients to place, time, and situation (Whitaker, 2010, p. 121 as cited in di Maria Nankervis et al., 2013). This art making helps clients process their experiences and, as a result, eco-art therapy can provide opportunities for clients to make choices, connect and communicate with others, and feel engaged and alive (Abraham, 2005 as cited in McMaster, 2013). Broadly speaking, eco-art therapy helps clients meet psychosocial goals by employing nature throughout art making within a professional relationship.

Defined clinically: *Eco-art therapy is a holistic, integrative mental health practice in which clients, facilitated by the therapist, use natural art materials and settings, the creative process, and the resulting artwork to improve mental, physical, and emotional health* (adapted from American Art Therapy Association [AATA], 2020).

From a clinical standpoint, eco-art therapy is a goal-oriented practice. To achieve clinical goals, therapists engage clients in activities such as exploring the natural world and its naturally occurring phenomena, including, but not limited to, living organisms, rocks and minerals, natural landscapes, or the sky (McMaster, 2013). Throughout eco-art therapy, therapists also guide clients in the use of natural resources—in other words, materials obtained from plants, animals, or the ground, such as clay, pine cones, shells, or wood. Beyond these activities and uses, educators and therapists have multiple avenues of integrating eco-art therapy practices, whether it be taking clients outdoors to collect natural art materials, teaching them to cultivate art-making resources, or utilizing metaphor to embody nature processes (Struckman, 2020). As a result, eco-art therapy approaches are three-fold: nature-as-subject, setting, material, or a combination of the three.

- **Nature-as-subject approaches** to eco-art therapy entail depicting nature in 2D or 3D forms such as by painting a landscape from observations or by memory.
- **Nature-as-setting approaches** to eco-art therapy entail visiting or recreating a blue or green space marked by biodiversity (e.g., plants, flowers, water, butterflies). Sessions use these settings for nature-based experiences and the cultivation and collection of materials. Setting examples include an onsite garden, state park, or even an office which has been converted into a "green space."
- **Nature-as-material approaches** to eco-art therapy entail using natural artifacts to create paint, clay, collage, paper, and more. Plants serve as dye, paint, or paper-making pulp, allowing the plant to become a conduit of creativity.

The benefits of eco-art therapy are in the expressive processes and include but are not limited to: 1) decreasing isolation, depression, and anxiety, 2) alleviating stress, and 3) increasing self-efficacy and social connectedness (Bessone, 2019; De Petrillo & Winner, 2005). However, eco-art therapy, given its art-making process, has many possible therapeutic benefits: It is a way to make meaning of an event, a way to communicate distress and thus provide some kind of relief, and a way to regulate emotions (Drake, Hastedt, & James, 2016). For these benefits to occur though, eco-art therapy sessions must promote safety and comfort and be client-centered (Cherdymova et al., 2019).

Safety and comfort is the highest priority in an eco-art therapy session. When clients feel safe, they are better able to communicate their experiences, thoughts, and feelings in ways which foster their well-being. This priority also reflects psychologist Abraham Maslow's theory of hierarchy of needs—basic needs, such as those for safety and comfort must be met first to allow clients to achieve their full potential for personal development. Client safety and comfort is enhanced through clear boundaries which help group members support one another. Clear boundaries in the form of rules increase demonstrations of mutual respect and appreciation for everyone's contribution and effort. Along these lines, basic rules may describe required group member behavior like: respecting all cultures, perspectives and feelings, and ensuring the confidentiality of anything shared in the sessions (Cherdymova et al., 2019). Confidentiality and privacy are also essential considerations to ensure clients remain engaged, especially when eco-art therapy sessions are outdoors.

Client-centered approaches entail empowering clients as "experts" with regard to their thoughts and feelings as well as the meanings represented in their artwork, including the latent and manifest content. Furthermore, all artworks are treated with equal respect, regardless of professionalism since the artwork is valued as a means of client self-expression. The quality is not judged and the content is not analyzed unless the client does so in tandem with the therapist.

Ultimately, we want to utilize eco-art therapy sessions to improve client mental health. To do this, we need to ensure clients fully engage in using nature as an opportunity for sensory experience. When processes are client-centered, safe, and comfortable, individuals more readily employ natural artifacts as metaphoric and symbolic elements in their art (Masterton, Carver, & Parkes, 2020).

Evidence Basis: "Why This Approach?"

Science

Neuroscience and Outcome Studies

Incorporating nature into art therapy through eco-art therapy aligns with research and neuroscience findings (Hermann, 2020). On a physical level, being in nature decreases the risk of chronic disease such as by decreasing blood pressure, risk of cardiovascular disease, anxiety, depression, chronic pain, and obesity (O'Malley, 2020). For instance, our skin receptors belong to the largest organ of the body and connect to the central nervous system (Kopytin & Rugh, 2017). The simple act of relishing a gentle breeze as it brushes against our skin can have a profound physiological impact on relaxing our nervous system. So much so, that a rising field of scientific inquiry called epigenetics explores how our environment, relationships, and experiences affect the very expression of our genetic coding (Kumsta, 2019).

Mentally, research shows that humans are drawn to interact with nature and create with it to process meaningful experiences, communicate, experience relief, and therefore regulate emotions (Drake, Hastedt, & James, 2016; Sweeney, 2001–2002). More specifically, current research in neuroscience reveals that the brain retains its plasticity, and that despite deterioration caused by everything from stress to dementia, people can form new neural pathways (Power, 2010 as cited in McMaster, 2013). Therapists can support this growth through eco-art therapy, help to improve brain function, and work to enhance client quality of life by targeting a variety of skills (Power, 2010 as cited in McMaster, 2013). For example, in the simple act of picking up a dried flower and gluing it to a canvas, the client is receiving tactile stimulation, planning and executing movement, and processing thoughts and emotion related to the experience including problem solving (Killick & Craig, 2011 as cited in McMaster, 2013).

These steps: planning, directing attention, and problem solving are aspects of higher cortical thinking (Hass-Cohen, 2008b as cited in Stace, 2016). With more narrative eco-art therapy creations, clients recall and describe different types of memories which engages both cognitive and perceptual neural pathways and expands personal agency (Vance & Wahlin, 2008 as cited in Stace, 2016). In other words, clients can "stand back and look at their lives as a whole," gaining insight into what could improve their quality of life and happiness (Stace, 2016).

Procedurally, a variety of mental abilities are put into practice throughout eco-art therapy practices. Clients rely on declarative memories for the identification of plants; they use perception, spatial navigation, and visuospatial skills when looking for art-making resources in a garden; they conceive, organize, and carry out new movements (praxis) when arranging and handling plants during art making; and finally clients exhibit cognitive control or executive functioning when they achieve expressive goals through focusing, self-monitoring, and planning (Larner, 2005, pp. 796–797 as cited in McMaster, 2013).

Using natural materials in art making can enhance therapeutic outcomes from a neuroscience standpoint without requiring clients to have artistic skills. The process of creating art such as during eco-art therapy triggers restorative neurochemicals, meaning the process in and of itself is relaxing and de-stresses clients (Williams, 2016). The human sensory system has developed a heightened sensitivity to the natural world (Coburn, Vartanian, & Chatterjee, 2017). Inherently fascinating visual stimuli in landscapes such as vegetation, wildlife, and "the motion of leaves in the breeze," capture the attention of our visual system (Coburn, Vartanian, & Chatterjee, 2017).

Consider collage once again and imagine a client who has a range of dried plants with a variety of colors and textures at their fingertips. The high-contrast plant colors capture attention and interest because they contain useful visual information for identification (Coburn, Vartanian, & Chatterjee, 2017). Grouping the collage materials by color, form, or texture activates associated neurons responsible for processing those features (Coburn, Vartanian, & Chatterjee, 2017). As the client arranges the materials into a pleasing pattern, the brain may release endorphins via the pleasure response, decreasing stress and experiences of physical pain (Coburn, Vartanian, & Chatterjee, 2017).

Using Eco-Art Therapy to Address Client Needs

In order for clients to overcome illness and maximize their potential, their basic human needs must be addressed first and foremost. Eco-art therapy practices can help with this. How can we expect clients to improve their lives in more abstract ways such through gainful employment and sustaining relationships if their basic needs like sunlight and sleep are not met? Often, it is not the symptoms or diagnosis at the heart of an issue, but the patterned lifestyle driving the symptoms. In eco-art therapy, clients are challenged with changing patterns of behavior, which includes reframing their current environment to achieve a more pleasant, less stressful, and more uplifting sense of being and quality of life (Saraceno, 2017). However, most clients struggle with this aspect of sustaining wellness and therapeutic outcomes. Many at-risk, or high-needs, clients are surrounded by home environments which drive destructive patterns by lacking basic fundamentals like clean air, organization, healthy food sources, supportive relationships, safe places, or peaceful, restful settings.

When a therapist helps clients introduce natural elements into their space, clients may gain insight into how to improve their lives. In nature, there is inherent organization, food sources, restful settings, and more. Most importantly, the quality of these therapeutic aspects is not linked to economic status. By bringing natural elements into a client's home, therapists inclusively broaden clients' perspectives. That said, whether the session is outdoors, in a client's home, virtual, or in-office, eco-art therapy requires an appropriately structured therapeutic process to help clients change destructive patterns (Kopytin & Rugh, 2017).

Each protocol included in Appendix A addresses one or more of Maslow's hierarchy of needs: physiological, safety, love and belonging, esteem, and self-actualization. Although clients should be free to create with minimal directive to explore creative responses, using the protocols within this book, when appropriate, offers a structured approach to ensuring clients address underlying causes of symptoms. Providing clients with an assessment such as using the *Maslow Assessment of Needs Scales* (MANS) can help determine if the structured protocols are most appropriate or if more open directives would better serve the client.

Biological and Physiological Needs

Because nature fulfills and helps regulate biological needs such as sleep, hunger, and oxygenation, research easily documents the benefits of maintaining a connection to nature; documented benefits include improved attention, decreased stress, shorter hospital stays, less pain medication, more positive mood, and many more (Huynh, 2017). On a practical level, trees and other plants create oxygen and their leaves trap pollution, keeping our air clean (Houghton & Worroll, 2016). Although 3.8 million people worldwide die prematurely each year from illnesses attributable to indoor air pollution, research clearly shows that plants reduce indoor and outdoor pollution, improving overall conditions (Han & Ruan, 2020; Nwanaji-Enwerem, Allen, & Beamer, 2020). Incorporating eco-art therapy directives which result in potted indoor plants or living artwork within client homes, or which expose clients to higher-quality air in institutional settings, serves their biological and physiological needs (see the *You Are Safe Here* and *Organic Collage* protocols in Appendix A).

Sleep is essential for quality of life and yet sleep problems are increasing all over the world (Knutson et al., 2017). Poor sleep can lead to impaired motivation, poor emotion regulation, and declines in cognitive functioning as well as increased risk for serious medical conditions like diabetes, cardiovascular disease, and cancer (Irish et al., 2015). Sleep is triggered internally by the release of neurotransmitters and is impacted by sun exposure given its role in maintaining a healthy circadian rhythm (Choi et al., 2020). For this reason, directives which encourage clients to go outdoors and experience nature and natural light play an important role in helping clients gain insight into healthy sleep patterns and sleep hygiene (see *Dream Catcher* and *Sunlight Portrait* in Appendix A).

Similarly, mental health impacts diet and hunger. Growing and harvesting food and herbs which simultaneously serve as art-making resources may help to encourage a healthier appetite among those who are losing an interest in food (McMaster, 2013). Directives which incorporate unprocessed, raw foodstuff offer clients an opportunity to learn about food in ways which foster insights into healthier lifestyles (see *Apple Doll, Sensory Still Life, Bread Sculpture*, and *Spore Print* in Appendix A).

Safety Needs

When a person feels unsafe, the stressful experience can be traumatic and this trauma lives in the body and can impact mind-body processes

(Jaworski, 2020). Our brains aren't tireless three-pound machines; they're easily fatigued (Williams, 2016). Stress and, subsequently, trauma, alters the physiology of our brains, rewiring them and changing how we store memories (Carey, 2006 as cited in Jaworski, 2020). Stress and trauma engage the sympathetic nervous system (SNS) by revving up heart rate, breathing, sweat production, and more (Slavich, 2020). When stress is chronic, long-term mental and physical health declines (Slavich, 2020). For instance, coronavirus disease (COVID-19) has rapidly emerged as a global pandemic, placing unprecedented stress on all aspects of society, exacerbating and increasing stress-related disorders for many throughout the world (Horesh & Brown, 2020).

In trauma theory, "grounding" and "anchoring" are outlined as methods for survivors to find safety in their bodies (Muller, 2018 as cited in Cauley, 2019). However, as Cauley (2019) notes, these approaches take on added significance when associated with actual places. Familiar forests, lakes, and lands can restore feelings and bodily sensations of safety. When clients activate sensory experiences by tuning into physical surroundings like connecting to nature, they better manage stress-related symptoms such as hyperarousal (Cauley, 2019). Ultimately, decreasing hyperarousal aids clients in restoring their overall well-being. This aligns with the Stress Reduction Theory (SRT), which states that certain environments either restore and enhance or decrease well-being (Berman, Jonides, & Kaplan, 2010 as cited in Huynh, 2017).

Restorative environments, whether it is a blue or green space in an office or a garden, reduce the effects of stressors on clients' overall health and well-being, helping clients feel energetic and more alive (Huynh, 2017; Summers & Vivian, 2018). Nature is a compelling antidote to the toxic physiological effects of stress (O'Malley, 2020). As a result, interaction and engagement with blue and green spaces have been linked with decreased risk of mental illness across a number of countries, reducing both psychopathology and physiological inflammatory responses; nature, when used in combination with therapeutic interventions, results in improvements in physical, mental, and emotional functioning (Berman, Stier, & Akcelik, 2019; Summers & Vivian, 2018).

During walks in nature such as when collecting art materials, clients are more likely to experience meditative-like brain waves which promote a regulation of attention, emotion, and self-awareness (Huskey, Wilcox, & Weber, 2018; Summers & Vivian, 2018). Eco-art therapy, by promoting relaxed and enjoyable experiences, helps clients decrease psychological stress, thereby engaging the restorative parasympathetic nervous system (PNS). Specifically, during sessions, the therapist guides clients towards experiencing flow and mindfulness to decrease stress responses (Jordan & Hinds, 2016). For instance, the physical engagement with art materials in a natural setting offers a sensory experience which can transform difficult traumatic material into tolerable content (Jaworski, 2020).

As described by an engineer who visits a healing forest in South Korea: *"When I'm in the wilderness and feel part of it… I'm in a state of flow, full of energy and passion and calm"* (as cited in Williams, 2016). Mindfulness promotes client awareness of the present moment, while facilitating a calm acknowledgement and acceptance of feelings, thoughts, and bodily sensations (Jordan & Hinds, 2016). Similarly, flow expands an individual's capabilities by increasing feelings of continuity and fluidity in attention and action (Cheron, 2016). Combined, mindfulness and flow enhance immune functioning, decreasing inflammation, and therefore promote mental, physical, and emotional well-being (Berman, Stier, & Akcelik, 2019; Cheron, 2016). Research describes a release of serotonin, also called the happy hormone, during these states (Muller & Cunningham, 2020). Directives which incorporate nature-as-setting within the directive optimize these positive environmental impacts while promoting flow and mindfulness (see *Four Emotions, Insect Movie,* and *Emotion Guest House* in Appendix A).

When working with clients who have mobility concerns, or within a large-scale facility, windows or access to the outdoors may be limited. Thankfully, images of a natural environment have been shown to lower stress levels after exposure to an anxiety-inducing situation (Hartig, Book, & Garvil, 1996 as cited in McMaster, 2013). Brain activity in clients viewing natural landscapes is marked by increased production of serotonin similar to being actually out in nature (Ulrich et al., 1991 as cited in Summers & Vivian, 2018). Directives which incorporate prompts to view and even depict natural scenes take a nature-as-subject approach and may promote this same serotonin release (see *Place Embroidered* and *Inspired* in Appendix A).

Love and Belonging Needs

Social support is critical to well-being and has been linked to improved cardiovascular health as well as enhanced immune function, mood, coping, and health behaviors (Cohen & Hoberman, 1983; Payne et al., 2012). Neuroscientists now have research to support the notion that physical and social pain are not that different from one another and that fostering a strong sense of belonging is critical to preventing or decreasing suicidal ideation (Allen, 2019; Wastler, Lucksted, Phalen, & Drapalski, 2020). Having a close, supportive relationship with the natural world results in an increased capacity to have close, supportive relationships with other human beings (O'Malley, 2020). This is because acknowledging our interconnection with nature can help those experiencing isolation feel part of something greater. Science demonstrates that everything is connected—air, water, soil, plants, animals, and humans (Houghton & Worroll, 2016). All the elements of life are bound together in a balanced system which has evolved to allow for our survival on this planet—the web of life (Houghton & Worroll, 2016). Consider this touching description of a researcher's connection with nature (Mosher, 2020):

> Before me lies acres of blooming paintbrushes... wild lupines... a line of blue iris. I break into a wide, uncontrollable smile. It's a pallet of color that pulls at a primal part of me... all measure of time is lost on me... I find myself thinking about the intricate relationships...

The biophilia hypothesis proposes that humans have had a long-established and positive relationship with nature as it played a key role in our ability to survive and thrive; as a result, this feeling of belonging in nature shows up in art across cultures and time periods (Kahn, 1997 as cited in Huynh, 2017). Spending time roaming though an undisturbed site can feel like being transported back in time, when civilization didn't encroach (Burroughs, 2020). Surrounded by nature, senses soften and attune to nature's quiet, and it provides both food for the body and nourishment for the soul (Burroughs, 2020); growing art materials requires clients to cultivate seedlings for example and by caring for plants, clients have the opportunity to embrace feelings of being needed (McMaster, 2013).

Nature's ability to support our "prosocial" human capacity for connection, helpfulness, and empathy is ever more important at a time when social isolation is epidemic and loneliness is a risk factor for disease and mortality (O'Malley, 2020). Having close, supportive relationships lowers markers of inflammation and results in a 50% reduction in mortality (Holt Lunstad et al., 2010 as cited in O'Malley, 2020).

Among children, impulse control, feelings of self-worth, motor ability, concentration, and social play are all positively influenced following interaction with nature (Fjortoft, 2001, 2004 as cited in Summers & Vivian, 2018). Exposure to an ordinary natural setting has proved effective in reducing attention deficit symptoms among children regardless of community size, geographic region, or household income (Kuo & Taylor, 2004 as cited in Summers & Vivian, 2018). During the COVID-19 lockdowns, as an example, younger people had higher rates of depression and anxiety symptoms than older people despite being hit less severely by the disease (Pouso et al., 2020). Although social media plays an essential role in socialization, younger clients have a heightened need for physical socialization (Pouso et al., 2020). A younger client's relationship with their environment is a vital factor in personality development, emotional bonds, and attachment style (Kopytin & Rugh, 2017). All of these are critical during childhood development. Children learn best from experience by using their senses actively rather than passively and nature provides a full sensory experience (Houghton & Worroll, 2016).

Incorporating nature, such as through eco-art therapy sessions, provides a platform for addressing client concerns such as feelings of belonging (Berger & McLeod, 2006 as cited in Berger & Tiry, 2012). Eco-art therapy processes allow people to connect with the life-cycle obvious in nature to which they inherently belong (e.g., seasons of life: birth, aging), helping clients to see themselves as part of a wider universal matrix (Berger, 2009a as cited in Berger & Tiry, 2012). This approach has a historical basis and may feel comfortable for clients across a wide range of cultures.

Humans have been using the creative arts in natural settings for social purposes for centuries (Belfiore, 2016 as cited in Toll & Mackintosh, 2020). For instance, consider the fiber arts. Textiles are one of the first ways humans overcame biological limitations and modified the planet to sustain themselves (Fagan, 2016 as cited in Skold, 2020). As a result, the fiber arts are associated with metaphors such as mending and weaving, the intention to create new and heal previously severed connections (Toll & Mackintosh, 2020). All of these metaphors are relevant in both educational and therapeutic sessions. Directives which incorporate themes of belonging through sensory experiences underscore elements of the biophilia hypothesis and promote learning and optimal functioning (see *Family Wind Chime, Bird's Nest*, and *Friendship Mural* in Appendix A).

Esteem Needs

Helping clients feel confident and believe in themselves is part of improving their mental health outcomes. In eco-art therapy, client identities are transformed from "patient" or "victim" to "artist" and the process enables clients to explore positive aspects of their identities, improving their capacity for critical reflection. So much so that the presence of blue and green spaces has been linked to a reduction in fatigue, stress, and aggression, and an improvement in social connections, feelings of well-being, and respect for the environment (McMaster, 2013). This respect for the environment simultaneously teaches clients self-respect. Through a sense of respect and reflection, the body, brain, and mind align as a synchronous force, grounded in making sense in the world (Kennedy & Villaverde, 2014).

When clients feel better and live a higher quality of life, they have a heightened sense of self-esteem. Lifestyle changes, such as spending more time outdoors, can be as beneficial as prescribed drugs in decreasing anxiety and depression (Walsh, 2011 as cited in McMaster, 2013). For instance, leisurely forest walks were shown to yield a 12.4% decrease in stress hormones, 7% decrease in sympathetic nervous system activity, 1.4% decrease in blood pressure, and 5.8% decrease in heart rate; overall, participants reported better moods and lower anxiety (William, 2012 as cited in McMaster, 2013). However, researchers have found that even simply viewing nature from a window can restore attention and reduce medical healing time (Ulrich, Lunden, & Eltinge, 1983 as cited in McMaster, 2013). Interventions which employ nature such as eco-art therapy provide an immune-enhancing mood boost. In a study on hospital patients recovering from surgery, art which depicted nature, such as flowers or landscapes, was preferred and decreased negative reactions towards self and others (Ulrich, Lunden, & Eltinge, 1993 as cited in McMaster, 2013).

Cultivating plant resources for art making offers a natural way for group members to help one another; through growing plants, clients can pass on both knowledge and life stories (EPA, 2011 as cited in McMaster, 2013). Through learning to care for plants and grow materials, clients demonstrate achievement and mastery which is valued by others within the community. Additionally, exercising skills of caring for nature reinforces self-care patterns of behavior. For that reason, eco-art therapy directives which focus on self-compassion, self-care, strengths, and abilities help clients fulfill esteem needs (see *Esteem Quilt, Shell Mirror, Person in the Rain*, and *Strengths Mask* in Appendix A).

Self-Actualization Needs

Aesthetics are an innate form of self-expression and a fundamental experience in life (Skold, 2020). By cultivating a blue or green space, whether it is through nature-as-setting, subject, or material, therapists create opportunities for an aesthetic experience linked with self-actualization (Chatterjee, 2013; Shimamura, 2013 as cited in Coburn, Vartanian, & Chatterjee, 2017). Three brain systems are activated during aesthetic experiences: sensorimotor, knowledge-meaning, and emotion-valuation systems (Coburn, Vartanian, & Chatterjee, 2017).

For example, as a client creates a dye using thawed blueberries, the stimulating smells and colors engage a client's sensorimotor systems. As a client uses that dye to create an image, their meaning-knowledge systems are informed by personal experiences, culture, and education (Leder et al., 2004 as cited in Coburn, Vartanian, & Chatterjee, 2017). Finally, when the client processes the feelings engendered by that image and art-making experience, their emotion-valuation networks are activated (Leder et al., 2004 as cited in Coburn, Vartanian, & Chatterjee, 2017).

Natural materials within an office can create an enriched environment—in other words, a setting which can promote enhanced formation, storage, and retrieval of memories to aid client decision making and their ability to fulfill their potential (Dominie, 2020). An enriched environment empowers clients to reflect on their values and embrace their acquired wisdom. Natural settings, including blue and green office spaces, are enriched with color, texture, and other sensory stimuli. Thanks to biology, humans are visual, tactile creatures; as a result, our sensory side is as much a part of our human nature as the capacity to speak or reason (as cited in Postrel, 2009, p. 15 as cited in Skold, 2020). When inspired by enriched environments, eco-art therapy products embody client sensations and affects, and therefore symbolize "becomings" and self-transformations (Kennedy & Villaverde, 2014).

Growth and discovery abound in nature as do symbols of death, dying, birth, and rebirth. Engaging with the fundamental questions of existence, such as the meaning of life and what happens after death, is valued in every culture, especially in areas such as the arts; this process of making sense of existence may be important for optimal human functioning and fulfillment (Allan & Shearer, 2012). From the existentialist perspective of eco-art therapy, humans have no predetermined existence but are endowed with the capacity and the capability to create and recreate purpose (Agbude, Obayan, Ademola, & Abasilim, 2017). When inspired to reflect on death, clients tend to report a greater sense of gratitude and they see life as a limited and valuable resource, which increases their inclination to create meaning from their experiences (Frias, Watkins, Webber, & Froh, 2011 as cited in Allan & Shearer, 2012). Directives which address aesthetics like life and death themes, here-and-now experiences, reflection, and mourning align with this existential perspective and can help clients explore self-actualization (see *Aromatic Mandala, Mourning Bracelet, Centered Coil Pot, Burning Interest*, and *Memory Orb* in Appendix A).

Overview of Practices

Although diagnosis of a disorder may be incorporated as required for insurance reimbursement and collaboration among a treatment team, eco-art therapy goes beyond diagnosis to center on addressing client needs which may underlie symptoms. Eco-art therapy processes focus on client strengths and abilities, using nature as a conduit of mindfulness and as a means of resilience and grit. Rather than landing on and remaining tied to a description of "What's wrong with the client?" eco-art therapy focuses sessions on "What potential sources of happiness exist for the client?"

In a fast-paced world whirring with distractions and anxieties, mindfulness in eco-art therapy can improve mood and feelings of vigor while decreasing symptoms of stress, addiction, medical symptoms, bodily pain, and psychological distress (Osman, Lamis, Bagge, Freedenthal, & Barnes, 2016; Vespini, 2019). Eco-art therapy is a means of success-oriented self-expression and the meaning of a client's creations may change over time, as the process evokes evolving feelings, thoughts, and reminiscences (McMaster, 2013). Ultimately, eco-art therapy engages clients in a creative process which involves decision making, stimulation of multiple senses, and a sense of self-worth (McMaster, 2013).

Take, for instance, working with clay. Much like mindfulness, the process of working with clay is an ancient practice (Vespini, 2019). The cool sensation of wet clay and the smell of earth activates the senses and boosts awareness of the here and now (Vespini, 2019). When working with clay, the clients are the masters; it bends how they want it to bend (Duckrow, 2017). The client is in charge, in control; and can create or express themselves with little fear of failure (Duckrow, 2017). As Seiden (2001) stated, "Clay always says, 'yes'" (Seiden, 2001, p. 44 as cited in Duckrow, 2017). Gratifications such as this can offer moments of relief and joy in an otherwise stressful life.

Outdoor Eco-Art Therapy Practices

Outdoor eco-art therapy sessions include practices such as cultivating plant materials through gardening and wildcrafting (also known as foraging). These practices promote client skill-building and functioning and provide a means of on-going informal assessment of client strengths (Abraham, 2005 as cited in McMaster, 2013). During outdoor eco-art therapy, both nature and human beings serve as therapists, orienting the client towards wellness (Summers & Vivian, 2018). Given the therapeutic experience of being outdoors when gathering materials or creating, practicing eco-art therapy with clients can simultaneously serve as professional self-care. As educators and therapists take time to process their own emotional response in nature, the prevalence of burn-out decreases (Carr, 2020).

The natural environment is a resource for coping; people can spend time in natural environments to improve their mood, to "clear their heads," or both (Huynh, 2017). In eco-art therapy sessions, encouraging clients to go on nature walks to collect a variety of natural materials, or even joining them in such walks during a session, can optimize therapeutic potential (Ankenman, 2010). Photography or videography may also be employed in such walks, whereby a client may deepen their observational skills of the world around them (Ankenman, 2010).

Despite the benefits of holding art therapy sessions in the outdoors, there are also challenges (Craig, 2012 as cited in McMaster, 2013). Researchers have outlined five obstacles to outdoor eco-art therapy (Clare, 2014): time and money, boundaries, confidentiality, and legal concerns, poor location choices, relevance to treatment goals, and lack of awareness or confidence. To overcome these obstacles, educators and therapists fine-tune processes based on assessment and client feedback (McMaster, 2013). In essence, sound eco-art therapy practices are guided by clear-minded goals and safety protocols.

For instance, an outdoor area may be inaccessible, unsafe, or too far from the residence for a given client so an indoor enriched environment may be more suitable (Craig, 2012 as cited in McMaster, 2013). Getting too cold, becoming overheated, getting sunburnt or lost, or falling while navigating uneven surfaces are real concerns which need to be addressed before such a venture can be considered (Craig, 2012 as cited in McMaster, 2013). Staff and caregivers worry about safety issues, and even the residents can feel uneasy about going outside if it is not a part of the institutional culture (Craig, 2012 as cited in McMaster, 2013). Consistency and routine are crucial in eco-art therapy and can help alleviate anxiety and confusion, affording sessions a sense of order (McMaster, 2013). A consistent outdoor location and a routine process of wildcrafting or cultivating materials helps ensure safety. Routines should also include a review of on-hand materials for personal safety and comfort, such as: sunblock, umbrellas, first aid kits, and blankets (Craig, 2012 as cited in McMaster, 2013).

In-Office Eco-Art Therapy Practices

If outdoor eco-art therapy is not feasible, clients can benefit from nature within clinical settings. By bringing plants into the office, therapists cultivate a green space, offering some of the positive impacts nature has to offer to clients in controlled indoor locations. For instance, potted plants can have a positive impact on mood, cognitive functioning, behavior, and mental health (Coburn, Vartanian, & Chatterjee, 2017). Scholars have noted that when clients are around plants, there is a decrease in self-reported illness, distress, and complaints (Huynh, 2017). A therapist who transforms a clinical space by growing plants and flowers for art making provides a critical service for their clients. The dynamic colors, sounds, textures, and smells of nature can be brought into an office or studio to make an institution appear more homey and create a calming ambiance (De Bruin et al., 2012 as cited in McMaster, 2013).

Converting a clinical office or studio into a blue or green space is increasingly easy. With technology advances, therapists and educators can introduce and cultivate natural art-making resources through hydroponic and aquaponic systems. Hydroponic systems use grow lights and nutrient solutions dissolved in water to create a green-space element. Aquaponic systems are similar but use fish to provide the nutrients as opposed to a formulated nutrient solution and result in a blue space element (Atkinson, 2018). Additionally, "found objects," from nature can be used to create still-life compositions in the office. Examples include driftwood with multiple, living air plants glued in place and misted with water weekly. Even simply hanging images of nature within an office space or having a television with soothing nature scenes playing has been shown to improve mental health outcomes, calm people down, and sharpen their performance (Williams, 2016). What's more, these images can serve as a means to simulate en plein air (outdoor) painting experiences indoors. Using digital images of nature such as on a widescreen television, clients can focus on capturing the spirit and essence of a landscape or animal, incorporating natural light, color, and movement into their work.

Virtual reality is increasingly becoming a viable option as well (Moller, Saynor, Chignell, & Waterworth, 2020). Researchers are beginning to incorporate 3D captures of majestic nature scenes as an affordable way to enhance well-being among clinical populations and to provide care to those lacking adequate access to outdoor leisure experiences (Moller, Saynor, Chignell, & Waterworth, 2020). The immersive media interface employs contemplative, mindfulness-based or mind/body awareness approaches (Moller, Saynor, Chignell, & Waterworth, 2020). In both cases, environmental cues allow individuals of all ages, means, and abilities to continue to enjoy an optimal level of presence and engagement with nature to preserve quality of life (Moller, Saynor, Chignell, & Waterworth, 2020).

Virtual and In-Home Eco-Art Therapy Practices

Having maps of where blue and green spaces are around the city can also prove effective for helping clients de-stress between visits but may also motivate them to independently collect art materials for sessions (Williams, 2016). Not all clients can afford to purchase art materials; many struggle just to purchase food so informing them of free natural areas which are safe to visit is a beneficial service.

When considering in-home sessions, an educator or therapist may be limited to using only materials which can be easily toted and packed up. When taking an eco-art therapy approach, everyday objects such as raw, unprocessed foodstuff can serve as art materials. For instance, a client may not be able to find the time or money to go to an art supply store but may be able to either pick or find an apple at a gas station or grocery store. That apple can then serve as a primary art-making material such as when creating apple dolls which are carved and then dehydrated. These types of ecologically sourced, readily accessible materials can also help to ensure that clients continue to engage in therapeutic activities outside of session.

Another means of empowering clients and facilitating in-home or virtual sessions is through simplified hydroponic use. A mason jar filled with water can be transformed during session time into a hydroponic container, enriching the home environment outside of session time and providing a means for on-going art-making materials. My favorite plant for this purpose is mint, which roots and grows easily in standing water; as a hardy, easy to cultivate aromatic edible, it lends itself to directives such as leaf rubbing where the leaves are picked, covered with paper, and then graphite, charcoal, or crayons are rubbed across the surface to reveal the texture of the plant. As the client rubs the plant, the smell of mint stimulates the senses, providing positive reinforcement for the creativity. However, client allergies should be assessed prior to introducing any plant; resources for assessing allergies are provided in later chapters. Mint is an easier plant to assess for allergies given the prevalence of mint toothpaste; as a result, clients will very likely know if they are allergic to mint.

Vignette: Structuring Sessions

A therapist's scope of practice typically includes goals such as psychoeducation, symptom management, or coping skills and so an eco-art therapy session will need to afford this focus (Spooner, 2016; Van Lith & Bullock, 2018). Along these lines, picture a group of adolescent males who have grown up in violent urban settings and who have been convicted of violent felonies. For this population, setting is at the core of their problems.

When I was working with this population, I began with inviting each one, individually, into my nature-enriched office. Promoting comfort, trust, and safety are essential when deciding how to implement eco-art therapy practices. I drew their portrait to show them the "good" I saw within them and listed clients' strengths, goals, and interests around the drawn portrait to build rapport while simultaneously observing symptom presentation. I assessed for unmet physiological, social, and psychological needs using elements from the *Maslow Assessment of Needs Scales* (MANS). Safety and sense of belonging were lacking for nearly all of these clients and many did not have their nutritional needs met at home.

I then determined each client's *Global Assessment of Functioning* (GAF), which is a 0 to 100 scale used to rate to what degree a person's symptoms affect day-to-day life (Aas, 2014). GAF is a widely applied, easy, and quick tool designed to help mental health providers understand how well a client can perform everyday activities (Aas, 2014). A children's version and a school-specific version of the GAF also exist and I use the GAF to assess which therapeutic directives are most appropriate for a given client or group. As a result, in each of the protocols within this book, you will see the GAF as a reference point. When working with clients who exhibit a GAF below 70, nature-as-setting may not be clinically appropriate unless the facility or agency has an onsite garden and staff members are available to assist as needed. These clients exhibited GAFs around 40 since their on-going violent behavior caused serious impairments in their school functioning. Taking this group off campus could trigger decompensation and create an unsafe situation so onsite directives were the ones I considered.

Once I understood each client's level of functioning and symptom presentation, I explored culture. The clients each talked a lot about respect. Signs of disrespect were commonly met with violence. I deemed an eco-art therapy approach as clinically appropriate in this context because eco-art making conveys a respect—respect for self, others, community, the world, and everything in it (Graham, 2007, p. 137 as cited in Lee, 2018). Additionally, these youth exhibited hyperarousal. Eco-art making is generally experienced as relaxing or even meditative. The process of creating art, especially eco-art, provides an opportunity to change one's level of arousal, and decrease hyperarousal (Spiegel, Malchiodi, Backos, & Collie, 2006, pp. 157–164).

Once it was clear that an eco-art therapy approach was clinically relevant, I selected rotating groups of between three and five participants to collaborate on an onsite, outdoor mural. The group format of an eco-art therapy session provided opportunities to address sense of belonging. I ensured all group members understood the rules and that each client knew how those rules would be enforced. Group members understood that non-compliance would result in their dismissal from the project.

Before beginning the creative aspect, I provided psychoeducation on the goals. I guided students towards collaborating on all steps, and together we drafted an image of nature centered on themes of safety, belonging, and nurturance. This directive is an example of using nature-as-subject. Although we were outdoors on a grassy knoll section of the campus, there was no biodiversity present to engage the clients. For that reason, I didn't consider this to be nature-as-setting.

By using a structured approach with clear rules and boundaries, the clients were able to experience a range of therapeutic benefits. Furthermore, by assessing clients carefully prior to incorporating eco-art therapy interventions, the session promoted client retention and measurable outcomes. For this reason, each of the protocols within this book are grounded in research-based directives, psychoeducation, and assessments.

Eco-Art Therapy Research-Based Interventions

Research-based eco-art therapy approaches involve steps such as having a clear rationale for treatment plans and collaborating with clients on treatment goals (King, Kaimal, Konopka, Belkofer, & Strang, 2019). More specifically, eco-art therapy sessions align with research-based interventions when they are (Perry, 2008): 1) relevant and appropriately matched to client needs, 2) pleasurable and rewarding, 3) rhythmic and stimulating, and 4) respectful towards clients and their cultures. Intervention relevance and match to client needs can be assessed prior to eco-art therapy onset. To ensure the process is pleasurable, clients can make choices and use their interests as guideposts for session content. Rhythm can be established through mindfulness exercises and careful routines throughout the eco-art therapy process.

For instance, by helping clients to stay aware of their breathing, heart rate, and other automatic functions, eco-art therapy can foster relaxation, client self-soothing, and increased resiliency. This process aligns with *Art Therapy Relational Neuroscience* (ATR-N), which is a system to compassionately adapt interventions to client needs (Hass-Cohen & Findlay, 2015). ATR-N is based on findings that responses of the autonomous nervous system (e.g., breathing and heart rate) can be placed under conscious control during the art-making process to decrease stress and enhance mood (Hass-Cohen, 2008). Through ATR-N, helping professionals can teach clients to synchronize bodily functions (e.g., breathing) with art-making activities to enhance the therapeutic effect of the session (Hass-Cohen, 2008). For example, a therapist may direct a client to listen to music and paint with a plant-based watercolor while practicing diaphragmatic or deep breathing in rhythm to the beat. By helping clients to stay aware of their breathing, heart rate, and other automatic functions, they can use the art making to relax, self-sooth, and engage comfortably in social settings. Throughout each protocol, ATR-N concepts help maintain a balance between a therapeutic process and necessary educational elements to guide clients towards a neurologically stimulating, aesthetically pleasing product. This means clients are encouraged towards a state of flow to achieve therapeutic outcomes while creating art with natural resources.

To foster respectful practices towards clients, families, and cultures, careful planning is needed. For instance, the protocols included in Appendix A are those centered on balancing a process and product focus to help clients routinely and repeatedly use life experiences as inspiration. When the creative process reflects client cultural and emotional needs, clients feel valued. As a result, clients may increasingly desire to share their personal stories and past experiences to connect with others, including family and community members (Alders, 2012).

Imagine guiding a meditative walkabout in a garden paired with breath work and a process of collecting found objects for art making (Kopytin & Rugh, 2017). Such a process employs restorative and rhythmic strategies which are a combination of physical activity, socialization, and problem solving, and have demonstrated among the greatest overall positive effect on mental health (Park, Gutchess, Meade, & Stine-Morrow, 2007). What research is teaching us is: Nature is restorative because it takes the load off all the inhibitory effort required in our modern world (Saraceno, 2017). Said differently, whereas in a city, a client may need to wear headphones to drown out the stressful noise when walking along a busy street, in nature the sounds are part of what relaxes and soothes.

In our fast-paced culture, the research-based goal of any eco-art therapy session is to help clients slow down enough to experience feelings of pleasure, self-esteem, relaxation, and therefore well-being. To illustrate this idea: Take a moment to imagine yourself on a warm, tropical beach. Close your eyes, and visualize yourself next to gentle rolling waves in the early evening collecting seashells for an artwork. During this exercise, your visual sense is engaged but most likely you may be imagining sounds and rhythms—even tastes and tactile sensations (Knill, 1995, p. 25 as cited in Ankenman, 2010). Engage all five senses. Can you:

- Feel the gentle warmth of the sun your skin?
- Taste the salty air?
- Smell the scent of the water?
- Hear seagulls calling?
- See the rolling motion of the waves lapping at the shore?

The visceral effects of this visualization reveal that imagination helps us create a therapeutic bond between ourselves and elements outside ourselves. The process of imagining is a biological activity in the same way the eye, tongue, ear, nose, and fingers enable us to see, taste, hear, smell, and feel (Burke, 1999, p. 12 as cited in Ankenman, 2010). By being deeply absorbed in imagining, cells are able to produce rehabilitative physiological change (Cardena et al., 2000, p. 377 as cited in Ankenman, 2010). By embracing the healing properties of the imagination during art making, eco-art therapy approaches support clients' journey towards wellness. Clients are able to reimagine and thus recreate their relationships with others and their environments such as home, community, and nature (Ankenman, 2010).

Vignette: Involuntary Memories and Neuronal Activity

When in nature, the smells, dappled light, and sensations may help clients recall memories at will; these are their voluntary memories. Yet, equally important are client involuntary memories, or those which simply pop up, in response to sensory stimuli. Involuntary memories tend to be much more vivid, emotional, cause bodily responses, and activate the visual system of the brain (Epstein, 2002 as cited in Pike, 2013). These memories include details like color, scent, and temperature, but more importantly, involuntary memories imbue a "feeling" (Epstein, 2002, p. 7 as cited in Pike, 2013).

Thanks to the sensory experiences afforded by nature, eco-art therapy processes easily evoke associations, triggering involuntary memories more readily than other approaches, allowing the client to re-experience details of the past. When therapists keep this in mind, they can use it to the client's advantage. Observing when the client is no longer visually responding to external stimuli and bringing them back to the present moment can offer rhythmically therapeutic experiences as the client cognitively and emotionally embraces the past, present, and future.

I once served a client who had had a stroke and exhibited symptoms of aphasia. Her mobility was limited as was her speech. Although she could comprehend what was said to her and nod or shake her head, she struggled with forming words and sentences. Death and dying were consistent themes in conversation with her facility caregivers since her health was declining. She was exhibiting decreases in fine and gross motor skills and increases in mood volatility—both of which were the focus of our sessions. Her anger outbursts seemed to be connected to the painful acknowledgement of how fragile and vulnerable she felt. During her art making, she demonstrated preferences to explore a connection to nature rather than people. Careful, onsite, nature-as-setting approaches were appropriate for this client as a means of sensory stimulation.

She was wheelchair bound but the onsite garden had an accessible path throughout. While exploring the large, forest-like onsite garden together, there were metaphors all around us. Closely observed, the apparently peaceful trees were caught in a slow-motion life and death struggle for sunlight. Yet, as the client looked around taking deep, belly breaths, she seemed to find nature's struggle life affirming. Leaves and flowers gently grazed my client's wheelchair, her shoulders, and legs. This provided her with touch and sensory stimulation which she had been lacking. We moved slowly and methodically past the trees. My hope was to help her experience a state of relaxation and comfort.

For several weeks thereafter, we collaborated bedside on a canvas collage using the orange and red leaves we collected. She smeared the glue with her fingertips rather than paintbrushes, smiling throughout the process. Using the sticks and twine we collected from the yard, we constructed a frame around the canvas. As the collage came together with the leaves scattered across the surface of the canvas framed by the sticks, she slowly whispered, "wow" and "fall." This vocalization was exciting to caregivers who remarked that she was typically unable to verbally express herself. The sensory stimulation helped and the emotional impact enabled her to momentarily bypass the limitations caused by the aphasia and vocalize.

In line with research, the collage process sparked involuntary memories, self-expression, and increased feelings of dignity and control (Woolhiser-Stallings, 2010). When clients create visual narratives which tell stories about their relationship with the environment, such as through collage, they have opportunities to rediscover, reinvent, and reconnect with positive aspects of their identity (Kopytin & Rugh, 2017, pp. 32–33). This experience of projecting a life-affirming identity can provide spiritual and emotional fulfillment (Postrel, 2009 as cited in Skold, 2020).

Models

Eco-art therapy is a holistic intervention, meaning it draws from a number of therapeutic models to target comprehensive wellness. Physical, mental, and emotional well-being are all addressed when sessions are guided by time-tested models. The European Care Farm Model informs practices given its blending of multifunctional agriculture with critical mental health services to support vulnerable populations (Bessone, 2019). In the U.S., community leaders have increasingly expressed substantial and increasing interest in therapeutic uses of nature as "green-care interventions" (Saraceno, 2017). These models center on empowering adults and children alike to experience enhanced quality of life (Berger & Tiry, 2012). This modern "green movement" has helped avail the arts as a means to re-establish healthy bonds with the environment (Kopytin & Rugh, 2017).

Beyond community care, three therapeutic models help educators and therapists facilitate sessions to foster client connection with nature; these are (Kopytin & Rugh, 2017): humanistic, existential, and transpersonal models.

- **Humanistic** perspectives help therapists focus eco-art therapy on client life goals (DeRobertis & Bland, 2018). In line with this model, art-making directives are planned according to client interests so they find them fulfilling and aligned with their values. As a result, humanistic models in eco-art therapy facilitate client intentionality, resilience, and on-going self-reflection (Farokhi, 2011).
- **Existential** viewpoints offer clients a chance to explore here-and-now meanings and the beauty within everyday life during eco-art therapy sessions (Correia, Cooper, Berdondini, & Correia, 2018). As a result of an existential influence, clients mindfully imbue works with symbolism specific to their life and experiences (Moon, 2007).
- **Transpersonal** approaches help clients balance concentration and relaxation to achieve flow (Vespa, Giulietti, Ottaviani, & Spatuzzi, 2018). Transpersonal art making in eco-art therapy addresses both the order and chaos found in nature and within clients (Taylor, 2016).

Humanistic Models in Eco-Art Therapy

As a species, humans have spent the majority of existence living in outdoor spaces (McNair, 2012). Although progress in industry and technology has removed us from fields and forests, the human body remains evolutionarily connected to nature (Conn, 1998; Sweeney, 2001–2002). Humanistic models bring this evolutionary reality into focus so clients can explore their strengths, inherent goodness, and abilities to find adaptive strategies to cope, trust, and derive satisfaction from life.

As a result of the humanistic model, the concept of "art" in eco-art therapy yields a personal representation of reality—one which may be so personal, emotional, and abstract that only the client who created it understands the meaning (Pike, 2013). Creating with natural materials can help clients explore their unique and authentic human experiences visually. Although a level of art education and guided steps are embedded in each session, when clients create, they control the material and metaphors as a means of self-governing and autonomy (Killick & Craig, 2011 as cited in McMaster, 2013). These metaphors can drive client insight and progress towards goals, self-esteem, and feelings of self-efficacy (Kopytin & Rugh, 2017; McMaster, 2013).

Existential Models in the Eco-Art Therapy

Much like a humanistic model, an existential approach assumes clients are continuously changing and evolving in response to life circumstances, including their environment (Kopytin & Rugh, 2017). An existential model provides the perspective that when clients witness beauty, awe, and symbolism inspired by nature, the experience can lead to personal and spiritual growth (Chalfont, 2007; McMaster, 2013). Existential therapy is a way of finding meaning in life to foster change, confront death, and accept death's inevitability (Harris, 2013, p. 354 as cited in Geha, 2019). These guiding principles allow for a more open and exploratory sessions, where the clients interpret emotional "unease" as acceptable and part of a life journey (Geha, 2019).

For example, when working with natural settings and materials, memories of loss, death, and dying may surface. As Freud put it, "Du bist der Natur einen Tod schuldig: thou owest nature a death" (Freud, 1930, p. 110 as cited in Barron et al., 1991). Eco-art therapy materials are subject to decomposition unless carefully preserved and the natural environment itself is rife with reminders of impermanence. Eco-art therapy embraces themes of impermanence to embed symbolic representations of birth, growth, death, and renewal, promoting psychosocial transitions (Hermann, 2020).

So often, people try to protect clients from unpleasantness (Riley, 2001 as cited in McMaster, 2013). However, if a plant dies or a material decomposes, from an existential model, therein lies an opportunity to discuss death; clients are then able to express their full range of emotions to feel heard and less isolated (McMaster, 2013). The therapist needs only to validate the client's experience, without projecting meaning (McMaster, 2013).

Clients often seek out therapy in order to receive emotional support during crises and as researchers explain, one shared community crisis relates to climate change (Ankenman, 2010). As a result of existentialism, eco-art therapy may help clients come together to explore feelings related to climate change, reframing individualistic questions such as "Who am I?" to more inclusive, place-based questions like "Where are we?" (Ankenman, 2010). Together, clients can learn to relate to one another based on "place" and "here-and-now" mindfulness, potentially sparking paradigm shifts and positive life changes (Ankenman, 2010). This existential process of centering sessions on gratitude, wonder, and above all, responsible action, furthers client well-being (Ankenman, 2010).

Transpersonal Models in the Eco-Art Therapy

Adding to humanistic and existential models, transpersonal perspectives encourage clients to work towards balancing mind, body, emotion, and spirit wellness (Geha, 2019). Utilizing a transpersonal model in eco-art therapy helps clients embrace their imagination to extend empathy and compassion towards themselves and others for personal transformation (Geha, 2019).

Transpersonal eco-art therapy facilitates client feelings of being connected to a greater reality by guiding clients across eight levels of consciousness (Kossak, 2009, p. 15 as cited in Geha, 2019):

- **Level one** involves pure physical interaction; this means eco-art therapy sessions involve physically manipulating natural resources such as by walking through a garden or picking plant resources for art making.
- **Level two** centers on exploring perception through sensory experiences including texture and aroma. For instance, during art making, clients may create a leaf rubbing of mint leaves, inhaling a stimulating aroma.
- **Level three** includes conscious drives. In other words, clients may have a goal of what they will create during the eco-art therapy session and may have hopes associated with outcomes.
- **Level four** incorporates embodied emotions. The client may have involuntary memories which trigger emotion-related brain chemicals such as serotonin.
- **Level five** relies on reflective awareness. During this level, the client reflects on their experience and may share disclosures regarding how it felt to reminisce in group.
- **Level six** fosters self-awareness where clients employ imagination. For instance, after reflecting on how it felt to reminisce in group, clients may realize they are becoming more trusting and less guarded. They may imagine what a future would be like if they could fully connect with others.
- **Level seven** refers to meta-cognition or the awareness of being aware. Once clients imagine a future different from their present circumstances, they can begin planning how to improve their lives in more tangible ways.
- **Level eight** empowers a transcendent consciousness in which clients begin to take action to transform their lives based on the insight and self-awareness gained in sessions. For instance, after envisioning ways to connect more authentically with others, the client may begin to prioritize time to call old friends rather than working long hours as a means to avoid relationships.

During eco-art therapy, clients have opportunities to gain a better understanding of themselves and their connection with the world beyond them.

Model Use Through Storytelling

All three models, humanistic, transpersonal, and existential, align with storytelling practices. Discussing the history of a natural material, using an analogy or metaphor, or explaining a myth associated with a place can embody a heightened sense of connection with nature. Imagine telling the following story while sitting under the shade of a tree to a group of clients in preparation for a shadow tracing directive. Shadow tracing entails placing paper on the ground where a shadow of a tree or other natural element is visible. Clients then trace the shadow, employing mindful breathing and thought awareness. The story is called "Flight from the Shadow," by Chuang Tzu (adapted from Merton, 2004):

> There once was a man who was so disturbed by his own shadow and the sound of his own footsteps that he tried to get away from them both. He decided to escape them, and so he got up and ran, but every time he put his foot down he heard another step. Everywhere he looked his shadow was there—behind him, chasing him relentlessly. He ran faster and faster, without stopping, without rest or food or even catching his breath. Eventually, he dropped dead. If he had merely stepped into the shade, his shadow would have vanished; if he simply sat down and stayed still, he would have escaped the sound of his own footsteps.

This story aligns with humanism viewpoints as it encourages a "slowing down" and client self-reflection; existentialism is reflected in the reference to shadow and death; transpersonal themes arise in the concept of self-compassion—rest offers solace. This story may resonate with modern clients as the session content relates to self-care and restful priorities, which would free the body and mind from the pattern of dependence on caffeine, energy drinks, constant amusements, or drugs (Saraceno, 2017). The "stillness" referenced in the story offers an opportunity for clients to develop emotional maturity and, therefore, coping and symptom management skills.

Coping and symptom management skills are clinically relevant goals regardless of diagnosis. Existential, humanistic, and transpersonal models align with modern treatment planning and goal setting while adding symbolism and meaning making into sessions. Along these lines, eco-art therapy uses nature analogies to inspire client interpretations. One that I have found relevant is the Lao-tzu, Tao Te Ching quote: "Men should learn from a pond of muddy water. No amount of stirring can clear it. But when it is left alone, it becomes clear by itself" (as cited in Ross & Hills, 2004).

Combined, the humanistic, transpersonal, and existential models in eco-art therapy sessions can help clients explore an integrated and authentic sense of self nested in relationships with others and the environment. With tragedy, loss, and trauma, identity can feel uncertain and this uncertainty can drive a relentless "busy-ness" and avoidance. By using metaphors in eco-art therapy, the therapist can honor a safe distance from direct confrontation of stressful, traumatic materials to gain insight in safe and comfortable ways (Carey, 2006 as cited in Jaworski, 2020).

The existential, humanistic, and transpersonal models help clients slow down and come to realize they are as much the environment as, say, a tree is and as clients see beauty in natural settings and materials, they are reminded of their own beauty (Neville & Varney, 2014). As one scholar put it, "where beauty is perceived, an integration of self takes place" (Hynes & Hynes-Berry, 1994, p. 27 as cited in Kopytin & Rugh, 2017). Nature boldly takes risks and unapologetically makes mistakes; when clients observe this phenomenon through the lens of humanistic, existential, or transpersonal models, the experience reinforces an important tenet: The goal in life is not perfection—mistakes lead to personal growth (Kopytin & Rugh, 2017).

Vignette: Slowing Down for Self-Care

The process of slowing down and focusing on personal growth and self-care is critical in nearly all sessions. For me this became apparent when I was assigned to a seven-year-old boy presenting with poor hygiene, severe anxiety, insomnia, and what appeared to be a developing eating disorder. I asked his mother to join the session to gain a family-systems perspective. Family involvement can help incorporate the three models into eco-art therapy since culture influences values and meaning making. After some effort, I was able to schedule the mother who sat nervously across from her son wearing a cotton t-shirt which had lost elasticity in the neckline and drooped below her collarbones. I could see blackened, circular sticky marks patterned across her chest just under her collar bone and when I inquired, she explained the marks were left-over glue from previously adhered EKG machine stickers.

A week earlier she had been hospitalized for heart attack symptoms but was released shortly after. The symptoms were psycho-somatic; she was actually having a panic attack. She expressed feelings of self-loathing, explaining that her adult son was incarcerated and she blamed herself. She went on to explain that she had not had time to shower in the week after hospitalization despite being unemployed. Her self-care had declined greatly since her older son was incarcerated several months prior and she suffered from intrusive thoughts. She felt paralyzed to do anything except wait for her son to be released. Her younger son, my client, was constantly worrying about his mom and that was why he couldn't sleep. Without a home routine, his eating and hygiene also suffered.

An eco-art therapy practice lends itself to multi-generational approaches given humanistic, existential, and transpersonal models. Nature-as-setting was not only clinically appropriate but greatly contributed to the process of achieving clinical goals. The client's mother described feeling as though the walls of her home were "closing in on her" but without a reason to go outdoors she simply sat on the sofa, smoking, the indoor air quality muddying her thinking and triggering recurring panic attacks. She was beginning to show symptoms of agoraphobia.

Natural distractions outdoors helped remove triggering reminders, calming the client's and his mother's nerves. The fresh air helped externalize their focus, decrease racing thoughts, and validate that they deserved to continue living a fulfilling life. Additionally, by caring for natural resources in the art-making process, growing and cultivating plants, both the mom and son were able to regain a sense of value. The plants "needed them"; the plants were flourishing because my clients "were there" for them. By fostering the mom's sense of self-worth, my seven-year-old client made notable therapeutic progress.

Through humanistic, existential, and transpersonal models in eco-art therapy, sessions convey a calming, inclusive message (Kopytin & Rugh, 2017, p. 29): "*We have made this world together; this means that we can make it differently... so can we leave to future generations a world which they will find worthy...*"

Frameworks

In modern healthcare settings, therapy must align with measurable goals to be reimbursable by insurance. Herein lies an opportunity for structure and relevance in eco-art therapy. Cognitive Behavioral Therapy (CBT) is considered a gold standard with its targeted goals and narrow focus and is favored in the healthcare marketplace since there is an outcome associated with a specific number of sessions (David, Cristea, & Hofmann, 2018). CBT frameworks within eco-art therapy demonstrate that a natural environment can successfully improve mood and positive emotions (Rosal, 2018; Saraceno, 2017). The act of "making something" in nature provides clients with a therapeutically productive experience, which, for those clients who "need" to be "busy," is simultaneously stimulating and relaxing (Stace, 2016).

CBT approaches are embedded into the eco-art therapy protocols found in Appendix A of this book through a focus on Acceptance and Commitment Therapy (ACT) interventions. ACT emerged as part of the third wave of CBT and provides a means to integrate humanistic, existential, and transpersonal models (Stockton et al., 2019). Empirical evidence suggests that ACT is effective with individuals, couples, families, and groups (Harris, 2013 as cited in Geha, 2019).

Applying ACT provides a structure while promoting client-centered ideals, such as "compassion, empathy, acceptance, and respect" (Harris, 2013, p. 356 as cited in Geha, 2019). These characteristics are considered fundamental to building a solid rapport with clients. Using the ACT framework affords a forgiving practice in which clients and therapists are both accepted as imperfect human beings who are navigating life together (Harris, 2013, p. 356 as cited in Geha, 2019). This mindset allows for a stronger sense of trust to be established between client and therapist.

Through the integration of humanistic, transpersonal, and existential influences, ACT is based on principles such as: acceptance, living in accordance with values, recognizing identity as contextual, and mindfulness (Harris, 2013, p. 356 as cited in Geha, 2019). Therapists who apply ACT within their practice help clients accept that life inevitably comes with unpleasant experiences. Validating clients' unpleasant thoughts and emotions is beneficial in helping them learn to honor all parts of themselves, and learn how to live more fully (Geha, 2019). This framework provides clients with a richer and more diverse repertoire of self-expression, leading to more freedom (Geha, 2019).

For instance, in eco-art therapy, this process of acceptance includes observing nature's unfolding without judgement such as by honoring all seasons and creating with materials which result from natural processes, with acceptance. An ACT framework within eco-art therapy provides clients with an added repertoire of sensory-based experiences, such as: the sounds of birds, the feeling of the wind, the smell of damp earth, and the view of flowers blooming (Geha, 2019). By providing a greater sense of freedom, flow, and insight, an ACT framework in eco-art therapy empowers a client to identify what is important to them in life, and what values are significant in leading a fulfilling life (Geha, 2019). In eco-art therapy sessions, the therapist models an acceptance for the unexpected and allows the clients creative control over the creative process, as long as safety and therapeutic goals are being met (McMaster, 2013).

Expressive Therapies Continuum in the Eco-Art Therapy Protocols

The Expressive Therapies Continuum (ETC) is a framework specific to art therapy which pairs nicely with CBT/ACT parameters and was developed by Vija Lusebrink. ETC provides an understanding of cerebral activity during creative experiences, aiding in structuring sessions so that clients may benefit cognitively from art making (Hinz, 2009; Kagin & Lusebrink, 1978). This framework is based on the idea that information is processed by the brain on three hierarchical levels of knowledge: (a) kinesthetic/sensory, (b) perceptual/affective, and (c) cognitive/symbolic.

The **kinesthetic/sensory (K/S) level** represents simple motor expression and sensory involvement such as viewing landscapes and smelling salt in the breeze (Lusebrink, 2010). At the kinesthetic/sensory level, the focus is on the release of energy through bodily action or movement. At this level, the material properties (e.g., fluidity or resistance) determine the scope of the action and type of interaction likely to be expected from the client (Kagin & Lusebrink, 1978, pp. 171–180).

At the **perceptual/affective (P/A) level,** the session addresses what the client perceives such as the colors in a sunset and the feelings aroused based on that perception which influence the subsequent interaction with art materials. These perceptions are experienced visually and through touch to help clients depict "forms" in their artwork, such as through differentiating figure and ground (Kagin & Lusebrink, 1978, pp. 171–180).

At the **cognitive/symbolic (C/Sy) level,** the client engages in more abstract thought such as through using natural artifacts to create a time-line of life-events. Both the cognitive and symbolic components of this level provide a release from the immediate present, and activate the imagination as the client explores metaphor and symbolism; this level helps clients process complex information such as the meaning of an experience and how that experience will help them lead a more fulfilling life (Kagin & Lusebrink, 1978, pp. 171–180).

ETC aims to assist clients in creating art with increasing levels of complexity, thereby stimulating diverse brain structures and functions (Lusebrink, 2004, 2010). In each protocol you will notice repeating cycles of each level over the course of the ten-week duration to promote flow and facilitate client gains in functioning. Repeating cycles of rhythmic stimulation helps to decrease feelings of frustration or being overwhelmed and can make it easier to modify and adapt the protocols to specific clients' symptoms and treatment goals (Finley, 2016; Pike, 2013). For instance, although each protocol is listed as a ten-week duration, each level of ETC can be a stand-alone session for high-turn-over clients such as those in crisis shelters or homeless shelters. Also, in each protocol, you will notice a breakdown which blends each framework and model with a means to assess progress, goal-set, and encourage reflection. Specifically, I've structured the eco-art therapy protocols so that the ETC levels of expressivity overlap with transpersonal levels of consciousness.

- Throughout weeks one and two, the K/S level prioritizes ritual openings and transpersonal levels I & II; the client engages physically with the materials as an exploration of sensory data.
- During weeks three and four, the P/A level explores cultural nuances, education including psychoeducation, and transpersonal levels III & IV; the client explores conscious drives and emotions.
- In weeks five and six, the C/Sy level affords metaphoric and symbolic meaning making, therapeutic themes, and transpersonal levels V & VI; the session prioritizes client self-awareness, cognition, and imagination.
- For weeks seven and eight, the P/A level encourages reflection and pattern recognition as the therapist rhythmically reincorporates education/psychoeducation and transpersonal levels VII & VIII;

clients are encouraged to process insights regarding self-awareness, self-monitoring, and interpersonal connections.

- Throughout weeks nine and ten, the K/S level centers on winding down and transpersonal levels I & II are revisited as clients preserve their work and prepare it for display. This serves as a grounding experience and closing to the protocol increment.

As shown in Figure 1.1, by including an assessment and goal review along with a rhythmic cycle of directives you can focus primarily on educating, promoting states of flow, and empowering clients. That way, each eco-art therapy session is tailored to client needs while centered on alleviating symptoms.

As therapists, we want our logic to be transparent to gain client trust. The easiest way to foster this transparency is through consistency and routine. Table 1.1 outlines the underlying elements which can foster this consistency within an eco-art therapy session. Additionally, the table highlights actions which ensure eco-art therapy sessions follow research-based approaches.

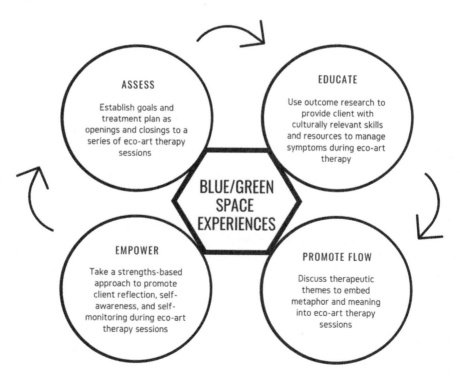

Figure 1.1 Eco-Art Therapy Research-Based Process
Note. This figure illustrates foundational components to align session content with client needs.

Table 1.1 Theory to Practice Quick Reference Table

Framework/Model	Key Concepts
CBT/ACT	**Respectfully set goals, address cognition,** and **validate emotions** through prompting clients to explain and describe artwork, establish standards of behavior, measure performance, and remain accountable for treatment progress.
ETC	**Rhythmically adapt** processes and procedures to client needs and to promote predictability and feelings of **safety and trust** while prioritizing the physical act of creating art.
Education	Incorporate **guided steps** which result in symptom management, model appropriate behavior, and verbally reinforce and praise **technical skills, integrate educational content** as appropriate, and use **cuing** to teach the use of natural materials, subjects, and settings.
ATR-N	Prioritize mind–body connections and gratifying experiences centered on a **process over product focus** where clients enter states of flow.
Humanistic	Encourage self-reflection, self-esteem, and pattern recognition to yield insight regarding **identity,** promote adapted viewpoints based on **shared perspectives** in **social interaction**, and plan **exhibits** to foster community.
Existential	Explore **meaningful** daily living, attribute and use **symbolism** to represent perceptions and emotional and spiritual experiences, dreams, and memories in art making.
Transpersonal	Address values and strengths which enhance connections with others, integrate **family-systems approaches** to understand client **role models** and **spiritual rites and rituals** embedded in **culture**.

As shown in Table 1.1, all of the protocols incorporate an educational component—be it art education or psych-education. More times than not, clients need assistance using art materials to confidently achieve therapeutic goals and so educating clients on methods and materials is an essential part of the process (Malchiodi, 2011; Rubin, 1999). Beyond art education though, each session offers clients opportunities to learn about focus, self control, forest ecology, mathematics (e.g., geometry, physics, fractals), science (e.g., botany, biology, oceanography), chemistry (e.g., mordants for dye, mineral components), language, teamwork, achievement, managing risks, responsibility, and resource sustainability (Houghton & Worroll, 2016).

In sessions, clients may solicit feedback on their art from you or other group members and responses typically fall into one of four categories (as cited in Anderson, 2003):

- **Emotional responses** as group members project their own self-concepts onto the image;
- **Interpretative responses** when group members make inferences about figures, images, style, and elements;
- **Critical responses** as group members make value judgements such as the effectiveness of an image; and
- **Evaluative responses** where group members take into consideration social factors like how well the piece represents a style or approach.

Teaching clients each type of response and when each type of response is appropriate may help the group support one another's therapeutic goals.

Chapter Summary

In modern healthcare settings, therapy must align with measurable goals and so when eco-art therapy practices are guided by models and frameworks, the resulting structure ensures that the process is a research-based, best practice. Ultimately, we want to be consistent. When we are, sessions convey a calming, inclusive message which encourages meaning making, and consequently, clients feel a greater sense of freedom, flow, and gain more insight. By respectfully setting goals, validating emotions, and prioritizing a mind–body connection, eco-art therapy empowers a client to explore what is important to them in life and make lasting changes to enhance their own happiness.

References

Aas, I. (2014). Collecting information for rating Global Assessment of Functioning (GAF): Sources of information and methods for information collection. *Current Psychiatry Reviews*, 10(4), 330–347.

Abbott, K., Shanahan, M., & Neufeld, R. (2013). Artistic tasks outperform nonartistic tasks for stress reduction. *Art Therapy*, 30, 71–78.

Agbude, G. A., Obayan, A., Ademola, L. L., & Abasilim, U. D. (2017). Leadership on trial: An existentialist assessment. *Covenant International Journal of Psychology*, 2(1).

Alders, A. (2012). *Effect of art therapy on cognitive performance among ethnically diverse older adults.* Doctoral dissertation: Florida State University. https://fsu.digital.flvc.org/islandora/object/fsu%3A183336/datastream/PDF/view.

Allan, B. A., & Shearer, C. B. (2012). The scale for existential thinking. *International Journal of Transpersonal Studies*, 31(1), 21–37.

Allen, K. A. (2019). Making sense of belonging. *InPsych*, 41(3). www.psychology.org.au/for-members/publications/inpsych/2019/june/Making-sense-of-belonging.

American Art Therapy Association (AATA) (2020). *About us: Art Therapy definition.* https://arttherapy.org/about-art-therapy/.

Anderson, T. (2003). Art education for life. *International Journal of Art & Design Education*, 22(1), 58–66.

Ankenman, N. (2010). An ecology of the imagination an ecology of the imagination: A theoretical and practical exploration of the imagination for holistic healing in the context of art therapy. *Eco Art Land: Landing in the Space Between Art and Ecology.* https://ecoartland.wordpress.com/an-ecology-of-the-imagination/.

Atkinson, N. (2018). Hydroponics: Should we think small? *CPQ Nutrition,* 1(3), 1–17. www.cientperiodique.com/article/CPQNN-1-3-15.pdf.

Barron, J. W., Beaumont, R., Goldsmith, G. N., Good, M. I., Pyles, R. L., Rizzuto, A. M., & Smith, H. F. (1991). Sigmund Freud: The secrets of nature and the nature of secrets. *International Review of Psycho-Analysis,* 18, 143–163.

Berger, R., & Tiry, M. (2012). The enchanting forest and the healing sand—Nature therapy with people coping with psychiatric difficulties. *The Arts in Psychotherapy,* 39(5), 412–416.

Berman, M. G., Stier, A. J., & Akcelik, G. N. (2019). Environmental neuroscience. *American Psychologist,* 74(9), 1039–1052. http://dx.doi.org/10.1037/amp0000583.

Bessone, E. (2019). *Implications and applications of eco-therapy on art therapy.* Expressive Therapies Capstone Theses: Lesley University. 155. https://digitalcommons.lesley.edu/expressive_theses/155.

Burroughs, G. (2020, January). Plant it and they will come. *2 Million Blossoms,* 1(2), 49–56.

Carr, S. M. (2020). Art therapy and COVID-19: Supporting ourselves to support others. *International Journal of Art Therapy,* 25(2), 49–51.

Cauley, N. (2019). *Trauma worlds: More-than-human stages of recovery.* Unpublished portfolio: York University. https://yorkspace.library.yorku.ca/xmlui/bitstream/handle/10315/36978/MESMP03274.pdf?sequence=1.

Chalfont, G. (2007). *Design for nature in dementia care.* Jessica Kingsley Publishers.

Chalquist, C. (2007). *Terrapsychology: Reengaging the soul of place.* Spring Journal Inc.

Cherdymova, E. I., Prokopyev, A. I., Karpenkova, T. V., Pravkin, S. A., Ponomareva, N. S., Kanyaeva, O. M., & Anufriev, A. F. (2019). EcoArt Therapy as a factor of students' environmental consciousness development. *Ekoloji Dergisi,* 28(107), 687–693.

Cheron, G. (2016). How to measure the psychological "flow"? A neuroscience perspective. *Frontiers in Psychology,* 7, 1823. https://doi.org/10.3389/fpsyg.2016.01823.

Choi, J. H., Lee, B., Lee, J. Y., Kim, C. H., Park, B., Kim, D. Y., & Park, D. Y. (2020). Relationship between sleep duration, sun exposure, and serum 25-hydroxyvitamin D status: A cross-sectional study. *Scientific Reports,* 10(1), 1–8.

Clare, S. (2014). *The eco-friendly therapist: An interpretative literature review of obstacles and solutions to practicing ecotherapy.* Doctoral dissertation: Auckland University of Technology. http://openrepository.aut.ac.nz/bitstream/handle/10292/7785/ClareS.pdf?sequence=3&isAllowed=y.

Coburn, A., Vartanian, O., & Chatterjee, A. (2017). Buildings, beauty, and brain: A neuroscience of architectural experience subject area. *Meteor Education.* https://meteoreducation.com/wp-content/uploads/Buildings-Beauty-and-the-Brainneuroscience.pdf.

Cohen, S., & Hoberman, H. M. (1983). Positive events and social supports as buffers of life change stress. *Journal of Applied Social Psychology,* 13(2), 99–125.

Conn, S. A. (1998). Living in the earth: Ecopsychology, health and psychotherapy. *The Humanistic Psychologist*, 26(1–3), 179–198.

Correia, E. A., Cooper, M., Berdondini, L., & Correia, K. (2018). Existential psychotherapies: Similarities and differences among the main branches. *Journal of Humanistic Psychology*, 58(2), 119–143.

Daughtry, K. M. (2018). *The effects of art therapy on the well-being of medical students in eastern North Carolina.* http://thescholarship.ecu.edu/handle/10342/6848.

David, D., Cristea, I., & Hofmann, S. G. (2018). Why cognitive behavioral therapy is the current gold standard of psychotherapy. *Frontiers in Psychiatry*, 9, 4. https://doi.org/10.3389/fpsyt.2018.00004.

De Petrillo, L., & Winner, E. (2005). Does art improve mood? A test of a key assumption underlying art therapy. *Art Therapy*, 22(4), 205–212.

DeRobertis, E. M., & Bland, A. M. (2018). Tapping the humanistic potential of self-determination theory: Awakening to paradox. *The Humanistic Psychologist*, 46(2), 105–128. https://doi.org/10.1037/hum0000087.

di Maria Nankervis, A., Tinnin, L., Malick, R., Madori, L. L., ter Maat, M. B., Dean, M. L., & Arrington, D. (2013). *Using art therapy with diverse populations: Crossing cultures and abilities.* Jessica Kingsley Publishers.

Dominie, R. (2020). *Rewiring the nervous system with art therapy: Advocating for an empirical, interdisciplinary neuroscience approach to art therapy treatment of traumatized children, a literature review.* Expressive Therapies Capstone Theses: Lesley University. 247. https://digitalcommons.lesley.edu/expressive_theses/247.

Drake, J. E., Hastedt, I., & James, C. (2016). Drawing to distract: Examining the psychological benefits of drawing over time. *Psychology of Aesthetics, Creativity, and the Arts*, 10(3), 325–331. http://dx.doi.org/10.1037/aca0000064.

Duckrow, S. (2017). *Filmmaking as artistic inquiry: An examination of ceramic art therapy in a maximum-security forensic psychiatric facility.* Expressive Therapies Dissertations: Lesley University. 30. https://digitalcommons.lesley.edu/expressive_dissertations/30.

Farokhi, M. (2011). Art therapy in humanistic psychiatry. *Procedia-Social and Behavioral Sciences*, 30, 2088–2092.

Finley, K. R. (2016). *Reimagining attunement: Perspectives on dyadic and family art therapy.* Research paper for the degree of Master of Arts: Concordia University. https://spectrum.library.concordia.ca/981786/1/Finley_MA_F2016.pdf.

Gardner, J. (2016). *Quilting a connection: The use of quilting in group art therapy to promote well-being for older women.* Unpublished research paper for the degree of Master of Arts: Concordia University. https://spectrum.library.concordia.ca/981561/1/Gardner_F2016.pdf.

Geha, J. (2019). *Nature as an impermanent canvas: An intergenerational nature-based art community engagement project.* Expressive Therapies Capstone Theses: Lesley University. 113. https://digitalcommons.lesley.edu/expressive_theses/113.

Han, K. T., & Ruan, L. W. (2020). Effects of indoor plants on air quality: A systematic review. *Environmental Science and Pollution Research*, 27, 16019–16051. https://doi.org/10.1007/s11356-020-08174-9.

Hass-Cohen, N. (2008). CREATE: Art therapy relational neurobiology principles (ATR-N). In N. Hass-Cohen & R. Carr (Eds.), *Art Therapy and clinical neuroscience* (pp. 283–309). Jessica Kingsley Publishers.

Hass-Cohen, N., & Findlay, J. C. (2015). *Art therapy and the neuroscience of relationships, creativity, and resiliency: Skills and practices.* WW Norton & Company.

Hermann, C. (2020). *Report on self-management of mental wellbeing using bonsai as an ecotherapeutic art tool.* www.preprints.org/manuscript/202008.0190.

Hinz, L. (2009). *Expressive therapies continuum: A framework for using art in therapy.* Routledge.

Horesh, D., & Brown, A. D. (2020). Traumatic stress in the age of COVID-19: A call to close critical gaps and adapt to new realities. *Psychological Trauma: Theory, Research, Practice, and Policy,* 12(4), 31–335. http://dx.doi.org/10.1037/tra0000592.

Houghton, P., & Worroll, J. (2016). *Play the forest school way: Woodland games, crafts and skills for adventurous kids.* Watkins Media Limited.

Huskey, R., Wilcox, S., & Weber, R. (2018). Network neuroscience reveals distinct neuromarkers of flow during media use. *Journal of Communication,* 68(5), 872–895.

Huynh, T. N. (2017). *Understanding the roles of connection to nature, mindfulness, and distress on psychological well-being.* Public Access Theses and Dissertations from the College of Education and Human Sciences: University of Nebraska–Lincoln, 296. http://digitalcommons.unl.edu/cehsdiss/296.

Irish, L. A., Kline, C. E., Gunn, H. E., Buysse, D. J., & Hall, M. H. (2015). The role of sleep hygiene in promoting public health: A review of empirical evidence. *Sleep Medicine Reviews,* 22, 23–36.

Iyengar, R., & Shin, H. (2020). Community-based programs to tackle environmental education and COVID-19: A case study from Millburn, New Jersey. *Prospects,* 1.

Jaworski, E. (2020). *Creating a space to externalize: Mindfulness based art therapy for childhood trauma, a literature review.* Expressive Therapies Capstone Theses: Lesley University. 328. https://digitalcommons.lesley.edu/expressive_theses/328.

Jordan, M., & Hinds, J. (2016). *Ecotherapy: Theory, research and practice.* Macmillan International Higher Education.

Kagin, S. L., & Lusebrink, V. B. (1978). The expressive therapies continuum. *Art Psychotherapy,* 5(4), 171–180. https://doi.org/10.1016/0090-9092(78)90031-5.

Kennedy, C. L., & Villaverde, L. (2014). *Mycological provisions: An A/r/tographic portraiture of four contemporary teaching artists.* Doctoral dissertation: University of North Carolina at Greensboro. https://libres.uncg.edu/ir/uncg/f/Kennedy_uncg_0154D_11412.pdf.

King, J. L., Kaimal, G., Konopka, L., Belkofer, C., & Strang, C. E. (2019). Practical applications of neuroscience-informed art therapy. *Art Therapy,* 36(3), 149–156.

Knutson, K. L., Phelan, J., Paskow, M. J., Roach, A., Whiton, K., Langer, G., & Lichstein, K. L. (2017). The National Sleep Foundation's sleep health index. *Sleep Health,* 3(4), 234–240.

Kopytin, A., & Rugh, M. (Eds.). (2017). *Environmental expressive therapies: Nature-assisted theory and practice.* Taylor & Francis.

Kumsta, R. (2019). The role of epigenetics for understanding mental health difficulties and its implications for psychotherapy research. *Psychology and Psychotherapy: Theory, Research and Practice,* 92(2), 190–207.

Lee, K. (2018). *Eco-Art Education in North America.* www.encyclopediaesd.com/blog-1/2018/10/31/eco-art-education-in-north-america.

Lee, M. S., Lee, J., Park, B. J., & Miyazaki, Y. (2015). Interaction with indoor plants may reduce psychological and physiological stress by suppressing autonomic nervous system activity in young adults: A randomized crossover study. *Journal of Physiological anthropology*, 34(1), 21. https://doi.org/10.1186/s40101-015-0060-8.

Li, C., Louis Kruger, P., & Krishnan, K. (2016). Empowering immigrant patients with disabilities: Advocating and self-advocating. *North American Journal of Medicine and Science*, 9(3), 116–122. doi:10.7156/najms.2016.0903116.

Lusebrink, V. B. (2004). Art therapy and the brain: An attempt to understand the underlying processes of art expression in therapy. *Art Therapy*, 21(3), 125–135.

Lusebrink, V. B. (2010). Assessment and therapeutic application of the expressive therapies continuum: Implications for brain structures and functions. *Art Therapy*, 27(4), 168–177.

Malchiodi, C. A. (Ed.). (2011). *Handbook of art therapy*. Guilford Press.

Masterton, W., Carver, H., & Parkes, T. (2020). *Parks and green spaces are important for our mental health–but we need to make sure that everyone can benefit*. https://dspace.stir.ac.uk/retrieve/af8d1ac4-b4d3-48b7-9060-d8143fb8e29b/Masterton-Carver-Parkes-Conversation-2020.pdf.

McMaster, M. (2013). *Integrating nature into group art therapy interventions for clients with dementia*. Unpublished research paper for the degree of Master of Arts: Concordia University. https://spectrum.library.concordia.ca/978027/1/McMaster_MA_F2013.pdf.

McNair, D. (2012). Sunlight and daylight. In J. Gillard & M. Marshall (Eds.), *Transforming the quality of life for people with dementia through contact with the natural world: Fresh air on my face*, (pp. 23–29). Jessica Kingsley Publishers.

Merton, T. (2004). *The way of Chuang Tzu*. Shambhala Publications.

Moller, H. J., Saynor, L., Chignell, M., & Waterworth, J. (2020) Nature and nurturance across the ages: Modest means for modern times. In A. Brooks & E. Brooks (Eds.), *Interactivity, game creation, design, learning, and innovation*. ArtsIT 2019, DLI 2019. Lecture notes of the Institute for Computer Sciences, Social Informatics and Telecommunications Engineering, vol 328. Springer. https://doi.org/10.1007/978-3-030-53294-9_39.

Moon, B. L. (2007). *The role of metaphor in art therapy: Theory, method, and experience*. Charles C Thomas Publisher.

Mosher, J. (2020, April). High country pollinators. *2 Million Blossoms*, 1(2).

Muller, C. P., & Cunningham, K. A. (2020). *Handbook of the behavioral neurobiology of serotonin*. Academic Press.

Neville, B., & Varney, H. (2014). Arts and health as an ecopsychological practice: Developing a conversation. *Journal of Applied Arts & Health*, 5(2), 273–280.

Nwanaji-Enwerem, J. C., Allen, J. G., & Beamer, P. I. (2020). Another invisible enemy indoors: COVID-19, human health, the home, and United States indoor air policy. *Journal of Exposure Science & Environmental Epidemiology*, 30, 773–775.

O'Malley, A. (2020). Nature as ally in our chronic disease epidemic. *Ecopsychology*, 12(3), 180–186.

Osman, A., Lamis, D. A., Bagge, C. L., Freedenthal, S., & Barnes, S. M. (2016). The mindful attention awareness scale: Further examination of dimensionality, reliability, and concurrent validity estimates. *Journal of Personality Assessment*, 98(2), 189–199.

Park, D. C., Gutchess, A. H., Meade, M. L., & Stine-Morrow, E. A. (2007). Improving cognitive function in older adults: Nontraditional approaches. *The Journals of Gerontology Series B: Psychological Sciences and Social Sciences*, 62(Special issue 1), 45–52.

Payne, T. J., Andrew, M., Butler, K. R., Wyatt, S. B., Dubbert, P. M., & Mosley, T. H. (2012). Psychometric evaluation of the interpersonal support evaluation list–short form in the ARIC study cohort. *Sage Open*, 2(3). https://doi.org/10.1177%2F2158244012461923.

Perry, B. D. (2008). Foreword. In C. A. Malchiodi (Ed.), *Creative interventions with traumatized children* (pp. ix–xi). The Guilford Press.

Pike, A. A. (2013). The effect of art therapy on cognitive performance among ethnically diverse older adults. *Art Therapy*, 30(4), 159–168.

Pouso, S., Borja, A., Fleming, L. E., Gómez-Baggethun, E., White, M. P., & Uyarra, M. C. (2020). *Maintaining contact with blue-green spaces during the COVID-19 pandemic associated with positive mental health.* https://osf.io/preprints/socarxiv/gpt3r/.

Pritchard, C. (2020). *Fostering hope in adolescents via art therapy teen group.* Expressive Therapies Capstone Theses: Lesley University. 267. https://digitalcommons.lesley.edu/expressive_theses/267.

Rosal, M. L. (2018). *Cognitive-behavioral art therapy: From behaviorism to the third wave.* Routledge.

Ross, F., & Hills, T. (2004). *Great religions.* www.budsas.org/uni/u-tongiao/mjrel-03.htm.

Rubin, J. A. (1999). *Art therapy: An introduction.* Psychology Press.

Saraceno, J. (2017). *CBT eco-art therapy: Mood regulation with young adults in nature.* Notre Dame de Namur University.

Scheirich, C. (2020). *Coping with the climate crisis: Exploring art therapy for sustainable mental health.* Unpublished research paper for the degree of Master of Arts: Concordia University. https://spectrum.library.concordia.ca/986936/1/Scheirich_MA_F2020.pdf.

Sheller, S. (2007). Understanding insecure attachment: A study using children's bird nest imagery. *Art Therapy*, 24(3), 119–127.

Skold, S. (2020). *Ecological art exhibition as transformative pedagogy.* Public Access Theses, Dissertations, and Student Research from the College of Education and Human Sciences: University of Nebraska–Lincoln. 363. https://digitalcommons.unl.edu/cehsdiss/363.

Slavich, G. M. (2020). Psychoneuroimmunology of stress and mental health. In K. Harkness & E. P. Hayden (Eds.), *The Oxford handbook of stress and mental health* (pp. 519–546). Oxford University Press.

Spiegel, D., Malchiodi, C., Backos, A., & Collie, K. (2006). Art therapy for combat-related PTSD: Recommendations for research and practice. *Art Therapy*, 23(4), 157–164.

Spooner, H. (2016). Embracing a full spectrum definition of art therapy. *Art Therapy*, 33(3), 163–166.

Stace, S. (2016). The use of sculptural lifelines in art psychotherapy. *Canadian Art Therapy Association Journal*, 29(1), 21–29.

Stockton, D., Kellett, S., Berrios, R., Sirois, F., Wilkinson, N., & Miles, G. (2019). Identifying the underlying mechanisms of change during acceptance and commitment therapy (ACT): A systematic review of contemporary mediation studies. *Behavioural and Cognitive Psychotherapy*, 47(3), 332–362.

Struckman, J. (2020). *Nature as metaphor in school art therapy: Development of a group method.* Expressive Therapies Capstone Theses: Lesley University. 235. https://digitalcommons.lesley.edu/expressive_theses/235.

Summers, J. K., & Vivian, D. N. (2018). Ecotherapy–A forgotten ecosystem service: A review. *Frontiers in Psychology,* 9, 1389. https://doi.org/10.3389/fpsyg.2018.01389.

Sweeney, T. (2001–2002, Winter). *Merging art therapy and applied ecopsychology for enhanced therapeutic benefit.* www.ecopsychology.org/journal/gatherings6/html/Overview/overview_art_therapy.html.

Sweeney, T. (2013a). Self-discovery through art and nature. *Eco-Art Therapy.* www.ecoarttherapy.com.

Sweeney, T. (2013b). *Eco-art therapy: Creative activities that let earth teach.* Theresa Sweeney.

Taylor, E. (2016). Mindfulness and flow in transpersonal art therapy: An excavation of creativity. In M. Powietrzynska & K. Tobin (Eds.), *Mindfulness and educating citizens for everyday life* (pp. 25–46). Sense Publishers.

Toll, H., & Mackintosh, D. (2020). Weaving community through creative expression in our home spaces (L'expression créative pour tisser la communauté à partir de nos espaces à la maison). *Canadian Journal of Art Therapy,* 33(1), 1–4. https://doi.org/10.1080/26907240.2020.1753480.

Van Lith, T., & Bullock, L. (2018). Do art therapists use vernacular? How art therapists communicate their scope of practice. *Art Therapy,* 35(4), 176–183.

Vespa, A., Giulietti, M. V., Ottaviani, M., & Spatuzzi, R. (2018). Mindfulness transpersonal psychology and tumors: This approach may be always suitable and effective with the patient. *Clinics in Oncology,* 3, 1489.

Vespini, S. (2019). *Clay work as a mindfulness-based practice.* Unpublished master's thesis: Indiana University. https://scholarworks.iupui.edu/bitstream/handle/1805/21208/Clay%20Work%20as%20a%20Mindfulness-Based%20Practice.pdf?sequence=1&isAllowed=y.

Wastler, H., Lucksted, A., Phalen, P., & Drapalski, A. (2020). Internalized stigma, sense of belonging, and suicidal ideation among veterans with serious mental illness. *Psychiatric Rehabilitation Journal,* 43(2), 91–96.

Williams, F. (2016). This is your brain on nature. *National Geographic,* 229(1), 48–69.

Woolhiser-Stallings, J. (2010). Collage as a therapeutic modality for reminiscence in patients with dementia. *Art Therapy,* 27(3), 136–140.

2 Professional Issues

We are all children of chance and none can say why some fields blossom while others lay brown beneath the harvest sun... Care less for the size of your harvest than for how it is shared, and your life will have meaning and your heart will have peace.

—Anonymous

Feasibility Considerations

As helping professionals, our work is meaningful when we make a positive difference in our clients' lives. To make this difference, we need to serve diverse clients with equal efficacy and juggle multiple priorities, such as: client safety, clinical outcomes, and agency rules and regulations. As caring individuals with a drive to help others, we can sometimes feel an overwhelming urge to meet client needs but if we want to be most effective over the long term, we must first take time to reflect (Carr, 2020). In addition to ensuring services are clinically appropriate for each individual client, we also want to make sure the approach is reasonable and sustainable so we can consistently provide the intervention. When considering the appropriate scope of eco-art therapy for you as a helping professional, consider three questions:

- **Nature-as-Setting Approach:** *Does your liability insurance cover outdoor interventions or does your agency or facility have an outdoor garden you can use for exploring, cultivating, or foraging for natural art materials?*
  - If not, you can bring the outdoors into the clinical setting through potted plants, windowsill gardens, living art, hydroponics, and aquaponics.
- **Nature-as-Material Approach:** *Are you familiar with plants to confidently identify them when foraging for use in art making?*
  - If not, you can purchase seeds, plants, or raw, unprocessed food-stuff such as blueberries for dye. However, be sure to assess

for client allergies before introducing new materials (see *Intake* in Appendix B).

- **Nature-as-Subject Approach:** *Which clients would specifically benefit from eco-art therapy approaches like depicting nature scenes and viewing images of nature as a source of inspiration?*

  - If you are not sure, you can use the intake form found in Appendix B of this book to explore client interests and strengths.

Essentially, by exploring these questions, you can decide to what degree to incorporate eco-art therapy, be it as a material, setting, or subject. This increases the feasibility.

As discussed in Chapter 1, growing literature shows that exposure to blue and green spaces (e.g., urban parks, woodlands, rivers, and the coast) has a range of potential benefits for mental health and well-being (Pouso et al., 2020). This exposure can come in three ways: *direct contact* through deliberately visiting a park for recreation; *indirect contact* such as enjoying window views of natural spaces; and *incidental contact* like passing through a park when commuting to work (Pouso et al., 2020). To date the strongest evidence in support of mental health benefits, for both general and clinical populations, has been for direct contact in natural settings (Pouso et al., 2020). So when clinically appropriate, outdoor eco-art therapy sessions will likely show the most impact. However, this is not always feasible and so to accommodate all clients, flexible approaches are necessary.

Containment is an important consideration in eco-art therapy as clients may have formed unpredictable associations with natural elements. Different environments, seasons, and plants will evoke varied emotional impacts among clients (Kopytin & Rugh, 2017). When outside at the seaside, for example, one client may feel freedom and relaxation, while another may experience anxiety and stress based on prior life experiences (Kopytin & Rugh, 2017). Creating art can help clients therapeutically address and explore these feelings. However, guiding clients towards depicting something positive or which allows the mind to concentrate on a neutral, relaxing external stimuli is highly effective at improving mood (Dalebroux, Goldstein, & Winner, 2008). For this reason, providing clients with directives which aim to provoke positive associations is a best practice (see all the protocols in Appendix A).

Directive and Protocol Elements: Models and Frameworks

With the therapeutic opportunity of working in and with nature during eco-art therapy comes a clinical responsibility. A holistic approach to eco-art therapy integrates the models and frameworks discussed in Chapter 1 to create a relevant treatment plan tailored to each client (Kopytin & Rugh, 2017). As Figure 2.1 illustrates, structuring sessions according to models, frameworks, and psychoeducational priorities creates a holistic series of eco-art therapy sessions which optimally focus on therapeutic goals and outcomes.

Gathering from and being inspired by nature is one aspect of eco-art therapy (Kopytin & Rugh, 2017). However, another aspect is the planning, which includes choosing the right space, method, and material according to the client's needs and clinical feasibility. For instance, a structured space may offer more emotional containment, in other words an atmosphere which helps clients process emotions in ways which feel safe (Case & Dalley, 2014). Choosing the space consciously and structuring the process optimizes therapeutic opportunities (Kopytin & Rugh, 2017).

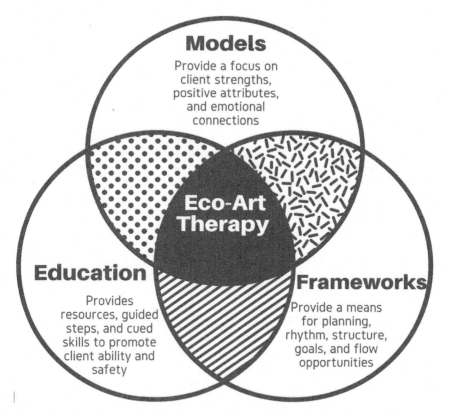

Figure 2.1 Combining Models, Frameworks, and Education in Eco-Art Therapy
Note. This figure illustrates the importance of integrating models and frameworks to ensure client outcomes.

Eco-art therapy can take place in whichever setting the client prefers (Saraceno, 2017). An unpredictable setting can make some clients feel exposed or even uneasy about their choice of participation and so a grounded therapeutic approach takes into account client preferences (Saraceno, 2017). As you increase the frequency of eco-art therapy practices with clients, make it a routine to document pleasant and unpleasant client responses to tailor your approaches (Kopytin & Rugh, 2016). Consider employing the *Nature-Relatedness Scale* as an initial assessment, which reveals a client's level of connectedness with the natural environment or a *Task Enjoyment Questionnaire* to maintain insight (e.g., Walter, 2015). The *Task Enjoyment Questionnaire* simply asks questions such as whether clients enjoyed the experience, if they would want to have another similar experience, and if they would recommend the experience to someone else. Another option is the *Ottawa Mood Scale* as a pre and post-session check-in. Sessions ideally improve client mood and client answers on these assessments help therapists tailor sessions to individualize the approach.

Vignette: Deviation from the Protocol

In eco-art therapy, as with other hands-on therapeutic approaches, directives provide a sense of direction or therapeutic holding (Abraham, 2005 as cited in McMaster, 2013). Having too many options can be overwhelming for clients and it is important to remember that a small choice is still a choice (McMaster, 2013). When nature is carefully selected as either a material, setting, or subject, the structure creates a sense of control. This opportunity for control and freedom simultaneously is what elevates eco-art therapy as a research-based practice.

Each session is an opportunity to encourage autonomy and flexibility; clients are free to deviate from a suggestion or specific directive (Riley, 2001 as cited in McMaster, 2013). Final art products which are unique or have a personal touch demonstrate a balance between structure and choice (Abraham, 2005 as cited in McMaster, 2013). Therefore, if a client were to depart from the proposed task due to personal choice or preference, their individual expression or contribution is not only acceptable but a sign of engagement (McMaster, 2013).

Consider for a moment online therapy sessions. I once served a 45-year-old woman virtually who was referred to me to target symptoms of depression which she had experienced on and off her whole life. My goal was to provide an enjoyable directive since helping clients to do something they truly enjoy can help overcome apathy and depression (Zoutewelle-Morris, 2013 as cited in McMaster, 2013). I introduced eco-art therapy based on her interests and she selected a nature-as-subject approach to depression symptom management using a protocol similar to the *Inspired* directive found in Appendix A. This directive would focus on viewing nature scenes and creating art based on those scenes as a positive distraction. She was excited to begin but immediately wanted to deviate from the protocol. She found a personal photo she wanted to replicate instead of the impressionistic images listed in *Inspired*. The photo she brought in showed two very large, sprawling trees: her backyard view growing up, as she explained. However, as we progressed, she began to miss sessions. She expressed doubt in herself and the process and later explained that the photo revealed a spot where she used to hide as a child to escape an alcoholic father's rampages. As the painting progressed, she remembered flashes of traumatic experiences underlying her depression.

Some clients suggest or even insist on modifications to directives, which inevitably lead to emotional flooding. As with any therapeutic approach, knowledge of models and frameworks are essential to navigating inevitable triggers as they arise throughout eco-art therapy sessions. The art-making process can trigger involuntary mental imagery and when this overwhelms a person's existing coping mechanisms, the client may need additional support or alternative interventions (Kapitan, 2011).

To continue therapeutic progress with this client, she and I shifted from a client-led, art-as-therapy exploratory approach to a therapist-facilitated, art-psychotherapy structured approach. We put aside the photo, discussed feelings of fear and anxiety, and selected ways to explicitly symbolize safety, acceptance, and unconditional love in the painting for the unseen little girl hiding in the woods (her childhood self). We also explored whether she wanted to make the invisible, hidden child seen in the painting. By re-establishing feelings of safety and containment in sessions, she was able to acknowledge an association between her depression and her childhood experiences of needing to "stay hidden."

This client vignette speaks to the importance of sequentially and gradually incorporating eco-art therapy practices to understand the full range of each client's associations with nature. By beginning with a nature-as-subject approach, I was able to understand the client's history associated with nature. Although a nature-as-setting approach seemed to be a viable option (GAF 70), if she had experienced these involuntary memories in an outdoor setting, we may not have been able to re-establish feelings of safety and trust. She may have been too emotionally flooded.

Professionally, you may decide to progressively incorporate eco-art therapy practices. For instance, perhaps you start with nature-as-subject to explore associations and then progress to nature-as-material. After exploring nature as a material and subject, you may be ready to move on to using nature-as-setting. However, guiding clients through a series of successive approximations or "baby steps" means introducing nature as first a subject, then a material, and last a setting to ensure client safety. Within each protocol included in this book, you will see a reference to the eco-art therapy approach, indicating whether nature-as-material, setting, or subject is prioritized.

Nature-as-Subject Approaches

When using nature-as-subject, clients may choose to use their imagination to draw a landscape or create a collage of nature scenes using digital tools such as an online collage-maker. However, to provide a sensory experience, a still life can be constructed from natural elements, potted plants, or even a hydroponic station. Drawing from observation, when paired with guided reflections on the process and product, can promote clients' emotional well-being (Wolk, Barak, & Yaniv, 2020). When having plants within a clinical setting isn't an option, including office paintings of nature or hanging a television screen depicting nature can provide clients with the stimuli needed to be inspired by nature-as-subject.

When deciding how to enrich an indoor space, using artist prints and paintings of nature as opposed to photos of nature scenes has a distinct advantage. These images introduce the idea that nature can be depicted subjectively rather than photo-realistically. Some paintings of nature scenes have been incorporated in research for stress reduction and include (Abbott, Shanahan, & Neufeld, 2013): *Ile St. Martin* by Claude Monet, *After the Rains* by Allan Stephenson, and *A River Through the Woods* by Christian Zacho. When clients view a painting of nature, they may interpret the artwork and project their own meanings and feelings, thereby initiating a therapeutic discussion. When choosing an artwork to show clients, consider those which may be ambiguous. More ambiguous images may illicit client interpretations which also reveal their viewpoints, personal circumstances, biases, and preferences. The overall process can serve as an informal assessment to determine if the client will respond well to other eco-art therapy approaches. For instance, prompt clients to explore the nature images visually and answer questions similar to those found in *Thematic Apperception Tests* (TAT) such as (Serfass & Sherman, 2013):

- Who or what do you notice in the image?
- What do you think led up to what is being shown?
- What do you think happened afterwards?

For clients who may need more sequential guidance, ask perception, interpretation, evaluation, and connection questions like (adapted from Milbrandt & Anderson, 2005):

- What lines, colors, and shapes do you see in this image?
- What do you think is going on in the image?
- How you feel viewing the image? What thoughts and feeling arise within you?
- How does the image relate to your past, present, or future life experiences?

The goal with using nature-as-subject in eco-art therapy is to employ methods to explore nature in metaphorical and symbolic ways (Kopytin & Rugh, 2017, p. 49).

Nature-as-Material Approaches

Using natural materials in eco-art therapy sessions helps clients remember that an emotional connection and attachment to nature is normal and healthy (Kopytin & Rugh, 2017). This attachment exploration may be relevant, especially in situations where clients have experienced insecure, anxious, or disorganized attachment styles. When using nature as a material, the artwork becomes a transitional object, or in other words, one which the client associates with psychological comfort and emotional security.

The longing for permanence, including an attachment to objects, is a perpetual desire in human beings (Geha, 2019). In the artistic world, the longing for permanence is reflected in the desire to conserve artworks forever (Geha, 2019). With eco-art therapy, the materials are subject to decomposition unless carefully preserved. Each protocol in Appendix A reserves the last week as a period of time when clients may "finish" the work with a varnish or UV protective coating to prolong the life of the work. This is an optional process but one which many clients may value.

When using a nature-as-material approach, I find it essential to identify the plant and understand the historical uses of all plant parts: leaf, fruit, seed, stem, root. I like to use the app *PlantSnap* (which is free to download) and cross-reference it with online searches and my books with plant Latin names since the common name may apply to several different species. For instance, I have Brazilian pepper (Latin name: *Schinus terebinthifolia*) growing wild on my farm and this plant is considered a prohibited, invasive plant. Prohibited plants are those considered a nuisance and are regulated and restricted within a specific area. Invasive plants are those which displace native plants and take over areas quickly.

I pull Brazilian pepper plants out of the ground as I see them for this reason to prevent their spread and have considered using them for art making. The bright red berries and glossy green foliage are beautiful. In other cultures, the plant is used medicinally and the berry is dried and used as pepper. However, the plant has the potential to cause dermatitis in those sensitive to poison ivy, oak, or sumac. Additionally, some have reported respiratory reactions to Brazilian pepper blooms. If I were to use this plant for art making, the choice may come with professional liabilities. Just because something is natural does not mean it is non-toxic or safe in clinical settings.

Choosing an invasive plant for art making can be a sound decision though as there are ethical reasons to use invasive and prohibited plants for art making. For one, picking these plants can decrease their ability to reproduce, helping to restore balance to eco-systems. Old World climbing fern (Latin name: *Lygodium microphyllum*) is another invasive, prohibited plant I see pop up on my farm which I need to prevent from spreading given its ability to smother trees and spread fire from the canopy level of a forest. Old World climbing fern has traditionally been used for weaving without any liabilities. As a result, I have deemed this plant to be an excellent foraged art material.

When choosing materials for art making, consider the impact if ingested. Some clients may have impulse control issues and habitually put things in their mouth. Materials brought in from nature or other sources should be deemed non-toxic and safe, especially in the case where clients may get the material on their hands and potentially in their mouth, or eyes. Some natural art materials are readily found in the grocery store. Just consider unprocessed and unrefined grains, fruits, and vegetables, for instance. Fruit and vegetables have cultural symbolism (e.g., apple for health, longevity, love; celery for tranquility, concentration) and using nature as a material provides an opportunity to therapeutically address home-life factors, like nutrition, contributing to symptoms. For instance, while working with a group of adolescents, I brought a sack of apples to use for an apple-doll directive on emotional expressivity but as I walked towards my office, clients saw me, ran to me and asked for an apple with a tone of desperation. Before I had a chance to explain that the apples were for art making, the sack of apples instantly got dispersed. These clients' homes were marked by food insecurity.

As therapists, our role and scope of practice may not include feeding our clients. We may not have the training, budget, or knowledge needed to ethically do so. Yet, we typically have mental health treatment goals directly linked to psychoeducation about self-care. Problematic school behavior and poor academic performance may very well relate to nutritional needs. By using nature as an art material, the final art product and process becomes much more relevant to clients. By using natural materials, which includes edibles, the art-making process can provide a means of art-as-therapy while simultaneously being a point of reference for psychoeducation.

The pervasiveness of hunger and food scarcity extends even to developed countries where one in six children experience food insecurity and famine (Galhena, Freed, & Maredia, 2013). To strengthen and intensify local food production, advocates are pointing out that home gardens are an integral part of local food systems, have endured the test of time, and enhance household food security and nutrition (Galhena, Freed, & Maredia, 2013). Eco-art therapy may indirectly teach life skills such as home gardening while simultaneously addressing mental health when using raw, unprocessed foodstuff as an art-making resource.

Incorporating natural, unprocessed edibles as an eco-art therapy material serves multiple purposes. The therapist can provide psychoeducation regarding self-care (e.g., nutrition, hygiene) within their scope of practice, the client may have access to the material outside of session or during virtual sessions and the material may be cheaper than commercial art materials. For example, a sack of 11 apples, the primary material for 11 apple dolls (1 per client) which take 10 sessions to create, costs $4 after tax. Comparably, using a more commercial art material such as a modeling clay could be as much as $24. With this directive, the client would carve a face into the apple. During an apple-doll session, a client experiencing food insecurity may eat the high fiber shavings during the carving process, possibly without asking or permission. A mental health therapist wouldn't likely be in the position to recommend or suggest the client eat these shavings. However, if a client did so, therein lies an opportunity for discussion and psychoeducation.

Using edible material in its original state, as with an apple, means nature is a central reference to the process and product and aligns with eco-art therapy core principles (Kopytin & Rugh, 2017). In terms of edible eco-art therapy options, some eco-artists may choose to use brewed coffee or black tea for ink, piped chocolate for drawing, marzipan or fondant for sculpture, or turbinado cane sugar mixed with food coloring for glitter. However, these materials could be considered stimulants, may come with ethical concerns, and are not in their raw, unprocessed state and therefore would not directly reference nature and the environment. As a result, materials like these may not align with eco-art therapy principles.

When choosing an eco-art therapy material with clients who may impulsively put the substance in their mouth or who may inadvertently splatter the substance, consider using natural resources which are highly unlikely to cause an allergic reaction (Easley & Horne, 2016). Along these lines, avoid stocking items which are most commonly associated with allergic reactions (e.g., tree nuts, peanuts, wheat, soybeans). For foodstuff which clients have never encountered or which is difficult to come by, clients will not know if they are allergic; using more common foodstuff items is likely safest. For instance, many sour herbs and berries (e.g., cranberry hibiscus, raspberries) are excellent sources of pigment and dye and allergic reactions are rare. Avoid citrus since skin exposure to the essential oils in the rind or even juice can increase the likelihood of sunburn. Salty herbs like alfalfa, seaweeds, and spinach are safe choices since they are highly unlikely to cause a reaction (Easley & Horne, 2016). Salty herbs are fun resources for collage and mixed media, especially when using leaves to make stamps, rubbings, and prints on canvas.

Flowers come in many colors and work readily as dyes for drawing, painting, sculpture, mixed media, and more. Some flowers are even root-to-flower edible, like cilantro, so these plants are generally safe for clients of all ages to handle since they will not likely cause a skin or respiratory reaction and creating art materials with all parts can be texturally interesting. For instance, I have used the white flowers on cilantro for collage but I have also dehydrated the roots and used them as tiny trees in dioramas or during sandplay where clients create miniature worlds, reflecting inner thoughts and feelings. The dehydrated stems work well as a drawing tool with ink.

Those with seasonal allergies may have a reaction to using flowers as an art material given the presence of pollen. In the intake form included in Appendix B, you will see that clients are asked if they have seasonal allergies. To safeguard sessions for those with allergies, I harvest each part of a plant separately, dehydrate the parts using a dehydrator or a microwave press, and store the parts separately in containers like mason jars out of direct light. Flowers in one jar, roots in another, leaves and stems in another, and finally, seeds in their own container as well. Then the plant can be used for years for collage, dye, or stamps as each part can serve a distinct purpose. When I provided in-home sessions across a tri-county area, my car was my art closet so I stored these dehydrated plants in small drawer systems which fit into a rolling cart. That way, I could take the materials into each client's home easily.

Along the same lines, and far more convenient, dye sources can include herbal teas. A caffeine-free tea is likely most appropriate in a therapeutic setting and choosing fruit-based herbal teas is a more viable clinical option since some clients are allergic to flowers in the daisy family such as chamomile. Teas can be purchased as a variety pack and sorted by the color produced with a water or oil infusion (a process of soaking herbs to extract a plant's essence). Another benefit of using herbal, fruit-based teas are the pleasing aromas they produce. I choose to purchase organic herbal teas with no added artificial colors or flavors/scents to prevent any unexpected skin reactions. These teas can make a nice watercolor paint and clients can explore associated artistic techniques (e.g., adding salt on watercolor painted paper to create texture).

In general, you may find you prefer simple media and processes to more complex ones for several reasons (Rubin, 1984 as cited in Pritchard, 2020). First, the more unstructured the material, the more an individual will be able to project on it. Since art therapists hope to evoke personally meaningful creations, the therapist must be comfortable with the idea that there may be no finished product and that some technical elements may be less than optimal. In sessions, the most natural way of helping clients experience a genuine creative process is to "create a physical and psychological environment in which... freedom becomes truly possible," encouraging exploration and non-judgemental playing which materials can enable (Rubin, p. 16 as cited in Pritchard, 2020). Allowing clients to explore and paint with nature-derived pigments like herbal teas offers this freedom of playful exploration.

Many natural materials come with a sensory stimulation element such as texture and smell, which are therapeutic in their own right. Table 2.1

Table 2.1 Eco-Art Therapy Material Substitution Examples

Material	Eco-Material
Watercolor	Flower/veggie dyes/spices like turmeric
Glitter	Quartz sand, pyrite rock pieces
Dye	Herbal teas, berries
Confetti	Seeds, spices, dried herbs
Paintbrushes	Bound pine needles, feathers
Stamps	Carved, starchy root vegetables, leaves
Paint pallet	Shells, slabs of bark
Collage images	Leaves, petals, bark, pods
Paper	Dried pulp of "weeds"
Glue	Tree sap
Twine	Dried vines
Pastel	Beeswax + seed oil infused with natural dye
ModelMagic	Fleshy fruits/vegetables
Slime	Hydrated chia or basil seed or psyllium husk
Painting Sponges	Sea sponges, luffas
Containers	Gourds

itemizes nature-based materials which could replace or supplement standard commercial art products to allow for a sufficiently organized selection to empower clients. These materials paired with a predictable routine and a supportive therapist will bolster client outcomes (Rubin, 1984, pp. 16–17 as cited in Pritchard, 2020). Although Table 2.1 itemizes some key examples, the list is far from exhaustive. Chapter 5 itemizes additional substitutions and reviews methods and materials in more depth.

Nature-as-Setting Approaches

Setting impacts therapists and their clients, whether or not anyone is aware of it (Ankenman, 2010). As researchers point out, six major environmental factors affect our physical and emotional well-being: light, color, sound, aroma, texture, and space (Gappell, 1993 as cited in Ankenman, 2010). Environments which do not therapeutically integrate these factors can increase stress, anxiety, and agitation, thereby reducing client ability to concentrate, think, learn, and sleep well (Ankenman, 2010). Considering these six factors and tailoring them to create a therapeutic eco-art therapy space is critical (Ankenman, 2010).

Light impacts mood and the ability to take in visual stimuli. When going outdoors, timing matters as the intensity of light and, therefore, heat, vary. A table positioned in the shade or under an umbrella is recommended to protect clients from direct midday sun (Craig, 2012 as cited in McMaster, 2013). Ideally, sessions take place in the morning to take advantage of the benefits that working in the morning sun can have on the circadian rhythm, cognition, and behavioral symptoms (McMaster, 2013). However, there are exceptions such as when reactions to morning medications might affect scheduling (Levine, 2010 as cited in McMaster, 2013). When converting an indoor setting into a green space, lighting can make all the difference. Using full-spectrum light or providing opportunities for clients to sit close to a window is ideal (McMaster, 2013). If your office doesn't have a window, using a grow light simulates outdoor sunlight and can provide a means to cultivate healthy indoor plants. These lights typically cost $10 for a single light or $35 for larger, multi-light units. Light Emitting Diodes (LEDs) are very energy efficient, generate a lot of light, produce minimal heat, and can even mimic natural sunlight in some instances (Baras, 2018). Although LEDs can come in various colors like red/blue, these can be overly stimulating and so full-spectrum white varieties may be the best choice. For client safety, light fixtures should always be oriented away from client eyes since directly looking into light can do physical harm.

Color can provide a sense of fascination and wonder. Outdoors, green is spliced with yellow, red, purple, blue, and red by flowers, bushes, butterflies, and more. Plants provide color. To bring natural color indoors, electrical hydroponic systems such as those offered by *AeroGarden* can provide controlled conditions for long-lasting growing periods. This particular brand offers seed pods and growing kits complete with seeds. I started out using these units because they were easy to use, self-watering, self-lighting, and the seeds came with the units. For instance, the flower, calendula, grows well in a hydroponic unit and can be used for dye or be dehydrated for collage. Much like hydroponics, aquaponics can offer another source of color and can be as simple as a fish tank housing a colorful beta fish with moss balls to help clean and oxygenate the water. Colorful succulents like aloe and air plants are easy to care for within a confined space, can be used in art making as they work well as wall hanging compositions within "living wall art." Moss, air plants, and aloe are low-maintenance plants and are also sound absorbing and air purifying. Living art can be created with clients regularly as a means to enhance both the clinical atmosphere as well as client home atmospheres. Color can also be added through window gardens with herbs and even orchids and violets which grow well in low light.

Sound helps to provide a means of positive distraction in sessions. When outdoors, the sound of birds singing, the wind blowing through trees, waves crashing, or insects chirping can stimulate a relaxation response. Indoors, forest or ocean sounds can serve as a background noise-maker. This provides added privacy for clients, but also exposure to nature sounds like singing birds has proven effective as a means to lower blood pressure and soothe clients (Williams, 2016). When selecting a soundtrack, choose one which is at least a 90-minute segment taken from a real outdoor location rather than a computer-generated loop of bird or waterfall sounds.

Aroma can remind clients to take deep, slow breaths and relish an experience. Outdoors, there are many smells like the ocean salts, or ripening fruit on a tree. Indoors, many therapists, like myself, incorporate essential oils into their practice. A diffuser can emit a therapeutic aroma continuously to enhance the olfactory ambiance during the session. Additionally, oils can be massaged into sculptural materials to promote a sensory effect during art making. As with all natural materials, caution is advised—if an essential oil is accidentally ingested or splattered into an eye, hospitalization may be necessary. Essential oils should be stored in a locked area to prevent any accidental exposures and taken out for topical use only; personally, I limit which essential oils I keep in my office and use only therapeutic-grade essential oils diluted with a non-allergenic carrier oil (e.g., coconut, olive, grapeseed). I keep on hand only essential oils which are suitable for the most vulnerable groups (e.g., young children aged two and over and pregnant clients) to decrease any likelihood of adverse reactions. Lavender is my primary go-to essential oil. I avoid pre-blended oils since they may have been diluted with peanut oil or other allergens and when I dilute an essential oil I add only one to two drops of essential oil per ounce of carrier oil.

Texture can cue memories and provide tactile stimulation. Outdoors, the variety of plants create this texture. Fuzzy ferns, prickly pines, and soft flowers together create a multitude of sensual experiences. Thanks to advances in technology like hydroponics, office settings can be equipped with a variety of textures. Plants improve the air quality in offices; as NASA research scientists suggest, include "two or three plants for every 100 square feet of floor area… The more plants, the cleaner the air—and the larger the plants, the better" (Clinebell, p. 164 as cited in Ankenman, 2010).

Space considerations can help clients feel relaxed or engaged. Outdoor spaces can seem limitless. However, indoors there are square footage constraints so by using resources such as vertical growing towers, wall hanging aquaponics, and table-top hydroponic systems, therapists can maximize space. Hanging low-light plants such as ferns from the ceiling can offer an additional means of maximizing natural elements within a confined area. Additionally, wall-mounted televisions showing natural scenes can serve as a digital window.

These six elements which help to foster a nature-as-setting experience—even within an office space—enliven the therapeutic experience and offer clients the chance to experience a health-enriching environment. When making an in-home visit, or serving clients remotely, providing psychoeducation on these six elements can also inspire clients to transform their living space into a therapeutically enriched environment.

As shown in Figure 2.2, because setting is central in eco-art therapy, even when simply using nature-as-subject or nature-as-material

QUEEN MARGARET UNIVERSITY LRC

Figure 2.2 Six Elements of Nature-as-Setting
Note. In this figure, the six major environmental factors which affect our physical and emotional well-being are illustrated: light, color, aroma, texture, sound, and space.

approaches in an indoor setting, embedding color, texture, space, sound, light, and aromas can help the process feel immersive.

For instance, when creating a paintbrush (nature-as-material) from pine needles, the smell of pine can permeate the room and the sound of the crackling needles can remind the client of walking in the forest. Taking the time to discuss these sensory experiences in session can elevate the experience and maximize the therapeutic potential.

Treatment Planning: "How is This Realistic?"

Therapists and educators are accountable for helping clients make measurable progress towards goals. Predetermined session goals help clients know what to expect, enable them to understand the purpose of the sessions, and empower them to fully participate. This process of establishing goals may also reveal the value of funding eco-art therapy spaces (e.g., gardens) among administrators. Clinical eco-art therapy may feel spontaneous, spiritual, and organic but is also SMART (Specific, Measurable, Achievable, Realistic, and Time-bound) just as with any other mental health intervention. In my clinical practice starting from the onset of therapy and periodically thereafter, I explicitly explore goals with clients beginning with questions on my intake form (see Appendix B):

INTAKE CONTENT

Motivation for session: Please describe the reason(s)/goal(s) for requesting services (be specific, if possible. When did the issue start? How does it affect you/their life?):

What goals do you have for therapy? _____
Put a check beside specific goals:

1. ___Stress reduction
2. ___Increased expressivity (non-verbal and verbal)
3. ___Improved self-esteem and self-worth
4. ___Identity and relationship exploration
5. ___Frustration tolerance/Anger management
6. ___Heightened emotional intelligence
7. ___Memory training
8. ___Relaxation and anxiety reduction
9. ___Enhanced fine/ gross motor coordination & visuospatial skills
10. ___Behavior regulation/ self-control/ autonomy
11. ___Coping skills/ self-soothing techniques
12. ___Improved social skills/ interpersonal skills
13. ___On-task behavioral skills/ concentration/ focus
14. ___Decision-making skills
15. ___Communication skills
16. ___ Other: _____

Figure 2.3 Intake Content

For clients to make progress though, the session duration, frequency, and format should be research-based, meaning pre-planned, and the process and outcomes should be well-documented. Decades of research demonstrate that sessions with declared goals and a definite schedule prove more effective because children and adults alike crave routine and structure (Norcross & Phillips, 2020). So do therapists and educators. The protocols included within this book all list the duration, frequency, and format to aid you in using, adapting, and modifying them when planning with clients.

Time and Schedule Efficiencies: Duration, Frequency, and Format

The eco-art therapy session durations will vary by goals and populations. The time it takes for individuals to engage with nature, sit, create art, share, and pack up at closing is going to depend on the directive as well as client engagement, attention span, and ability (McMaster, 2013). Ultimately, the goal is to plan session durations to afford enough time for clients to experience a state of flow and mindfulness within the session (McMaster, 2013).

A recent study found that people who spent at least two hours in nature per week were consistently more likely to report higher levels of health and well-being (Masterton, Carver, & Parkes, 2020). Given this, providing more than one weekly session or providing on-going weekly sessions may help promote therapeutic outcomes and allow clients to have the two full hours of time with nature per week. In the Appendix A protocols, the 90-minute session duration assumes clients commute or transition to and from session (e.g., 30 minutes total), which would result in two hours per week.

That said, some clients do not have the choice of staying in therapy over the long term either for financial or scheduling reasons. Depending on the population served, eco-art therapy session frequency can be anywhere from a single session to years of on-going sessions. The protocols in Appendix A are all ten weeks in duration with a weekly frequency to allow for continuity, routine, and structure, but each protocol segment (e.g., K/S, P/A, C/S) can be broken down into stand-alone sessions.

With many clients, stress can delay information processing speed, learning rate, and the ability to filter out distractions (Schwabe et al., 2012). Additionally, studies show that depression can lead to even more slowed processing speed (Gilley, Wilson, Bienias, Bennett, & Evans, 2004 in Pike, 2013). For this reason, session length within each Appendix A protocol is 90 minutes (1.5 hours) so clients who need the additional processing time have it. A once-a-week, 90-minute therapy frequency and duration has consistently demonstrated success in improving client functioning and progress (Pike, 2013).

Beyond planning the duration and frequency of sessions, the format will influence client outcomes. Eco-art therapy session format can be individual, dyad, family, or group. Individual eco-art therapy is suggested for first-time clients to fully introduce the therapy experience in a gentle, personal manner. Later, group-work limited to under ten participants may be a therapeutic ideal.

Facility Considerations: Funding and Budgeting

Facility administrators differ in their ability to support initiatives and so having a clear idea of the funding and budgeting necessary to implement eco-art therapy practices will provide administrators with insight into program feasibility. When collaborating with administrators on creating an onsite garden, many find that it's getting easier to convince higher-ups to hire a professional landscaper (Flottum, 2020). City, county, and even state governments are finally getting the message that setting aside a portion of land towards pollinator-plant gardens (which provide excellent art-making resources) is not only good for their image but when done right, it actually enhances the budget by cutting down on weekly mowing (Flottum, 2020).

In onsite gardens, pruning and trimming is a necessary process which results in routine harvesting of free art materials for the eco-art therapy sessions. As a result, many of the protocols potentially have a "0" dollar cost if natural materials are available for foraging. Natural materials are readily found for free outdoors in these gardens and include items such as: sand, clay, stone, shells, pine cones and needles, flowers, leaves, fruit, feathers, nuts, lichen, bark, wood, and straw (Whitaker, 2010, p. 123 as cited in McMaster, 2013).

Within the protocols in Appendix A, the budget listed references portion costs when items are purchased in bulk and do not include "extras" which carry non-recurring costs such as tools or equipment. Table 2.2 itemizes some of those "extras" which are good to have on hand within a clinical

Table 2.2 Budget for Non-Recurring Expenses

Optional Items	Cost	Example of Eco-Art Therapy Use
Microwave	$50	Dehydrating plants, thawing frozen berries for dye
Microwave dehydrator press	$50	Dry flowers and plants in under 5 minutes
Pyrography kit	$30	Burning designs into wood, gourds, and more
Convection oven	$75	Baking bread sculptures, plant-based clays
Hydroponic unit	$50	Growing flowers or plants indoors
Mini-refrigerator/freezer	$110	Preserving dyes or to help seeds germinate
Counter dehydrator	$60	Drying bark, roots, stems, and flowers in 3D shape
Coffee grinder	$15	Grinding seeds to create dye
Blender	$30	Creating pulp from plants to make paper
Silica in bulk – 5lbs	$10	Drying plant materials such as twigs, stems, leaves
Juicer	$70	Extracting pigmented juice for painting (e.g., beets)
Seedling trays in bulk	$10	Growing plants from seeds
Storage containers – 120 ct	$30	Organizing dehydrated plants and found objects
Mason jars of various sizes	$100	Extracting and storing pigment including iron/rust
Bulk sets of spices – 20ct	$45	Creating watercolors or aromatic mandala collages
Bulk sets of herbal teas – 50ct	$20	Infusing in water or oil with color for painting
Food powders – five colors, 10ct	$30	Infusing in water or oil for dying or painting
Bulk perennial wildflower seed	$40	Growing flowers for dye, collage, paper making
Pots and seedling trays, hand shovels, watering cans, and spray bottles	$100	Growing art materials

office setting to preserve natural resources and utilize a wider range of natural materials. These items require a one-time budget and may already be available in client homes or can be found second-hand for a lower cost.

In the budget table, I also include things like a hydroponic unit, mini-refrigerator, juicer, blender, and coffee grinder. These materials have a one-time cost but can make practicing eco-art therapy more convenient in clinical settings. For instance, when making natural dye by infusing teas in water, freezing the pigment in an ice cube tray will help make the dye last longer without any additives or preservatives. These items are optional and you may choose to get only one or two of the items.

For instance, drying flowers in silica can be cheaper than using a dehydrator so you may choose one over the other. Additionally, preserving art materials can be as simple as pressing flowers between the pages of a book, or hanging plants upside down to dry. However, I have found that timing is important when serving a variety of clients. I need to make sure I can quickly restock materials. A dehydrator or a microwave press can help ensure natural materials are always on hand. As an example, a microwave press can dry flowers and herbs in as little as 20 seconds. I also have a table-top dehydrator which I use for seeds, roots, vines, and other found objects which I want to maintain a 3D shape. For small objects which I want to be in 3D, I use silica. In silica, flowers and buds typically dry with color intact within three to five days. I like to use this between sessions since it requires no electricity and can be easily mobile. I have multiple-compartment storage bins with lids filled with silica to stay organized. If you decide to do the same, choose containers with a dark or opaque base to protect dried flowers from UV damage.

Planning an Eco-Art Therapy Resource Garden

Creating an onsite garden can save quite a bit of money on materials in the long run and creating an initial garden area for art material cultivation can cost as little as $5. The materials needed to create this garden include yellow and blue color pencils ($1), the *PlantSnap* app (free), marking spray paint ($2), and paper ($2). The first step is to collaborate with the facility manager to select an area away from sidewalks and buildings to designate as "no mow" for a minimum of three weeks but up to three months. After the no-mow period ends, document answers to the following questions using plant identification resources including apps like *PlantSnap*. All that is needed is time for observation, a willingness to take a chance, and being creative.

- Is the **no-mow zone** producing flowers or plants other than sod?
- Based on **positive identification**, can these plants be used in art making?
- What type of art making would be most appropriate given **historical uses** of the plants identified?

Plants will grow without human intervention and can serve as art-making resources. I have personally been guilty of viewing the presence of "weeds" as a sign that I am failing in the garden. However, throughout the pre-technological era, humans built their homes, made their clothing, grew their food, and produced crafts with "weeds," and the concept of some plant being "useless" did not exist. Ralph Waldo Emerson said that weeds are plants "whose virtues have yet to be discovered" (as cited in Easley & Horne, 2016). For example, common nettles which we humans consider a weed are the primary food source of the larvae of the breath-taking peacock butterfly, whose appearance in spring can offer clients joy (Houghton & Worroll, 2016). These same nettles are also the basis of myth and folklore, including the fairy tale of *The Wild Swans* by Hans Christian Andersen; they grow without any pesticides or fertilizer, through rain or drought, and under every fence, and in art, nettles have served as an indispensable material for textile creation (Blakeley, 2019).

Understanding what is growing naturally without interference can help create a vibrant and beautiful eco-system. Who doesn't enjoy seeing a butterfly?! In my own garden, I regularly find scattered butterfly wings and use them in collage—all thanks to "weeds." As a result, some people choose to abolish the four-letter word "weed" from their vocabulary altogether (Wiggins, 2020). Instead, identifying each plant and understanding its role may lead to a greater appreciation of what grows without effort!

Destroying or displacing what naturally grows may seem easier than identifying and using naturally occurring plants. However, I have found this to be an expensive and often unproductive practice. Identifying what grows naturally can be a way to quickly establish a garden. For instance, when I created a "no-mow" section to observe what would grow without intervention on my farm, periwinkles and marigold were among the plants! These flowers quickly took over the entire section and were beautiful. I quickly stocked materials and all I had to do was designate an area to stop mowing. The point is, you don't need to go out into the wilderness to find art-making plants (Easley & Horne, 2016). You may not even have to purchase plants or seeds. Most common lawn and garden "weeds" have art-making value.

If you decide to add to what is growing naturally on your site, many useful plants can be found at garden nurseries so you can easily plant them in your yard or grow them in pots as houseplants (Easley & Horne, 2016). If you believe clients will delight in seeing butterflies, plant their favorites like fruiting bushes, Mexican sunflowers, zinnia, holy basil, and native milkweed among existing flora (Burroughs, 2020). When buying seeds or plants to put in my garden for art making, I like to do a cost/benefit analysis and consider plant life span and growth rate, the fiscal investment, and eco-art therapy applications. For instance, I ask myself:

- *Is the plant a perennial, meaning it will grow for multiple years?*
- Perennials may take longer to establish but will not need to be replanted each year, therefore saving me time and money. I like to start with perennials and fill in with annuals. If I add annuals, I choose those which "readily reseed" so there is no recurring cost. In general, cottage-garden perennials are easiest, cheapest, and more environmentally friendly since they should last forever (Goulson, 2020).
- *How fast does the plant grow?*
- Some plants take years to reach maturity or even to germinate! When cultivating plants for art making, I need plants which grow quickly and which reseed themselves to produce more plants. To conserve budgets, plants which grow from cuttings or have seeds with high germination rates are good choices. These plants can be propagated quickly to provide many clients with plant material for their home gardens or to enrich agency settings.
- *What is the cost of a one-pound bag of seed?*
- Buying in bulk allows me to cover a large section of land but also enables me to share resources with clients so they can grow their own art materials.
- *Does the plant have multiple purposes and uses?*
- Some plants have many different uses. If my client cannot afford to cover material costs, it works to my advantage to grow plants which are multipurpose. For instance, some plants are edibles but also serve as dyes, pulp for paper making, fiber for weaving, flowers for collage, and more. That way, I can still use the plant personally for its edible value while dehydrating and saving the remaining parts for art making with clients. I see gardening as self-care so when the plant is multipurpose, my self-care serves me professionally and personally. If an edible plant, like fennel, is also a butterfly host plant (those which adult butterflies use to raise their larval young), I get even more joy while in the garden. I enjoy seeing a variety of butterflies while collecting art materials and the only way for this to happen is if there are multipurpose plants throughout the garden.

Personally, when I first set up an eco-art therapy resource garden, I used a cost/benefit analysis and decided to begin cultivating perennial, edible wildflowers. They were beautiful, edible as garnishes, required little to no care or maintenance, grew in poor soils, were drought tolerant, and served as both nectar and host plants for butterflies! These flowers also provided multiple materials including gnarled roots which looked like trees; flowers of many colors and shapes for dying, stamping, and collage-making; sturdy tall stems for coiling into containers and pulping into paper; and leaves for resist paintings, leaf sewing, and more. If you go looking, you can find bags and bags of wildflower or pollinator seed packets online selected by experts to grow in your area and specifically equipped to thrive (Flottum, 2020).

When managing an eco-art therapy garden, mulching is key to preparing an area for seeds and limiting plants which may appear unsightly to decision-makers (Flottum, 2020). Creating an area which appears planned is key to avoiding the "abandoned lot" look and continuing to receive funding (Flottum, 2020). When planting, clump plants close together so they shade out unwanted plants and conserve moisture (Lanza, 2020). Lay cardboard over unwanted plants and then cover the cardboard in mulch. As researchers and gardeners alike will tell you, using cardboard and mulch together to prevent unwanted growth is very efficient (Wiggins, 2020). Cardboard serves a dual purpose; in addition to suppressing unwanted growth, it retains moisture (Wiggins, 2020).

Chapter Summary

Sessions with declared goals and a definite schedule prove more effective and so, although gathering from and being inspired by nature is one aspect of eco-art therapy, another critical aspect is the planning. Choosing the right environment, method, and material according to the client's needs will influence outcomes. For that reason, eco-art therapy is most feasible when therapists and clients decide together among the three approaches: nature-as-setting, material, and/or subject. To make eco-art therapy even more feasible, plan eco-art therapy session durations to afford enough time for the individual client to experience a state of flow and mindfulness. Beyond planning the duration and frequency of sessions, the format will influence client outcomes. Introducing eco-art therapy as an individual intervention may help you to evaluate client needs and responses to understand what type of group would be the best fit. Another key feasibility consideration is material and associated costs. You don't need to go out into the wilderness to find art-making plants since a backyard no-mow zone, window garden, or hydroponic station is often sufficient. However, if you decide to cultivate a resource garden, buying seeds or plants in bulk based on plant life span and growth rate is a good idea.

References

Abbott, K., Shanahan, M., & Neufeld, R. (2013). Artistic tasks outperform nonartistic tasks for stress reduction. *Art Therapy*, 30, 71–78.

Ankenman, N. (2010). *An ecology of the imagination an ecology of the imagination: A theoretical and practical exploration of the imagination for holistic healing in the context of art therapy.* Eco Art Land: Landing in the Space Between Art and Ecology. https://ecoartland.wordpress.com/an-ecology-of-the-imagination/.

Baras, T. (2018). *DIY hydroponic gardens: How to design and build an inexpensive system for growing plants in water.* Quatro Publishing Group, USA Inc.

Blakeley, D. (2019). In textile arts. *Feuer und Wasser*. www.feuer-und-wasser.com/blog.

Burroughs, G. (2020, January). Plant it and they will come. *2 Million Blossoms*, 1(2), 49–56.

Carr, S. M. (2020). Art therapy and COVID-19: Supporting ourselves to support others. *International Journal of Art Therapy*, 25(2), 49–51.

Case, C., & Dalley, T. (2014). *The handbook of art therapy*. Routledge.

Dalebroux, A., Goldstein, T. R., & Winner, E. (2008). Short-term mood repair through art-making: Positive emotion is more effective than venting. *Motivation and Emotion*, 32(4), 288–295.

Easley, T., & Horne, S. (2016). *The modern herbal dispensatory: A medicine-making guide*. North Atlantic Books.

Flottum, K. (2020, January). The good, the bad, and the ugly. *2 Million Blossoms*, 1(2), 29–32.

Galhena, D. H., Freed, R., & Maredia, K. M. (2013). Home gardens: A promising approach to enhance household food security and wellbeing. *Agriculture & Food Security*, 2(1), 8.

Geha, J. (2019). *Nature as an impermanent canvas: An intergenerational nature-based art community engagement project*. Expressive Therapies Capstone Theses: Lesley University. 113. https://digitalcommons.lesley.edu/expressive_theses/113.

Goulson, D. (2020, January). Gardening for pollinators. *2 Million Blossoms*, 1(2), 90–95.

Houghton, P., & Worroll, J. (2016). *Play the forest school way: Woodland games, crafts and skills for adventurous kids*. Watkins Media Limited.

Kapitan, L. (2011). "But is it ethical?" Articulating an art therapy ethos. *Art Therapy*, 28(4), 150–151. https://doi.org/10.1080/07421656.2011.624930.

Kopytin, A. I., & Rugh, M. M. (Eds.). (2016). *Green Studio: Nature and the arts in therapy*. Nova Science Publishers, Incorporated.

Kopytin, A., & Rugh, M. (Eds.). (2017). *Environmental expressive therapies: Nature-assisted theory and practice*. Taylor & Francis.

Lanza, J. (2020, January). The parsley plant and the swallowtail. *2 Million Blossoms*, 1(2), 33–38.

Masterton, W., Carver, H., & Parkes, T. (2020). *Parks and green spaces are important for our mental health–but we need to make sure that everyone can benefit*. https://dspace.stir.ac.uk/retrieve/af8d1ac4-b4d3-48b7-9060-d8143fb8e29b/Masterton-Carver-Parkes-Conversation-2020.pdf.

McMaster, M. (2013). *Integrating nature into group art therapy interventions for clients with dementia*. Unpublished research paper for the degree of Master of Arts: Concordia University. https://spectrum.library.concordia.ca/978027/1/McMaster_MA_F2013.pdf.

Milbrandt, M. K., & Anderson, T. (2005). *Art for life: Authentic instruction in art*. McGraw-Hill.

Norcross, J. C., & Phillips, C. M. (2020). Psychologist self-care during the pandemic: Now more than ever. *Journal of Health Service Psychology*, 1–5.

Pike, A. A. (2013). The effect of art therapy on cognitive performance among ethnically diverse older adults. *Art Therapy*, 30(4), 159–168.

Pouso, S., Borja, A., Fleming, L. E., Gómez-Baggethun, E., White, M. P., & Uyarra, M. C. (2020). *Maintaining contact with blue-green spaces during the*

COVID-19 pandemic associated with positive mental health. https://osf.io/prep rints/socarxiv/gpt3r/.

Pritchard, C. (2020). *Fostering hope in adolescents via art therapy teen group.* Expressive Therapies Capstone Theses: Lesley University. 267. https://digita lcommons.lesley.edu/expressive_theses/267.

Saraceno, J. (2017). *CBT eco-art therapy: Mood regulation with young adults in nature.* Notre Dame de Namur University.

Schwabe, L., Joëls, M., Roozendaal, B., Wolf, O. T., & Oitzl, M. S. (2012). Stress effects on memory: An update and integration. *Neuroscience & Biobehavioral Reviews,* 36(7), 1740–1749.

Serfass, D. G., & Sherman, R. A. (2013). Personality and perceptions of situations from the Thematic Apperception Test. *Journal of Research in Personality,* 47(6), 708–718.

Walter, Z. K. (2015). *The outer limits of cognitive processing: A closer look at what is desirable.* Undergraduate Honors Thesis Collection: Butler University. 253. https://digitalcommons.butler.edu/ugtheses/253.

Wiggins, C. (2020, January). Cardboard flowerbed. *2 Million Blossoms,* 1(2), 81–84.

Williams, F. (2016). This is your brain on nature. *National Geographic,* 229(1), 48–69.

Wolk, N., Barak, A., & Yaniv, D. (2020). Different shades of beauty: Adolescents' perspectives on drawing from observation. *Frontiers in Psychology,* 11, 687. https://doi.org/10.3389/fpsyg.2020.00687.

3 Assessment and Ethics

Clinical Considerations

As professionals, we build authentic relationships with our clients while also being responsible and accountable for our clinical choices which impact those clients. Because each client is unique and each clinical situation distinct, confident decision making grounded in preserving client dignity is essential. Many ethical dilemmas lack obvious right or wrong answers, and so we may lack an external "compass" outside of our own moral code, ideals, virtues, and conscience to make the right decision. Yet, trusting ourselves and using professional ethical codes and standards as guidelines are critical steps to provide clear-minded eco-art therapy sessions.

Teachers and therapists are societal leaders helping to better the community, especially in times of uncertainty when many look to us when striving to overcome fear and anxiety. As described in research, upheavals in society energize demands for authentic leaders; COVID-19, the destruction on 9/11, corporate scandals at companies like WorldCom and Enron, and massive failures in the banking industry all inspire people to look for those they can trust and for leaders who are honest and good (Northouse, 2010, p. 205 as cited in Agbude, Obayan, Ademola, & Abasilim, 2017). Helping professionals strive to be those trustworthy light posts.

As helping professionals, we need to be sure of ourselves, particularly when taking clients into nature or using new materials with clients. Eco-art therapy practices inherently incorporate positive approaches to ethical decision making (Hinz, 2011, p. 185–186). This approach emphasizes our own as well as client strengths and virtues, fostering empowerment while embracing limits within a trusting relationship (Hinz, 2011, p. 185–186). Through an ethic-of-care for self, others, and the natural world, eco-art therapy can support clients in becoming emotionally, socially, and environmentally aware (Steele & Scott, 2014, p. 237 as cited in Struckman, 2020). Keeping ethics in the forefront of eco-art therapy practices through a positive approach empowers us as helping professionals and positions clients to become active partners in formulating treatment goals and making decisions, reducing fear and instilling self-confidence. (Hinz, 2011, pp. 185–186).

Many eco-art therapy directives are readily adapted with modified approaches and materials to serve a wide range of clients. For instance, modern materials complement eco-art therapy practices. Using a video app on a phone, clients can capture experiences in nature during sessions and the inclusion of technology may decrease resistance. However, with these modifications come ethical considerations (Alders, Beck, Allen, & Mosinski, 2011). iPads, digital photography, and videography make it easy to post therapy content to social media. This may have positive social implications but may also come with over-disclosure so clients should be advised to post with caution or simply keep content private (Alders, Beck, Allen, & Mosinski, 2011).

As another example, when going out into nature with a client or incorporating found objects, the therapist along with the client may have a physiological reaction to the beauty or the natural stimuli. An important clinical consideration then lies in the concept of boundary crossing (D'Souza & De Sousa, 2017). Going beyond a clinical setting or going beyond using sterile commercial materials can feel personal and meaningful—as it should. That said, professional boundaries are critical to ensuring client symptoms remain contained. Boundary crossing may be inevitable when traveling to a natural park or even when walking in a garden with a client (D'Souza & De Sousa, 2017). There is spontaneity and unpredictability for both the therapist and client.

As D'Souza and De Sousa (2017) note, boundary crossings are benign when they are grounded in respect for client dignity, are openly discussed with clients, and are non-exploitative. In some cultures, it is not unusual for clients to enquire about the therapist's or educator's likes and dislikes or to ask certain questions which may be personal. Many therapists are trained to safeguard against boundary crossing to such an extent that they sometimes come off cold, rigid, formal, and inapproachable. In this case, clients may reject such therapists who behave more professional than human because in some therapeutic moments, good rapport with a client involves careful boundary crossing (D'Souza & De Sousa, 2017).

Certain boundary crossings by therapists, such as incorporating setting within an eco-art therapy approach, can be in the client's best interest. In this setting, a higher level of authenticity and "realness" may be experienced by both the therapist and the client. Staying mindful and grounding practices in a therapeutic rationale ensures boundary crossing does not lead to a boundary violation. Boundary violations are events which are harmful to the client and exploitative of the client's vulnerable position in therapy (D'Souza & De Sousa, 2017). During eco-art therapy, the following should be strictly avoided: accepting gifts, excessive and on-going physical touch, any sexual or romantic interaction, excessive therapist disclosure, meeting outside the therapy times, having lunch or dinner with clients, and confidentiality violations (D'Souza & De Sousa, 2017).

Codes of ethics specific to your field will reinforce these safety guidelines. These documents reinforce the importance of practices or procedures which fit a therapist's scope of practice, experience, training, and education. Within the field of art therapy, the professional documents which provide content regarding professional standards and ethics include (but are not limited to):

- Art Therapy Credentials Board (ATCB)—Code of Ethics, Conduct, and Disciplinary Procedures; and
- American Art Therapy Association (AATA)—Ethical Principles for Art Therapists

If going outdoors is clinically appropriate, foraging is such a wonderful experience and truly connects us and our clients to natural surroundings but caution is necessary (Houghton & Worroll, 2016). When selecting artifacts like feathers and shells, ensure the object is sterilized prior to use among clients. Know your local area and wildlife to understand the risks associated with certain artifacts (e.g., avian flu virus). When selecting plants, some can be toxic, rare, or poisonous and so only pick what you can positively identify. If in doubt, leave it alone and follow local regulations about what you can and cannot pick (Houghton & Worroll, 2016).

Therapist experience and training is essential for positively identifying plants. Accidentally choosing plants which cause dermatitis or respiratory ills would impede therapeutic outcomes and may cause the client harm. Additionally, if a therapist and client are in a public outdoor area like a natural park, confidentiality may be a concern and so therapists will want to know the location well prior to bringing a client. Know which areas are densely populated and those which are not to promote client comfort with sharing and disclosing life experiences.

Before taking a client into a natural setting offsite, make sure the client is likely to therapeutically benefit. For instance, taking a client who is actively experiencing psychosis into an offsite park would place that client and therapist in danger. Therefore, conducting a *Global Assessment of Functioning* on an on-going basis can help determine the appropriate scope of eco-art therapy, be it nature-as-setting, material, or subject. Personally, I ensure clients are functioning at a minimum of a 70 on this scale with no active psychosis, suicide ideation, or active self-harm tendencies before incorporating setting within my eco-art therapy practice. The only exception is if the agency or facility has an onsite garden and there are available staff members to ensure the client-to-therapist ratio remains therapeutic.

Also, whenever possible, a photographic representation should be maintained for all eco-art therapy artwork created by the client.

INTAKE CONSENT CONTENT

I give permission to: (Check all that apply.)

1. _____ *Have my artwork photographed for documentation/ record-keeping purposes.*

OPTIONAL
Confidentiality of Records: *If any of the following are indicated, your identity will be kept confidential. Your name will be kept private.*

2. _____ *Have the information from sessions used in professional publications and presentations.*
3. _____ *Have my artwork used in professional presentations and publications*
4. _____ *Have photos/video content posted online on websites to promote sessions.*

I understand that:

_____ *Artwork and information that is posted online, even when visibly removed from a website, remain accessible indefinitely.*

Figure 3.1 Intake Consent Content

Photographic representation ensures documentation, especially when the original artwork may be difficult to preserve such as when constructing an outdoor mandala, rock sculpture, or raked sand design at the beach. Additionally, eco-art therapy materials may age poorly if not preserved using pH-neutral glue or acid-free paper, and so a photograph would be essential to preserving the original creation. I have used a consent form template for discussing this process with clients and it includes an explicit consent for photographing artwork and confidentiality (see *Intake* in Appendix B):

A final element to consider is that art therapists should use names or designations for their practices which accurately inform the public concerning their educational background, identity, and status. In the case of someone practicing eco-art therapy, this person would not be an "eco-art therapist" since there is no governing body for "eco-art therapy" specifically, but instead a therapist/educator may "specialize in eco-art therapy practices." For example, I am an art therapist and educator and I practice eco-art therapy. Another person might be a counselor, a psychologist, or other trained professional. The practice is nested within the profession.

Ethics of Sustainability in Eco-Art Therapy

Eco-art therapy practices offer new ways of thinking and interacting with the environment (Ankenman, 2010). The process embodies sustainable practices like respecting biodiversity and avoiding the depletion of natural resources (Everden 1978, p. 20 as cited in Ankenman, 2010). Genetic diversity is a trusted metric of how well a species is doing and eco-art therapy can provide a means of amplifying this diversity. For example, while foraging for art resources, therapists can choose non-native, invasive plants as often as possible to help keep those plants limited in number (Brown, 2020). By choosing non-native, invasive plants for art making, you will create an opportunity for native plants to grow in their place. Native plants are those which occurred and evolved prior to colonization. By removing non-natives, you help to restore eco-systems and feeding wildlife (Jiménez-Alfaro, Frischie, Stolz, & Gálvez-Ramírez, 2020).

Eco-art therapy may facilitate engagement in pro-environmental behavior when sessions provide an opportunity for clients to learn how to engage respectfully with nature through actions aimed at preservation and cultivation (Kopytin & Rugh, 2017; Scheirich, 2020). This process models an effort to promote durable living on a finite planet (Kopytin & Rugh, 2017). To promote preservation and cultivation, teach clients ethical wildcrafting practices formally before going outdoors.

For instance, when collecting materials for art making, only pick flowers or dig up roots for plants which are in abundance. If collecting shells from the beach, collect in places and during times which will not disturb vulnerable wildlife like nesting turtles. Also, choose shells which are unsuitable habitats for crabs or other creatures. When collecting materials, consider the wildlife which will be impacted by the choices you and clients make. Therapists and educators can advise clients to avoid taking branches which have flowers or berries on them, as these provide food for wildlife and the seeds of future trees. When foraging for materials during sessions, clients should look first to the forest floor for materials (Houghton & Worroll, 2016). Also, when preparing for sessions, therapists and educators may want to check on the United Plant Savers website (www.unitedplantsavers.org) for a list of plants which are at risk of depletion and are suffering from habitat loss to avoid picking those plants (Easley & Horne, 2016). More specifically, we can follow some simple guidelines to ensure sustainable practices. Those include: avoiding depletion, ensuring regrowth, seeking permission, and staying organized (Easley & Horne, 2016):

Avoiding depletion entails a careful approach to foraging such as selecting plants which can naturally reproduce and continue providing food for wildlife. So if there is only one flower, don't pick it. Otherwise, that flower cannot create seeds to produce more flowers. Gather plants only where they are abundant. Never take more than 10% of the plants in a given area. Always leave plenty of plants so that nature can replenish its supply. Know what you will be using the plant for before you gather it to prevent waste and only harvest the part of the plant you intend to use. Also, try not to gather from wet ground, where footprints can damage the soil and make future growth more challenging. Leave an area in better shape than you left it.

Ensuring regrowth entails keen decision making such as gathering leaves, seeds, and flowers which grow back easily rather than barks and roots, since the loss of these may kill the plant. Harvest bark with respect for the needs of the tree and preferably from recently pruned or fallen branches. For example, if you cut bark off around the circumference of a tree, you will kill it. Instead, look for branches and bark which are on the ground. When you harvest plants on a hill, leave the plants at the top of the hill untouched so seeds and roots wash downhill to replenish the slope.

Seeking permission may seem easy for therapists and educators who have community partnerships and allies. However, for clients, they may need to be taught and directly told to ask before picking plants. For instance, clients shouldn't harvest plants from other people's property without their permission. If you or clients are harvesting from government land, make sure you know what the laws and regulations are as it's illegal to harvest plants from some countries' national parks (e.g., United States).

Staying organized decreases the likelihood of waste. To ensure you maximize the use of what you gather, harvest only one species of plant at a time to avoid confusion. Individual plant parts like leaves are easy to get mixed up among different species. Label everything carefully as soon as you get home. Dry or process plants as quickly as possible to ensure that the plants you do harvest are put to good use rather than wasted. For instance, Easley and Horne (2016) provide the following advice: Keep fresh flowers loose and in open containers so they do not congeal and mold. When flowers are dry (crumble when rubbed between fingers), store them whole in dark, airtight containers. Succulent leaves should be frozen and not dried. Roots can be difficult or even impossible to cut when dry so chop large roots into small pieces while still fresh.

Incorporating sustainability concepts within sessions is a means of modeling empathy, respect, place-based social action, and environmental activism (Inwood & Kennedy, 2020). As a result, the eco-art therapy process can help beautify and enhance areas. For instance, by selecting a non-native, invasive plant for art making, you remove a plant which is taking over an area, limiting biodiversity and displacing food sources for wildlife. Additionally, therapists may choose to strive towards a zero-waste approach as part of their eco-art therapy practices. Using a preservation mindset, a therapist or educator may also choose to use all parts of the plant or to cultivate only plants which are root-to-flower useful for therapeutic purposes so no part is wasted. Another option would be to compost plant parts left unused. A more creative example entails using (instead of throwing away) scrap paper; a therapist may shred that paper, mix it with water, seeds, and some soil to create seed balls which the client could plant in their home garden. The paper then becomes mulch to help conserve water for the plant as it grows. This process serves as a reminder to appreciate the natural world and acknowledge how our actions of either wasting or reusing directly affect it. Hopefully, our approaches within eco-art therapy sessions can serve as a role model to others around us and inspire them to conserve and cultivate natural settings.

Using only what you need and knowing what is "enough" is integral to eco-art therapy processes. Knowing when you have "enough" is a therapeutic process and is illustrated nicely in a classic fable, present in numerous cultures, called the *Fisherman and the Businessman* (adapted from Coehlo, 2015, original source unknown):

> Once upon a time a businessman sat on a beach where he saw a villager quickly catch a large fish and pack to leave. The businessman excitedly approached the fisherman.
>
> "Leaving so soon?" the businessman inquired.
>
> "This is plenty to feed my family," shrugged the fisherman.
>
> "But what do you do the rest of the day?" stuttered the businessman in disbelief.
>
> The fisherman smiled, "Go home, play with my kids, nap with my wife, and then join friends to play guitar, sing and dance."
>
> The businessman scratched his head, "I could help you to be successful. From now on, work day and night catching as much as possible. Save, buy a big boat, catch even more, and use that money to set up a company to can fish. Then you can retire, play with your kids, nap with your wife... join friends to play guitar, sing and dance!"
>
> The fisherman laughed, walking away "I do that already!"

In Western society, researchers easily document patterns of people wanting more, more, more, and this is where neurochemistry comes in. Studies show that the pleasure center of our brain lights up more during giving and sharing than when acquiring and winning. The reason "more" doesn't satisfy is because of a missing experience—one rooted in a caring connection and a meaningful life based on doing something prosocial or creative (Eisler, 2019). The preoccupation with getting and wasting is often a means of seeking a substitute for unmet emotional needs (Eisler, 2019).

Quality of life often involves being happy with what you have rather than constantly yearning for something more. This feeling of being satiated is exemplified in eco-art therapy when a *Reduce, Reuse, and Recycle* motto is applied in sessions (Kopytin & Rugh, 2016; Scheirich, 2020). For instance, using thrifted, recycled, or found objects (i.e., natural or re-used manmade objects) minimizes single-use art materials (Scheirich, 2020). Beyond this, eco-art therapy practices ideally incorporate the basics: recycling bins, mindful and proper disposal of art supplies, non-toxic paints and supplies, and modeled conservational behaviors for clients (Ankenman, 2010). These foundational practices provide many benefits for the environment and session outcomes. Utilizing recycled materials can help cut costs, both financial and ecological, may help clients to become more conscious of consumerist habits, and empower clients to increase imaginative abilities more adeptly (Ankenman, 2010).

By taking a zero-waste approach, eco-art therapy practices demonstrate a respect for the environment while creating an opportunity for clients to reconnect to nature in times of increasing ecological loss (Ankenman, 2010). Given this loss, themes of preservation, cultivation, and sustainability may be met with expressions of grief and fear (Ankenman, 2010). Chellis Glendinning's book, entitled *My Name is Chellis & I'm in Recovery from Western Civilization*, addresses this concept of ecological grief (Glendinning, 1994 as cited in Ankenman, 2010). From this perspective, "weeping about injured seals is as healthy and normal as weeping about one's injured childhood" (Glendinning, 1994, p. 163 as cited in Ankenman, 2010). In sessions and particularly groups, a shared acknowledgment of ecological loss and the resulting grief may serve as a step towards ethical action and a starting point to process eco-historical traumas (Ankenman, 2010).

As eco-art therapy gains in popularity, places will be transformed along with the people within them. However, the practice of eco-art therapy itself is visionary and relies on an ethical and sustainable concept of quality of life. Whatever we can each do to strengthen the community and enrich relationships is truly worthwhile and while eco-art therapy is simply one means, it truly fulfills an increasing human need.

Informal and Formal Assessment: "When is This Safe?"

Assessing Client-Approach Fit

Safety applies to multiple areas since a therapeutic experience should be both emotionally as well as physically safe. Candid discussions with clients are necessary to understand whether an eco-art therapy approach is a fit for any given client and whether going outdoors or bringing nature inside is the best approach to meet therapeutic goals.

As mentioned in Chapter 1, the *Maslow Assessment of Needs Scales* (MANS), *Global Assessment of Functioning, Ottawa Mood Scale*, and *Nature-Relatedness Scale* may serve well as an initial assessment. Additionally, a *Task Enjoyment Questionnaire* after each session can provide insight into which directives are most congruent with client culture and interests.

Two informal drawing assessments may help explore clients' relationship with nature alongside the *Ottawa Mood Scale* and *Nature-Relatedness Scale*. Those are: *Safe Place Drawing and A Favorite Kind of Day* (AFKOD; Manning Rauch, 1987 as cited in Betts, 2016). AFKOD considers the weather to gain an understanding of how a client views their interpersonal environment. The *Safe Place Drawing* explores a real or imaginary "safe place," where the client could go when afraid or upset (Gantt & Greenstone, 2016). When used as informal assessments, these directives can help therapists and educators explore client interests and perceptions as a precursor to eco-art therapy session planning.

Some clients may naturally imagine an outdoor place as a safe and favored place to go. Others, even if prompted, would struggle with the mere idea of feeling safe outdoors and their favorite kind of day may be restricted to indoor settings. This preference and emotional reaction to the outdoors and to nature is important to explore early on. Additionally, a literal "safe place" creation can be integrated into sessions such as through creating an outdoor structure. Along these lines, as seen in Figure 3.2, there are several areas to consider to evaluate safety for clients. This includes client perceptions and history. If a client has a trauma history, immersive, nature-as-setting approaches may not be emotionally safe but nature-as-subject or nature-as-material may be.

Some cultures have generational fears related to outdoor settings. For instance, I worked with a client from South Africa who compared nature parks in the U.S. to farms in South Africa where farmers were slaughtered due to on-going unrest caused by apartheid horrors. This client was comfortable using dried flowers indoors but was not comfortable collecting those flowers or visiting open areas with neighboring

Figure 3.2 Outdoor Eco-Art Therapy Safety Quick Reference
Note. In this figure, some considerations for client safety are presented as a quick reference. However, client safety is a multifaceted consideration which extends beyond these items and requires an individualized assessment.

forests. Similarly, one of my African American clients described stories her grandmother told her of black people being violently targeted in outdoor areas. She had no interest in going outdoors, even to the front garden of the facility. However, she was very interested in hammering flowers to create prints on fabric for a quilt we were sewing together. In my intake form, I include key questions to begin a dialogue with clients regarding whether eco-art therapy practices will be a good fit (see Figure 3.3).

Asking clients about allergies, and allowing them to freely associate as related to nature and their past experiences will help you understand if eco-art therapy is appropriate for a client and which approach is the best fit (e.g., nature-as-material, setting, or subject).

Beyond the initial intake, to further explore which intervention category of eco-art therapy is safest and most appropriate for each individual client, consider using some classic art therapy projective assessments. These assessments can facilitate conversations with clients about eco-art therapy approaches. Projective drawing assessments are based on the assumption that people "project" their own needs, feelings, and thoughts. However, I prefer to use these assessments informally given significant variations attributed to age, race, and culture (Betts, 2003). Instead, I use many art therapy assessments as part of a more in-depth assessment process to (Betts, 2003):

- Determine a client's level of functioning;
- Formulate treatment objectives;
- Assess a client's strengths;
- Gain a deeper understanding of a client's presenting problems; and
- Evaluate client progress.

For instance, the *Draw a Person in the Rain* (DAPR) assessment has been used to elicit information about client stress levels and defenses (Lichtenberg, 2014). Evaluation of the drawing involves examining specific environmental elements (e.g., number of raindrops, lightning bolts) and their relationship to the human figure in the drawing (Lichtenberg, 2014). However, the drawing or painted version can simply be a point of reference during a conversation about being outdoors and the client's comfort level with unpredictability. Nature-as-setting approaches may include rainy weather even if the forecast predicted otherwise. Discussing this reality with clients is an important preparation element.

Another assessment which includes ecological elements is *Picking an Apple from a Tree* (PPAT). This assessment is scored using the *Formal Elements Art Therapy Scale* (FEATS) which quantifies and correlates components of the picture and picture plane with mental health symptoms (Gantt, 2016). However, when used more informally to engage

INTAKE QUESTIONNAIRE

Have you/ the client experienced any of the following? *(Put a check by those which apply)*

____*Seasonal allergies. Explain:*

_____.

____*Allergies to certain plants. Explain:*

_____.

____*Allergies to insect bites or stings. Explain:*

_____.

____*A past experience involving a strong emotional experience while in nature. Explain:*

_____.

____*Childhood memories related to the outdoors. Explain:*

_____.

Complete each sentence.

I find outdoor, natural areas like _____ *very relaxing.*

Being in the wilderness is

_____.

When I see an insect or reptile I

_____.

One of my memories being outdoors alone is

_____.

When I see landscape paintings in a museum or as a home decor, I think

_____.

Outdoors, people collect things such as _____ *to*

_____.

People who paint outdoors are probably _____.

Using nature as an art material is _____.

In my home, I have _____ *from nature.*

Figure 3.3 Intake Questionnaire

clients in dialogue, the directive can provide insight into culture, life experiences, and life skills such as problem solving and logic (Gantt & Tabone, 1998). In my particular area in South Florida, for instance, my clients are more likely to have picked a coconut, avocado, lychee, or mango from a tree than an apple and discussing these regional attributes can reveal a client's background as well as their familiarity with outdoor settings and materials.

Beyond culture, I have found that the PPAT assessment, when used as an directive, allows for conversations regarding nature as a food source, a place of comfort, and as inspiration for spiritual and religious beliefs. For instance, during the PPAT assessment, I once had a client associate "picking an apple from a tree" with Eve's eating the "forbidden fruit" from Christian depictions of Genesis 3:7, *Tree of the Knowledge of Good and Evil*. This client's religious beliefs interpreted the biblical Genesis story in ways which reinforced her interest in eco-art therapy. Cultivating an Eden-like garden was therapeutic for her, aligned with her religious values, and facilitated our eco-art therapy sessions. For her, immersive, nature-as-setting was very appropriate.

If you plan to take a client into a natural setting, you may want to determine the client's level of motor coordination and visuospatial skills. Visuospatial skills allow clients to perceive objects in relation to each other and to themselves and are essential skills when navigating a natural setting to avoid undue risks related to tripping or falling. Visuospatial skills include figure–ground perception, such as the ability to separate the foreground from the background when depicting landscape scenes in art, and is a skill needed in daily living (Pike, 2014). Showing a client an image and exploring *Visual Thinking Strategies* is an informal way to assess visual spatial skills and the process would include questions like (Ishiguro et al., 2019): *What do you think is going on in this image?* More formally, the *Bender Visual Motor Gestalt Test* (abbreviated as Bender-Gestalt test) is a psychological test used by mental health practitioners (Piotrowski, 2016). This test assesses visual-motor functioning, developmental disorders, and neurological impairments in children and adults (Piotrowski, 2016).

Beyond assessment, to ensure safety when collecting art materials outdoors, have a route in mind for your walk with a beginning and an end point (Houghton & Worroll, 2016). Offer a walking stick as a staff to help clients' walking stability. Also, start with short walks lasting no more than 15 minutes in total and increase the time outdoors from there as appropriate.

Risk Management

When working indoors with natural materials, moderate risks by ensuring proper ventilation, adequate lighting, access to water, knowledge of hazards or toxicity, and confidentiality (AATA, 2013). As a quick reference, within each protocol in Appendix A there is a section entitled, *Safety and Ethics: Modifications.* For instance, within the protocol, *Inspired*, the following safety and ethics considerations are referenced:

- **Material Toxicity or Allergens:** *Use non-toxic paint sources*
- **Client History Considerations:** *Discuss associations with images to assess potential trauma history in natural settings*

Safety of materials is an on-going consideration for art therapists as we judge the appropriateness of various media for clients based on age, ability, allergies, and other relevant considerations. This is even more important with eco-art therapy practices since you may be foraging or wildcrafting materials. Introducing clients to the names of plants can enhance memory and language skills but can also enhance the likelihood of positive identification, and therefore ensure client safety during art making (Houghton & Worroll, 2016).

Some saps are corrosive (including celandine and fig sap), so wear protective gloves before cutting, pruning, or harvesting plants (Easley & Horne, 2016). Materials used in art making must be non-toxic since clients may have an undeniable urge to taste things or their muscle memory may cause them to inadvertently place something in their mouth (McMaster, 2013). If a sealant or glaze is required for weather-proofing artwork, application must occur outside in well-ventilated areas (McMaster, 2013).

If using potting soils or mulch, a mask may be an important consideration. Potting soil and mulch have become my essentials for growing my own material since, from a permaculture perspective, mulch rebuilds soil and can restore eco-systems in line with sustainability values (Lawton, 2008; Luna, Dávila, & Reynoso-Morris, 2018). However, mulch is host for many micro-organisms, which serves the plants well but can be stressful for the body when exposure is long term. To prevent health problems, I wear a mask while moving mulch and do not involve clients in this task. Some recommend a mask when handling soil and potting mix as well and so use potting soil in an open space to ensure client safety.

Toxicity and Positive Identification

Before heading out into the wilds to learn to identify plants, start by becoming acquainted with the art resources growing in your own backyard (Easley & Horne, 2016). Take a series of walks in your own backyard or onsite garden with a skilled herbalist or botanist. Take classes in the field of botany; there are many free resources and your local *Native Plant Society* may be able to make practical recommendations. Learn to identify the poisonous plants in your area so you do not confuse any other plant with them (Easley & Horne, 2016).

Before you start harvesting anything, you need to make sure you have properly identified the plant. Plants should be identified by their Latin names rather than their common names as the same common name is often given to more than one species of plant (Easley & Horne, 2016). If you're not absolutely sure what plant the plant is, don't harvest it. Plants change throughout their life and with the seasons; also, the plant kingdom is full of look-a-likes and sometimes the differences between an art-making resource and a toxic species are very subtle. Health concerns are an important consideration so cautious wildcrafting is fundamental to eco-art therapy session safety. Plants which cannot be positively identified are good candidates for photography or drawings from observation. That way, they remain untouched but are studied for later identification.

To ensure positive identification, incorporate multiple checks using information such as the location where the plant is growing, leaf shape, quantity of leaves, and texture, and chemical indicators like smell and color. Using several sources such as an app, a field guide, and expert knowledge together can ensure positive identification. By growing or cultivating a particular species throughout a year, you will learn to recognize plant life-cycle and reactions to the seasons. I like to plant from seed in pots and also throughout my garden; that way, I can watch the plant progress through life cycles in multiple settings to observe how external influences alter appearance. One example is sunlight; plants which crave full sun and are grown in part shade grow very "leggy" or have yellowed leaves, appearing quite different from those grown in preferable conditions.

Toxicity considerations are essential when bringing materials into the office from the outdoors. With commercially purchased materials, you can simply check the labels to ensure the product creates no health hazards and is non-toxic. Similarly, when foraging, collecting, purchasing, or using natural materials for art making, maintain this same standard by ensuring each plant is non-toxic and poses no health hazards. When foraging, this requires accurate identification, which comes with practice. Personally, I like to research very common wild edibles including wild-flowers since these are deemed "safe" and I use these in art making since the toxicity and allergic reaction risk is very low. Additionally, if a plant is a known edible, there is research available online and in books about safety and probable reactions. Edible wildflowers often grow easily in very poor soil with minimal care and come in so many shapes and sizes. As a result, growing these for art making ensures success with minimal effort and cost.

In addition to selecting low-risk materials like edible wildflowers, specific guidelines are important for the proper storage and handling of art materials (adapted from AATA, 2013):

- Label all containers, itemizing contents, hazards, and the date collected and stored;
- Keep containers closed with airtight lids to prevent problems with dust or vapors;
- Maintain an inventory to enable disposal of items with a limited shelf life;
- Have non-toxic cleaning supplies, masks, gloves, and other protective equipment on hand; and
- Avoid keeping flammable, combustible materials, or chemical corrosives.

Clothing and Wildlife Considerations

If foraging materials in the outdoors with clients, you may want to recommend clients wear their hair up and use a hat to deflect the sun out of the eyes. Additionally, you may want to recommend clients wear light-colored, breathable clothing such as cotton or linen long-sleeved shirts and pants. This type of clothing protects clients from the elements but also can protect them from insect bites. Not all clients can afford natural fibered clothing so I like to have one-size-fits-all extra clothing on hand such as drawstring pants. I stock this extra clothing from the only online store I have found which allows me to filter by clothing fabric, price, and color: *thredUP*.

I've had clients nervously ask me about snakes or other wildlife perceived as dangerous when deciding whether eco-art therapy practices were for them. Often, the only difference between fear and respect is knowledge, and so when presenting eco-art therapy as an option for clients, help them understand the site. Know what can be expected so you can inform clients and achieve accurate informed consent. National and state parks may have a brochure listing the wildlife. My local one does and I used their brochure as inspiration to make my own. In my brochure I list the cottontail and marsh rabbits, eight species of butterflies, eleven species of birds, three species of frogs, the black racer snakes, and more which frequent the two acres.

On my farm, I have snakes, namely, black racers, which are non-venomous, very shy, and harmless if not attacked or threatened. So when I propose a meeting or session on my farm, I inform clients of the wildlife they may encounter. That said, many people are deathly afraid of snakes for cultural and evolutionary reasons. Snakes are sensitive to smell so wearing an essential oil may announce your presence to a snake and give the shy creature a chance to leave before you notice them. Additionally, singing is both therapeutic and helps to scare away wildlife. Just think of all the Disney princes and princesses singing in the forest—there is a practical reason to do this. Also, bringing a walking stick to shift grass in front of you as you walk is another precautionary step. Some therapists incorporate pet therapy and bring their dog while outdoors with clients; there are breeds of dogs which smell and detect snakes so they may also help additionally preserve safety.

Safety Protocol

Consider a brief walk outside to the far end of a garden to collect coriander flowers to press for a collage. Feelings such as anticipation, excitement, and even disappointment are unavoidable, unpredictable, but safe within a therapeutic context (Saraceno, 2017). Nature itself is healing so creating art within it amplifies the therapeutic potential (Brazier, 2011). However, when going out in nature with a client, it is critical to establish a safety protocol. Clients should be educated against "tasting" unidentified plants. Additionally, client and therapist collaboration should result in positive plant identification prior to touching or picking.

Safety rules and physical boundaries are essential throughout eco-art therapy sessions. Keeping on hand a first-aid kit, supply of water, soap, and towels for cleaning hands can help clients feel secure and allow them to get dirty without having to worry about it. Eco-art therapy may incorporate all weathers as part as the therapeutic experience (apart from high winds in the woods since tree limbs may fall) so appropriate clothing is always an important consideration. Harvesting wild plants can easily lead to trespassing on someone else's land so therapists should educate clients about this so they do not independently get themselves in trouble (Murphy-Hiscock, 2017). When taking clients into an outdoor setting there are many ways to ensure safety. To name a few: know all roads and paths, research the region, make an itinerary, tell others where you are going, give a copy of the itinerary to staff, carry a phone, keep track of time, bring a compass, wear appropriate clothing/shoes, carry nutritious snacks, and bring plenty of water. These safeguards are critical to ensuring your own and client safety.

Even with safety in mind, there is always an element of unpredictability when outdoors, which is why having a safety protocol and liability insurance in place is essential. For instance, the following checklist is a means to ensure safety and serves as an initial safety protocol:

Eco-Art Therapy Outdoor Safety Protocol Checklist

Check all that apply:
___*Client GAF and other assessments demonstrate therapeutic appropriateness of outing*
___*Therapist educated client regarding therapeutic purpose of outing and has informed consent*
___*Therapist is knowledgeable in first aid and CPR*
___*Epinephrine auto-injectors (EpiPen) are on hand*

___*Therapist is trained in group management, conflict resolution, and crisis prevention*

___*A contingency plan is in place for weather-related challenges*

___*Therapist has necessary navigation skills and equipment (e.g.,GPS, map, compass)*

___*Therapist assessed local environmental risks (e.g., terrain, weather, wildlife, plants)*

___*Therapist has prepared a planned response to adverse situations or emergency evacuations*

___*Water, toilet, and shelter are accessible at the location*

___*Sites are within 30 minutes by an ambulance to a hospital*

___*Groups maintain a three to one ratio, client to staff, when in an outdoor, offsite setting*

___*Client is low risk for run-away, aggression, or self-harm*

___*Client is dressed in appropriate clothing for outdoor setting or is provided with clothing*

___*Client agrees to comply with state, federal, and local regulations at location*

Table 3.1 summarizes the ethical and safety considerations discussed throughout this chapter by category.

By considering ethical and safety considerations by category, therapists can systematically self-check to ensure client safety throughout each category of eco-art therapy.

Chapter Summary

As helping professionals, we strive to build authentic and ethical relationships with our clients while ensuring client safety and dignity. This ethical approach to eco-art therapy emphasizes our own as well as client strengths and virtues, fostering empowerment while embracing limits. Through an ethic-of-care for self, others, and the natural world, eco-art therapy can support clients in enhancing their quality of life. Along these lines, quality of life requires being happy with what you have rather than constantly yearning for something more; having "enough" is exemplified in eco-art therapy when a *Reduce, Reuse, and Recycle* motto is applied in sessions. This motto can be applied to any eco-art therapy directives as interventions can be adapted with modified approaches and materials to serve a wide range of clients. In planning, erring on the side of caution applies to all aspects of eco-art therapy. Before taking a client offsite, make sure the client is likely to therapeutically benefit by exploring informal and formal assessments with them. When working indoors, moderate risk by ensuring proper ventilation, adequate lighting, access to water, knowledge of hazards or toxicity, and confidentiality. When foraging for art resources, properly identify the plant by the Latin name and if you're not absolutely sure what plant the plant is, leave it alone.

Table 3.1 Safety Protocol and Ethics Quick Reference

Assessment Area	Eco-Art Therapy Precautions
Global Assessment of Functioning	Assess for 70+ GAF for eco-art therapy "setting" approach unless using onsite garden accompanied by staff.
Client allergies	Ask clients if they have seasonal, insect, or plant/sap allergies.
Client history	Assess client associations to nature and any past trauma in nature to ensure eco-interventions will be therapeutic.
Toxicity	Limit eco-materials to those you have positively identified, researched, and determined to be safe for skin and respiratory exposure and know effects if accidentally ingested.
Client mobility/visuospatial skills	Ensure clients can cognitively decipher foreground, middle-ground, and background to verify they can ambulate a natural setting. Otherwise, ensure wheelchair access.
Client resources	Confirm clients have the ability to dress appropriately if going into an outdoor setting or be prepared to provide a change of clothes for their protection.
Safety protocol relevance	Evaluate if your safety protocol addresses clients' needs and the situational context. New situations may warrant an update to the protocol.
Liability insurance	Contact your professional liability insurance company to confirm coverage for outdoor interventions if planning excursions offsite with clients.
First Aid	Check your first-aid kit prior to any outing to restock as needed; keep your CPR certification up to date or have an assistant onsite; be within a reasonable distance to a medical facility in the case of emergency.
Location	Verify that site locations have facilities such as a drinking water source, covered shelter, and a bathroom; plan the outing nearby these facilities to accommodate client needs.

References

Agbude, G. A., Obayan, A., Ademola, L. L., & Abasilim, U. D. (2017). Leadership on trial: An existentialist assessment. *Covenant International Journal of Psychology*, 2(1), 46–62.

Alders, A., Beck, L., Allen, P. B., & Mosinski, B. B. (2011). Technology in art therapy: Ethical challenges. *Art Therapy*, 28(4), 165–170.

American Art Therapy Association [AATA] (2013). *Ethical principles for art therapists.* https://arttherapy.org/wp-content/uploads/2017/06/Ethical-Principles-for-Art-Therapists.pdf.

Ankenman, N. (2010). *An ecology of the imagination an ecology of the imagination: A theoretical and practical exploration of the imagination for holistic healing in the context of art therapy.* Eco Art Land: Landing in the Space Between Art and Ecology. https://ecoartland.wordpress.com/an-ecology-of-the-imagination/.

Betts, D. (2013). A review of the principles for culturally appropriate art therapy assessment tools. *Art Therapy*, 30(3), 98–106.

Betts, D. J. (2016). Art therapy assessments: An overview. In D. E. Gussak & M. L. Rosal (Eds.), *The Wiley handbook of art therapy* (1st ed., pp. 501–513). John Wiley & Sons.

Brazier, C. (2011). *Acorns among the grass: Adventures in eco-therapy.* John Hunt Publishing.

Brown, S. (2020, April). Hawaii's endangered bee. *2 Million Blossoms*, 1(2), 74–76.

Coehlo, P. (2015). *The fisherman and the businessman.* Paulo Coelho blog. https://paulocoelhoblog.com/2015/09/04/the-fisherman-and-the-businessman/.

D'Souza, R., & De Sousa, A. (2017). The concept of 'professional boundary' in psychotherapy. *Global Bioethics Enquiry*, 5(1), 1–51.

Easley, T., & Horne, S. (2016). *The modern herbal dispensatory: A medicine-making guide.* North Atlantic Books.

Eisler, R. (2019, February). Early partnership societies: How the collaborative generation is not just a trend. (Interviewer: Bowie, S.) *Autre Magazine*. https://autre.love/new-products/pre-order-autre-volume-2-issue-9-maurizio-cattelan-banan-art-basel.

Gantt, L. (2016). The formal elements art therapy scale (FEATS). In D. Gussak & M. Rosal (Ed.), *The Wiley handbook of art therapy* (pp. 569–578). Wiley-Blackwell.

Gantt, L., & Greenstone, L. (2016). Narrative art therapy in trauma treatment. In J. A. Rubin (Ed.), *Approaches to art therapy: Theory and technique* (3rd ed., pp. 353–370). Routledge.

Gantt, L., & Tabone, C. (1998). *Formal elements art therapy scale: The rating manual.* Gargoyle Press. https://helpfortrauma.com/wp-content/uploads/2018/11/FEATS-Manual.pdf.

Hinz, L. D. (2011). Embracing excellence: A positive approach to ethical decision making. *Art Therapy*, 28(4), 185–188.

Houghton, P., & Worroll, J. (2016). *Play the forest school way: Woodland games, crafts and skills for adventurous kids.* Watkins Media Limited.

Inwood, H., & Kennedy, A. (2020). Conceptualising art education as environmental activism in preservice teacher education. *International Journal of Art & Design Education*, 39(3), 585–599.

Ishiguro, C., Takagishi, H., Sato, Y., Seow, A. W., Takahashi, A., Abe, Y., & Kato, E. (2019). Effect of dialogical appreciation based on visual thinking strategies on art-viewing strategies. *Psychology of Aesthetics, Creativity, and the Arts.* Advance online publication. https://doi.org/10.1037/aca0000258.

Jiménez-Alfaro, B., Frischie, S., Stolz, J., & Gálvez-Ramírez, C. (2020). Native plants for greening Mediterranean agroecosystems. *Nature Plants*, 6(3), 209–214.

Kopytin, A. I., & Rugh, M. M. (Eds.). (2016). *Green Studio: Nature and the arts in therapy.* Nova Science Publishers, Incorporated.

Kopytin, A., & Rugh, M. (Eds.). (2017). *Environmental expressive therapies: Nature-assisted theory and practice.* Taylor & Francis.

Lawton, G. (2008). *Establishing a food forest the permaculture way.* Eco Films Australia.

Lichtenberg, E. F. (2014). Draw-a-Person-in-the Rain Test. In L. Handler & A. D. Thomas (Eds.), *Drawings in assessment and psychotherapy: Research and application* (pp. 164–183). Routledge/Taylor & Francis Group.

Luna, J. M., Dávila, E. R., & Reynoso-Morris, A. (2018). Pedagogy of permaculture and food justice. *Educational Foundations*, 31, 57–85.

McMaster, M. (2013). *Integrating nature into group art therapy interventions for clients with dementia.* Unpublished research paper for the degree of Master of Arts: Concordia University. https://spectrum.library.concordia.ca/978027/1/McMaster_MA_F2013.pdf.

Murphy-Hiscock, A. (2017). *The green witch: Your complete guide to the natural magic of herbs, flowers, essential oils, and more.* Simon & Schuster.

Pike, A. (2014). *Improving memory through creativity: A professional's guide to culturally sensitive cognitive training with older adults.* Jessica Kingsley Publishers.

Piotrowski, C. (2016). Bender-gestalt test usage worldwide: A review of 30 practice-based studies. *SIS Journal of Projective Psychology & Mental Health*, 23(2), 73–81.

Saraceno, J. (2017). *CBT eco-art therapy: Mood regulation with young adults in nature.* Notre Dame de Namur University.

Scheirich, C. (2020). *Coping with the climate crisis: Exploring art therapy for sustainable mental health.* Unpublished research paper for the degree of Master of Arts: Concordia University. https://spectrum.library.concordia.ca/986936/1/Scheirich_MA_F2020.pdf.

Struckman, J. (2020). *Nature as metaphor in school art therapy: Development of a group method.* Expressive Therapies Capstone Theses: Lesley University. 235. https://digitalcommons.lesley.edu/expressive_theses/235.

4 Client and Multicultural Competence

The boiling water that softens the carrot hardens the egg.

—Unknown

Empowering Techniques: Serving Diverse Clients

The word "therapy" comes from the Greek word *therapeia*, which means 'to be attentive to.' In the case of eco-art therapy, remaining attentive to each client's individualized reactions to natural settings, materials, and subjects ensures the experience is therapeutic. Eco-art therapy techniques and interventions are often informed by agricultural calendars, seasonal shifts, weather patterns, and historically relevant cultural practices. Planning according to these cycles can incorporate a consistent routine which will yield insight. For some clients, the cool of the fall with its winds and colors invigorates and inspires. However, for clients originally from a warmer, tropical climate, colder temperatures may be uncomfortable and stressful. Likewise, the early summer mornings with its lushness and abundant growth may energize some while an experience of sweating and heat might be an unwelcome experience for others. Paying attention to natural cycles as well as clients' diverse needs helps therapists tailor eco-art therapy practices to make sessions relevant, respectful, pleasurable, and stimulating. Eco-art therapy practices rely on the supportive nature of the client–therapist relationship so the art-making experience can help clients find meaning unique to their culture and background.

Recently, COVID-19 revealed inequalities in access to blue and green spaces (Masterton, Carver, & Parkes, 2020). Although green and blue spaces serve as places of solace, respite, exercise, and relaxation, access to these locations was restricted to enforce social distancing and limit the spread of the virus (Ugolini et al., 2020). There were many petitions to keep parks and gardens open for public use, with blue and green spaces described as crucial for well-being (Masterton, Carver, & Parkes, 2020). However, the availability of blue or green space differs depending on location; affluence allows people to buy homes in areas with more blue and green spaces, less air pollution, and more room for physical activity (Masterton, Carver, & Parkes, 2020). During the lockdowns, there was a sudden increase in Google search requests to find where to "go for a walk" (Kleinschroth & Kowarik, 2020). The surge in interest in walks was not matched by supply as neighborhoods vary in green and blue space quantity by social and economic status (Kleinschroth & Kowarik, 2020). If someone has less access to local parks, gardens, and playing fields, they are far less likely to gain the therapeutic benefits that those spaces provide (Masterton, Carver, & Parkes, 2020). These inequalities clearly existed before COVID-19, but the pandemic brought a wider awareness to a problem: easy access to nature is not an opportunity available to everyone. Using London as an example, the wealthiest areas have around 10% more public space compared to the most deprived areas (Masterton, Carver, & Parkes, 2020). Approximately half of the residents in the most deprived areas of London are from minority backgrounds (Masterton, Carver, & Parkes, 2020). Eco-art therapy practices can help equalize this disparity by ensuring all clients have access to nature during sessions. By providing access to green and blue spaces, helping professionals promote physical and psychological well-being, which in turn improves client resistance to and ability to cope with new pathogens and life stressors (Kleinschroth & Kowarik, 2020).

Empowered by humanism models, eco-art therapy practices involve a social action—a participatory, collaborative process which emphasizes art making as a vehicle to understand client realities, identify their needs and strengths, and enhance quality of life (Morris & Willis-Rauch, 2014, pp. 28–36). The art created with ecologically sourced materials is a platform for communication (Morris & Willis-Rauch, 2014, pp. 28–36). In this way, by acknowledging human needs as related to the environment and using nature to promote client potential, communication, and well-being, sessions can contribute to what some researchers call "human capacity development" (Eisler, 2019).

Eco-art therapy helps to develop client capacity through attentive observation, which then informs client self-knowledge in addition to therapist understanding. Ever since the inscription "know thyself" was carved into the facade of the temple of Apollo at Delphi, self-exploration has been recognized as the key to authenticity and quality of life (as cited in Figueroa, 2020). By spending time in nature, clients witness nature's unfolding such as when watching the sun rise and set, noting seasonal changes, observing and contemplating surroundings, and creating impermanent art from natural elements (Geha, 2019). When clients connect with nature in this way, they learn to recognize phenomena beyond and within themselves, orienting to the "here and now" but more than that, they experience validation which inspires the creative process (Geha, 2019). As a result, eco-art therapy helps to promote cultural exchanges, feelings of belonging, identity transformation, strengthened family ties, and healthy socialization and community living (DeSouza, 2015 as cited in Speert, 2016).

Population Accommodations: "Who Benefits?"

Humans have an inherent and evolutionary connection to nature which spans cultures, age groups, and socio-economic backgrounds. Therapists and clients alike benefit from the eco-art therapy approach. "*El duende*" is a Spanish term used in the arts to mean an experience which, like the wind, is shared but not always visible or explainable (Miller, 2012, pp. 166–173 as cited in Figueroa, 2020). Whether client or therapist, all humans feel vulnerable at times and may find comfort in peaceful natural surroundings and artifacts. We all struggle in different ways regardless of circumstances and, as therapists, compassion fatigue and burn-out are ever-present realities. With a transpersonal lens, therapists can embrace nature alongside clients as a means of self-care as well as a strategy to hone their skills and abilities, honestly exploring their own vulnerabilities and needs (De Souza, 2015). Indeed, understanding ourselves as a part of nature provides a way to integrate mixed cultural identities, the need to belong, and find our "place" in the world (Figueroa, 2020).

As one art therapist explained, "… through exploring my relationship with nature and nature's relationship with me … I perceive a greater understanding of place and belonging" (Figueroa, 2020). Observation and engagement with nature enhances our own capacity to support clients. Through observing nature's resiliency and adaptability, a client, and even a therapist, is reminded of their own resiliency and adaptability. This is because, through eco-art therapy practices, there is an opportunity for understanding the self and others simultaneously (Figueroa, 2020). Take, for instance, an arts-based project centered on a series of outdoor meditation and mask-making workshops (Wycks, 2016). This project was based on research which presented storytelling as a means of connecting with others and transforming perceptions of individualism through a collective sense of place. A collective perspective may enhance cultural sensitivity in sessions with some clients.

Cultural Sensitivity

Clients come to us from all backgrounds and life circumstances and it's not always obvious what their culture is and how that will influence their interests in eco-art therapy. Ultimately, we want sessions to feel culturally sensitive, meaning sessions allow the therapist to adapt services to meet individual client needs (Betancourt et al., 2016). This process of adapting services requires developing awareness and knowledge of ourselves and other cultures' beliefs and behaviors, cultural dynamics and interactions, and skills and interventions which are ethical and appropriate for clients with cultural backgrounds which differ from our own (ter Maat, 2011, p. 9). Beyond these steps, including a social justice vision elevates eco-art therapy endeavors (Talwar, 2017). As Figure 4.1 illustrates, integrating culturally sensitive strategies is possible in many different ways which have been touched upon so far

Figure 4.1 Eco-Art Therapy and Cultural Sensitivity
Note. In this figure, elements which help to enhance cultural sensitivity are outlined according to research and practice considerations.

within this book, including storytelling, a strength-based focus, belief and meaning symbolism, structure, ritual, discussed goals, and more.

Although specific techniques and strategies help to imbue a session with inclusive elements, the underlying practices which make eco-art therapy culturally sensitive session-to-session rely on the skill and compassion of each therapist. When I have discussed cultural competency with my interns, I have used an analogy of plants:

> *Some plants need full sun and are drought tolerant. Other plants need partial shade and constant moisture. Still others thrive in full shade and require excellent drainage. The goal is to find a fit between conditions and plants. If a plant which needs full shade is placed in full sun, it will suffer and have symptoms. In life, clients may experience conditions which cause them symptoms and then come to believe that something is inherently wrong with them. Each client will have unique needs and particular conditions may not meet those needs. As a therapist, we can help clients gain self-awareness and insight so they can adapt to conditions or take action to change their living conditions. Helping clients understand their inherent worth and explore what will help them thrive is part of the therapeutic relationship. Because of this, a one-size-fits-all approach to therapy is not effective. Flexibility in materials, interventions, conditions, and focus ensure client needs guide the session.*

To help foster client insight in eco-art therapy, we can apply culturally grounded strategies such as formal directives paired with psychoeducation, delayed formal assessments, explanations of what can be expected in session, assured confidentiality, solution-focused, strengths-based sessions, structured processes, and metaphoric speech (Bermudez & ter Maat, 2006; Boston, 2016; Moon & Nolan, 2019; see *Strengths Mask* in Appendix A as an example). Some examples of ways to explore culture include working with clients to construct coats of arms and family portraits. Another means to explore culture involves creating genograms which represent a family tree and display detailed information on relationships, hereditary patterns, and psychological factors (Gatfield, 2017). Aligned with eco-art therapy practices, clients create these representations using natural materials. For example, clients may select natural artifacts and use those artifacts to represent their immediate family members in a mobile genogram (see *Family Wind Chime* in Appendix A).

Yet another culturally congruent approach to eco-art therapy includes a process of "creative personalization" of the environment. This involves selecting objects to create visual narratives as markers of identity within the environment (Kopytin & Rugh, 2017; see *Memory Orb* in Appendix A). Clients can also personalize the environment by building homes in nature and creating environmental art such as designing, creating, and maintaining green spaces like gardens (Kopytin & Rugh, 2017; see *Emotion Guest House* in Appendix A). This process of personalizing the environment involves self-reflection and can be cued with a simple opening exercise such as: "Close your eyes and remember a happy time which relates to the object that you are holding in your hand. Visualize that memory. What colors are present? What textures?" (Alders, 2012). Then clients can influence their environment to embed positive visual reminders of that memory.

Cuing a positive or "happy" memory aligns with research on enhancing mood—a foundational goal of eco-art therapy. While exploring negative thoughts and feelings can be a form of "venting," it often negatively impacts mood in the short term and so focusing client attention on the present moment can offer clients relief. The physical act of creating can be quite pleasurable when it is directly related to the senses (e.g., touch, sight) and does not require extensive thought, planning, or skill. Bodily pleasures throughout the art-making process are fleeting, but can quickly enhance mood and facilitate emotional expressivity, bypassing deficits and, in some cases, rehabilitating functioning (Alders, 2012). Directives such as visual journaling outdoors, creating botanical arrangements, sculpting with found objects from nature, and taking outdoor photography and videography help calm clients' racing mind while revealing culture and promoting self-expression and rehabilitation (Kopytin & Rugh, 2017; see *Insect Movie* in Appendix A). These directives aim to relax clients to allow both their body and mind to experience therapeutic benefits. As described by one research participant: *"I'm fully washed over with peace... I feel my whole body react. My shoulders drop their tension, my breathing deepens and slows... I feel still"* (Journal entry, October 31, 2011 as cited in Flowers, Lipsett, & Barrett, 2014).

Religious Beliefs and Cultural Congruence

Nature teaches us that there is nothing to fear in difference because difference ensures survival of the species as a whole and is therefore one of the healthiest and most invigorating aspects of life. Yet, as humans search for the "right" relationships to themselves, others, and the world, commonalities are what is often sought. When considering cross-cultural commonalities, scholars point to a universal human need for quiet, meditative spaces to help connect to imagination, a sense of wonder, and hope (Wycks, 2016). This universal human need is sometimes reflected in religious and cultural rituals.

For instance, I've had clients consult their holy book to decide which plants are relevant to use to express different experiences and feelings in an eco-art therapy session. Most religious texts explicitly mention plants, including 120 plants in the Bible and 20 in the Qur'an (Zagonari, 2020). In the Bible, saffron is referenced as a dye, but more symbolically, in James 1:9–10, lupin flowers are referenced. The symbolism of passing lupin flowers was said to be a reminder of mortality, and the passing nature of power and wealth: "Let the believer who is lowly boast in being raised up, and the rich in being brought low, because the rich will disappear like a flower in the field" (Whitehead, 2020). For a religious client experiencing loss, this symbolism and reference may be relevant.

In therapy, clients may reference their own and their families' ritualized, structured, social practices related to spiritual beliefs. These practices may include more new-aged celebrations of winter solstice, cosmology, or astrology as well as more mainstream religious celebrations. Given the variety of potential religious and spiritual associations with nature, the *Belief Art Therapy Assessment (BATA)* may be a relevant means of beginning important dialogues with clients in addition to those listed in Chapter 3 (Betts, 2016; Horovitz, 2017). The BATA assessment instrument is used for assessing a client's spiritual beliefs and how those beliefs impact their life, families, and society (Betts, 2016; Horovitz, 2017). This assessment aligns with research that what is good for our spiritual journey is good for our relationships and our immune system (Shattuck & Muehlenbein, 2020). Additionally, the BATA may shed insight into whether eco-art therapy practices are culturally congruent or if eco-art therapy practices would be therapeutic as an intervention following the conclusion of a more traditional battery of assessments.

Consider that in many cultures metaphors and rituals related to nature are embedded in social practices such as when burying the dead beneath soil to commence formal bereavement, lighting candles to remember the

INTAKE CULTURAL INQUIRY

Optional section: The following questions will help me provide meaningful directives centered around your life milestones. Completing this section is optional. Please indicate which holidays you celebrate:

Winter holidays (e.g., Christmas, Martin Luther King Day, Hanukah, Winter Solstice, Purim):

_____

Spring holidays (e.g., Ramanavami, Easter, Passover, Edi al-Fitr, Spring Equinox):

_____

Summer holidays (e.g., Lailat Ul Qadr, Independence Day, Summer Solstice):

_____

Fall holidays (e.g., Veteran's Day, Eid al-Adha, Rosh Hashanah, Diwali, Thanksgiving):

_____

Figure 4.2 Intake Cultural Inquiry

deceased, or throwing flowers on a grave site (Kopytin & Rugh, 2017). Because spirituality and religion may intertwine with eco-art therapy practices, in my intake materials. I ask about holidays rather than religion because many families represent multiple religions and holiday celebrations can be an initial means to explore this (see Figure 4.2).

Through culturally sensitive eco-art therapy practices, a therapist is able to show clients respect and inclusivity. This respect is amplified by the ethical guidelines discussed in previous chapters which align with many different religious moral codes throughout cultures across the world (Zagonari, 2020). For instance:

- Hinduism emphasizes stewardship, viewing Mother Earth as an extended family (Zagonari, 2020). This stewardship is apparent in eco-art therapy when carefully choosing which plants or materials to collect for art making.
- Buddhism includes an emphasis on nature for aesthetic value (Zagonari, 2020). During eco-art therapy clients readily explore this aesthetic value to create meaningful and symbolic works.
- Daoism focuses on human health, which is perceived as a sustainable equilibrium between the body and its environment (Zagonari, 2020). In eco-art therapy, the environment is a primary consideration and aligns with therapeutic models and frameworks centering sessions on health goals and outcomes.

- In Judaism, humans are "stewards" for future generations with preservation emphasized, such as through conserving nature's biodiversity (Zagonari, 2020). Through eco-art therapy, multiple generations of family members can come together to cultivate art materials and practice conservation. Also, eco-art therapy sessions promote biodiversity when therapists and clients select non-native, invasive plants as an art resource.
- Christianity teaches an admiration of Earth's goods as resources while acknowledging imperfections inherent in nature (Zagonari, 2020). Embracing our own and nature's imperfection occurs throughout eco-art therapy. In session, nature is admired as a creative resource.
- Islam discusses impermanence, parsimony, and natural conservation (Zagonari, 2020). This value of avoiding waste is apparent in eco-art therapy through zero-waste practices. Additionally, impermanence is addressed throughout each protocol when deciding whether or not to take steps to preserve artworks from decompensation (e.g., using sealants).

In summary, eco-art therapy practices align with diverse cultural beliefs through an appreciation of nature's beauty, health-enhancing properties, and its use as a finite resource. By integrating eco-art therapy practices, therapists can utilize nature as a means to align with diverse cultural values.

Practical Techniques

To extend cultural sensitivity within eco-art therapy, the therapist's primary task is to create an experience grounded in acceptance, respect, encouragement, and safety—in other words, a holding environment (McMaster, 2013). Central to creating a holding environment is placing an emphasis on the process of creating rather than the product as a "fine art" (McMaster, 2013). However, the product is a means of communication and an accomplishment which does needs acknowledgment (Stewart, 2006 as cited in McMaster, 2013).

Another practical technique to foster cultural sensitivity is through collaboration. No matter what the client's cognitive awareness or verbal ability, all group and staff members should communicate directly with clients and not about them in their presence (Tyler, 2002 as cited in McMaster, 2013). Therapists should train staff members on how to be encouraging and supportive since positive staff attitude is associated with higher attendance, lower resistance, and greater improvements among clients (Waller, 2002b as cited in McMaster, 2013). Staff members have a crucial role since eco-art therapy may require high levels of prompting and support such as through verbal cues, step-by-step instructions, gestural explanations, and hand-over-hand assistance (Stewart, 2006, p. 117 as cited in McMaster, 2013). Additionally, if planning a group format, ensuring the group size is small will promote authentic connections and safety among members (e.g., under ten members).

Some cultures will predispose a client to wanting to watch a technique prior to attempting it while other cultures may influence clients to want to dive into experimentation and innovation. That's why within each protocol the level of engagement is scaled up and down using ETC to help clients warm up to the idea of fully engaging. The K/S level of engagement is procedural and does not require disclosure or risk-taking and so may be a more comfortable warm-up. For clients who are immediately responsive and engaged, steps may be combined. As clients progress through ETC levels, they increasingly have opportunities for imagination, cooperative interaction, and skill development.

Throughout each protocol and nearly any eco-art therapy session in general, clients will exercise critical life skills regardless of cultural background, age, or diagnosis. These life skills apply to nearly any eco-art therapy directive universally and include:

- *Gross Motor Skills*, which relate to movements of the large muscles in the arms, legs, and trunk, and are needed for activities like exploring a garden;
- *Fine Motor Skills*, which pertain to movement and dexterity of the small muscles in the hands and fingers, and are needed for activities like picking up small plants, holding a paintbrush, or pinching a slab of clay;
- *Visual Motor Skills*, which relate to client's ability to decide on movement based on the perception of visual information, and are needed to paint an object, glue natural artifacts onto a collage, or dip a paintbrush into a bowl of paint;
- *Self-Care Skills*, which include rinsing hands after painting, wearing protective clothing such as a facemask, or avoiding tasting or eating plant materials during foraging;
- *Sensory Integration Skills*, which involve the ability to take in, process, and respond to information in the environment, and is especially important in clients who are under- or over-sensitive to sound, light, touch, noise, etc. (e.g., those with autism); and
- *Motor Planning Skills*, which involve the ability to plan and sequence motor tasks such as drawing a circle for a head and then planning out the body of a person or extracting dye from berries and then mixing the colors on a palette to apply the colors to a canvas.

Beyond these life skills, eco-art therapy directives will fall into specific goal categories and themes and will have associated psychoeducational components needed to help clients individually. For instance, the protocol entitled *Inspired* found in Appendix A provides the following information on how the directive is planned to benefit clients:

- **Therapeutic Themes**: *Stress reduction; catharsis; mindfulness; self-monitoring; positive distraction; breathing as coping*
- **Goal Category**: *Affective*
- **Psychoeducation**: *Diaphragmic breathing; color as metaphor*

Art Education as a Facilitation Technique

When creating art during eco-art therapy, art education components are naturally embedded. This is because clients may need to be guided sequentially. This art education component draws on the wealth of historical practices well-documented across cultures. Nature was the original setting, material, and subject of artists. Just think of murals found in caves done in prehistoric times or Native American and indigenous art. Nearly every natural material has been explored and mastered by indigenous populations so eco-art therapy draws from this wealth of knowledge and history. Additionally, Native American art often centers attention on the process while honoring interaction with materials throughout each stage of the creation (Kaimal & Arslanbek, 2020). Additionally, rituals associated with the creative process are of equal if not more importance than the artistic skill (Kaimal & Arslanbek, 2020). This focus on process over product tightly aligns with eco-art therapy best practices.

For instance, mask-making is a cross-cultural tradition, employing natural materials and has proved therapeutic especially for veterans and military personnel (Alexander, 2020). Creating containers, such as by using gourds, is another cross-cultural and historically grounded art-making process which has proven effective to address therapeutic themes such as boundaries (Reis, 2019). Fiberwork with natural materials and textiles also has roots in Native American traditions and is employed by therapists for goals such as community cohesion and bereavement (Wood, Jacobson, & Cridford, 2019). Ceramics and pottery are yet another example of cultural art which has become embedded in therapy with research describing goals such as anger management (Moula, 2020). Shell-engraving, stone glyphic writing, murals, woodcarving, mosaics, embroidery, and birch-bark boxes all have indigenous cultural roots and can have a place within eco-art therapy sessions to target therapeutic outcomes.

More recently, a number of art movements have relied on nature-derived pigments and have used nature as a subject of the artwork itself. Using nature as a material, subject or setting is a time-honored tradition among artists. Table 4.1 shows an overview of art movements and their relevance to eco-art therapy.

Table 4.1 Art Movements and Eco-Art Therapy Techniques

Movement	Description	Eco-Art therapy Use Example
Impression-ism	Atmospheric effect with color and form; reflects vagaries of perception (e.g., Monet's art)	Painting a natural scene from observation while employing mindfulness techniques
Pointillism	Contrasting hues; colors mix in the retina of the viewer's eye (e.g., Georges Seurat's art)	Using a cattail as a paintbrush to blot color while employing coping techniques like breathing in rhythm with movement
Early Modernism	"Speaks" with color and form; uses agitated lines and intensified color schemes (e.g., Van Gogh's art)	Representing extreme experiences and emotions using naturally derived pigments as means to gain insight and vent
International Modern Art	Conscious design through organized color schemes and defined spaces (e.g., Cezanne's art)	Planning and measuring forms to represent nature with geometrical shapes to explore self-determination and achievement orientation
Symbolism	Visual elements convey thoughts and sensations; links to math, music, and literature; metaphysical and spiritual themes (e.g., Moreau's art)	Reading plant symbolism books to select artifacts to collage a representation while listening to music to inspire rhythmic arrangements based on the notes and chords
Les Nabis	Applies 2D ornamentation inspired by Japanese prints; celebrates leisure/pleasures of the good life	Decreasing depression symptoms through using nature-based myths, legends, and cultural/religious stories to explore gratitude and pleasures
Parallelism	Symmetrical compositions with parallel arrangements; serene pathos/contained passions; allegory and anecdotal details (e.g., Hodler's art)	Narrating work/life balance goals using two side-by-side scenes of nature, one symbolizing "work" and the other "life"
Art Nouveau	Playful use of plant-like, intertwining lines; employs a stylistic masquerade (e.g., Klimt's art)	Depicting individualism, identity, and differentiation of self from family using woven vines to address generational cycles (e.g., abuse)
Expression-ism	Brilliant colors on white canvas; confessional art; swirling, swaying, and exaggerated brushstrokes (e.g., Munch's art)	Taking a strengths-based perspective when selecting a plant or animal "totem" to represent as self in a self-portrait
Fauves	Colors like bombshells; savage-like; represents simplified and abstracted everyday experiences; mentally soothing (e.g., Matisse's art)	Engaging in self-soothing techniques via immediate gratification such as through pounding/hammering freshly picked flowers onto fabric to stain abstracted forms

By referencing these movements, therapists can tailor and structure eco-art therapy approaches to enhance the cultural sensitivity. For instance, a therapist may present clients with Table 4.1, *Art Movements and Eco-Art Therapy Techniques*, so clients can choose the movement which they believe will allow greatest expression given their life circumstances and interests. Then the clients can use natural materials, subjects, and settings to complete the artwork.

Aligning Expectations: "Where Should I Do This?"

Many locations are appropriate settings for eco-art therapy sessions, including: mental health facilities and agencies such as homeless shelters, eating disorder clinics, substance abuse recovery centers, private practice offices, studios, and academic locations. However, best practices for deciding where to do eco-art therapy is grounded in what would be most therapeutic for clients. Taking clients outdoors is one opportunity to enliven therapeutic sessions but in the 21st century many clients may be accustomed to constant technology use. By employing technology, therapists can help clients enjoy outdoor settings by using what is familiar. For example, clients may use their phone to artistically video an unscripted documentary of wildlife, employ apps to photograph nature, or even grow art-making materials such as flowers within indoor settings using hydroponics linked to phone-based monitoring apps. These digital techniques can assist clients with externalizing their focus, processing emotions, and developing coping skills (Bogan, 2019).

Foraging within an onsite or personally maintained garden for art materials may be a viable option for some. However, for those who do not have access to a managed outdoor space, state or national parks can be alluring. That said, in these parks, it may be illegal to forage, or foraging may be limited to a specific quantity or type of plant to ensure quantities of plants sustain over time. Be sure to research the laws of your local area before foraging. This research may prove useful and to your advantage. For instance, conscientious foragers can actually work with parks to remove invasive or prohibited species, making a positive impact on the environment. Some invasive or prohibited species are found all over the world and are excellent resources for art making. While foraging for these invasives, you will be doing your natural area a great service. Consider asking a park representative for a list of invasive which are OK'd for picking.

Indoor eco-art therapy has many advantages. While some clients and therapists may prefer to be surrounded by the dynamic colors, sounds, textures, and smells of nature outdoors, others may need the structure and stability of experiencing nature within a controlled setting (Speert, 2016). Likewise, although there is a joy to being able to feel the temperature and texture of the earth outdoors, therapists can bring the natural world to the client indoors when clinically appropriate (Speert, 2016). For instance, within an open-studio approach to eco-art therapy the focus on "art" is central (Kopytin & Rugh, 2017). An open-studio, eco-art therapy session can help therapists employ their very specialized visual-art knowledge to empower and inspire client creativity (Fish, 2019). In this setting, the client becomes an "artist" and can bypass some of the stigma associated with illness (Carr, 2014, pp. 54–70 as cited in Fish, 2019). In studio environments, there are open hours whereas clients can come and go with a sign-in sheet. Some therapists choose to incorporate a recurring monthly fee which incorporates a set number of sessions or hours that clients can attend at their convenience.

In academic settings, *Waldorf* and *Reggio Emilia* schools prioritize natural and environmentally sourced materials in education and early childhood development, and encourage family and community partner-ships. In these and other school settings, outdoor murals can expose stu-dents to natural elements while still providing structure and safety. When creating a mural, nature is easily the subject and setting but can also be the material. For instance, picking flowers and plants, covering them with paint, and stamping the plants onto the wall to create a silhouette creates a pleasing effect. This exercise promotes cooperation, group unity, as well as individualism and self- expression. In some activities on school grounds, group members can be asked to create a mural together, working together silently, without the use of words, which allows group members to practice their non-verbal communication skills and to break through barriers of distrust and isolation (Fish, 2019).

Community-based, arts-for-health locations like community centers and yoga studios can maximize the impact of cultural programs (e.g., mandala painting) on the general and mental health of persons. Such settings may provide a more casual and informal atmosphere for thera-pists. However, a lot of advocacy may be needed at the community centers to maintain attendance (Alders, 2012). Creative professionals may find that clients attend community centers irregularly or experience transpor-tation issues (Alders, 2012). Using eco-art therapy in these locations may be well-received but sessions will likely need to be self-contained/beginning and ending in a single session and be longer in duration to compensate for irregular attendance. For instance, when referencing the protocols included within this book, each step could be a stand-alone session or several steps can be shortened to create a finished product within a longer workshop-style session (e.g., six-hour/day-long workshop).

Balancing Process and Product Priorities

Eco-art therapy approaches are often process-driven since clients work continuously on one product for a prolonged period, layering in ideas and themes (see all protocols within Appendix A). There is no rush to have a final product. Throughout sessions, self-understanding as well as feelings of self-judgement can arise; to prepare clients to accept both of these experiences, encourage clients to "work with" whatever emerges and embrace all aspects of themselves to have a more authentic and transformative experience (Geha, 2019). Progress requires error—our response to our imperfection is the very thing that can make us more perfect.

Similarly, at the heart of analytical thinking is a willingness to learn over and over that the process is as important as the product. In therapy, thinking analytically includes reflecting on values and relationships which are the invisible influencers of the art-making process. Although some cultures place higher priority on the aesthetic outcome of a work of art, engaging clients in Socratic questioning can help them remember that not all artwork is intended to be beautiful. Sometimes clients need permission to create something portraying ugliness to communicate unmet needs. Socratic questioning involves supporting clients through an analytical thinking process during art making by asking clear, concise, purposeful yet neutral questions, meaning there are no "right" answers (Neenan, 2009). Examples include:

- What do you think would happen if you let yourself experiment and play (in the art-making process) without judgement?
- Why do you think I've chosen to ask you that question?
- When will you know that you have done enough to call the work "finished"?
- Can you describe how the metaphor in the artwork applies to your life?

To help balance priorities between process and product, openings and closings can establish a ritual to emphasize a respect for the creative process (Alders, 2012). Rituals are an integral part of establishing structure and can start simple and evolve into what is most meaningful for each client (McMaster, 2013). For instance, at the onset of a group, openings and closings can help create standards for socially acceptable behavior. Specifically, non-verbal opening and closings can help therapists avoid linguistic biases since culture affects how clients will communicate (Alders, 2012). As a non-verbal opening and closing, therapists and clients could create natural pigments or collect nature-based art materials. This process would be a kinesthetic and sensory experience and would prepare clients for subsequent sessions and art making.

Each protocol within Appendix A has an overview of therapeutic themes which can be discussed with clients as a ritual opening. Another opening can be stating a very brief overview of what will happen in the session before beginning the art-making process or reviewing what happened in the previous session to provide a sense of continuity (McMaster, 2013; Pike, 2013). The opening ideally presents "happenings" in ways which are success-oriented and clearly defined (Stewart, 2006 as cited in McMaster, 2013).

Opening and closing rituals need not be complicated and can be based on session logistics and practicalities (Suchostawski, 2018). Cleaning up is a good closing ritual since it naturally suggests that something is finished (McMaster, 2013). Among clients with severe symptoms, clean-up responsibilities may be a welcome way of demonstrating capabilities (McMaster, 2013). Anything that group members can do should be encouraged so each client contributes to the group or session being successful (McMaster, 2013). As an example, simply wiping soil and paint off a tablecloth and folding it, can reinforce life skills and therefore may translate into greater independence over time (McMaster, 2013). With a task like clean-up, the closing is simple and straightforward. As a result, the closing can provide an opportunity for therapists and educators to observe client energy levels (Strongwater, 2018). If clients are engaged in a repetitive task which occurs each session, variations in mood and behavior are more apparent. Some professionals use this time to jot down notes as a quick and easy way to review session outcomes until there is a chance to sit down to write formal progress notes (Strongwater, 2018). Following this ritual, when the session is coming to an end, thank clients for their participation and efforts, wish them a good day, and remind them that the next session will be in a week's time to ensure sessions end on a positive note (McMaster, 2013).

Whatever the ritual, openings and closings ideally incorporate a quick process which aims to enhance mood and heighten a client's awareness of their surroundings so they can externalize their focus and fully engage in the session (Alders, 2012). By repeating openings and closings every session, therapists can evoke a sense of predictability, routine, and enjoyment while orienting the client to therapeutic goals (Alders, 2012). Ultimately, openings and closings center attention on a creative process and can alleviate anxieties regarding the product outcomes.

Another means of balancing a focus on process and product includes planning out when to plant, harvest, or cultivate art-making materials. This approach can create a cyclical timing and establish feelings of familiarity and routine. For instance, in the spring afternoons, flowers are usually harvested since the dew has dried (Easley & Horne, 2016). In the early to mid-summer mornings, leaves are harvested because their chlorophyll and their aromatic constituents are at their peak (Easley & Horne, 2016). In contrast, bark, roots, and tree resin are typically gathered in the fall and in the evening hours when the plant is pulling its energies downward. In late fall, in the mid-morning, seeds are best harvested before the weather turns wet or the snow starts to fall (Easley & Horne, 2016). Planning activities such as these with clients based on the seasons and time of day can help provide a sense of connection to nature and also provide a means of orienting clients to place, time, and situation.

For some, paying attention to the phases of the moon is an important agricultural practice. Dates in a farmer's almanac can be a valuable

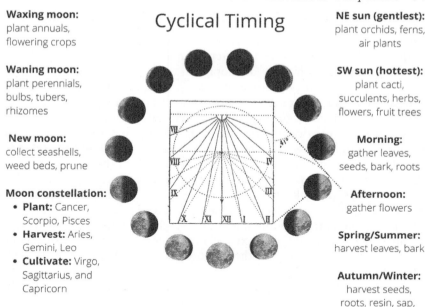

Waxing moon:
plant annuals,
flowering crops

Waning moon:
plant perennials,
bulbs, tubers,
rhizomes

New moon:
collect seashells,
weed beds, prune

Moon constellation:
- **Plant:** Cancer,
  Scorpio, Pisces
- **Harvest:** Aries,
  Gemini, Leo
- **Cultivate:** Virgo,
  Sagittarius, and
  Capricorn

Cyclical Timing

NE sun (gentlest):
plant orchids, ferns,
air plants

SW sun (hottest):
plant cacti,
succulents, herbs,
flowers, fruit trees

Morning:
gather leaves,
seeds, bark, roots

Afternoon:
gather flowers

Spring/Summer:
harvest leaves, bark

Autumn/Winter:
harvest seeds,
roots, resin, sap,

Figure 4.3 Eco-Art Therapy Cyclical Timing
Note. In this figure, some farmer's almanac concepts are embedded to help create rhythmic directives in eco-art therapy.

resource for eco-art therapy sessions for this reason. This reference can also spark rich discussions on how the plant world responds to the lunar cycle and how, historically, sowing and harvesting was done according to moon phases (e.g., plant things that exhibit strength above ground—like fruit trees—on waxing moons and plant things that have strength below ground—like potatoes—on waning moons). As you will see in Figure 4.3, you can provide clients with resources and visual aids to collaborate with them on eco-art therapy session activities according to time of year and time of day.

Another consideration rich with metaphor is the fact that humans share the same chemical components found on the earth and in the stars (e.g., carbon, oxygen, nitrogen; Metzner, 1995, p. 67 as cited in Ankenman, 2010). Incorporating references to the sky within eco-art therapy may appeal to many clients and align with their cultural practices. For instance, the moon moves through constellations just as the sun does. The moon appears to pass through all 12 zodiac constellations and farmers use these phases to plan action steps (e.g., plant when the moon is in Cancer, Scorpio, and Pisces; harvest when the moon is in Aries, Gemini, and Leo; cultivate when the moon is in Virgo, Sagittarius, and Capricorn). By having eco-art therapy relate to seasons, phases, and natural phenomena, directives have greater metaphoric potential.

Directive and Protocol Elements: Play as an Embedded Social Skill

Throughout eco-art therapy practices, clients of all ages will be engaging in the creative process—which is often compared to a form of play. Play is an integral part of human development throughout the lifespan, and facilitates opportunities to learn technical and social skills (e.g., sharing, turn-taking) and to exercise cognitive, emotional, and communication abilities (e.g., sequencing, planning, and self-regulation; Courtney, 2020). Play is a form of work and provides a means of flow and immersion in the art-making process, facilitating emotional processing and the reforming of a life narrative (Lloyd, Press, & Usiskin, 2018). In eco-art therapy, the process is not necessarily about making sense of an experience, as this is not always possible, but instead provides a means to look at an experience in a number of different ways (Lloyd, Press, & Usiskin, 2018). The hope here is that by looking at an experience differently, clients will be able to live with difficult experiences without allowing those experiences to define them or limit their future choices and enjoyment (Lloyd, Press, & Usiskin, 2018).

In eco-art therapy sessions, play is a means of creative expression regardless of age, culture, or background and occurs across a spectrum of

Table 4.2 Social Interaction Levels and Eco-Art Therapy Engagement

Social Skill Level	Interactive Roles	Eco-Art Therapy Example
Solitary (S)	Therapist provides a verbal directive and materials for client independent creation	Clients explore the texture and sensory elements alone
Spectator (Sp)	Therapist/group member models use of material for client to replicate or client observes natural phenomenon as an art study without taking immediate action	Clients sit together and direct visual attention based on sounds and other stimuli but don't interact
Parallel (P)	Therapist/group member creates alongside client on separate work with minimal verbal directive or assessment of client's work	Clients sit beside one another using shared resources and work on the same directive but have separate artworks they create
Associative (A)	Therapist/group member and client create a single combined artwork contributing according to therapist prompts	Clients cluster around materials and simultaneously create an artwork, contributing one at a time
Co-operative (C)	Therapist/group member and client plan and execute an artwork through dialogue and compromise	Clients create by taking turns, sharing, observing each other, and providing feedback to accomplish shared goals

five stages or social skill levels: Solitary, Spectator, Parallel, Associative, and Cooperative (Fehr, Boog, & Leraas, 2019). These stages typically fall into five ascending categories with solitary play being the lowest developmental level and cooperative play being the highest (Fehr, Boog, & Leraas, 2019). At any given time, clients may fluctuate between different stages based on their emotional state and comfort level. Table 4.2 outlines these roles and levels.

Within the protocols in Appendix A, you will notice a reference to each stage shown in Table 4.2, denoting therapist and group member roles. For instance, in the protocol, *Inspired*, the social skill level is listed as *Parallel* as the therapist may want to model techniques which clients all practice simultaneously but independently (e.g., breath work as coping skill). In this case, the clients would sit beside one another in a group setting using shared resources and work on the same directive but will have separate works of art.

Chapter Summary

A sense of belonging is critical for mental and emotional health. In eco-art therapy, social skills and interpersonal connections are cultivated through playful engagement with nature. By integrating eco-art therapy practices, therapists and educators can utilize cultural connections to nature as a means to serve a wide range of clients. Nature changes and is different every day. In this way, nature teaches us that there is nothing to fear in change or difference because it is one of the healthiest and most invigorating aspects of life. All humans feel vulnerable at times and may find comfort in peaceful, natural surroundings and artifacts. By paying attention to natural cycles as well as clients' diverse needs, therapists and educators can tailor eco-art therapy practices to make sessions relevant, respectful, pleasurable, and stimulating. One need which is becoming more obvious is equal access to nature since affluence allows people to buy homes in areas with more blue and green spaces. Eco-art therapy practices can help equalize this disparity by ensuring all clients have access to nature during sessions. Beyond taking clients into parks or onsite gardens, many formal locations are appropriate settings for eco-art therapy, including: mental health facilities and agencies such as homeless shelters, eating disorder clinics, substance abuse recovery centers, private practice offices, studios, and academic locations. However, best practices for deciding where to do eco-art therapy is grounded in what would be most therapeutic for clients and requires developing awareness and knowledge of ourselves and other cultures. No matter where eco-art therapy is practiced, culturally sensitive sessions rely on the skill and compassion of each therapist and so by consciously applying culturally grounded strategies day-to-day, we can better serve clients.

References

Alders, A. (2012). *The effect of art therapy on cognitive performance among ethnically diverse older adults.* Unpublished doctoral dissertation: Florida State University. https://fsu.digital.flvc.org/islandora/object/fsu%3A183336/datastream/PDF/view.

Alexander, A. (2020). The Artopia program: An examination of art therapy's effect on veterans' moods. *Art Therapy*, 37(3), 155–161.

Ankenman, N. (2010). *An ecology of the imagination an ecology of the imagination: A theoretical and practical exploration of the imagination for holistic healing in the context of art therapy.* Eco Art Land: Landing in the Space Between Art and Ecology. https://ecoartland.wordpress.com/an-ecology-of-the-imagination/.

Bermudez, D., & ter Maat, M. (2006). Art therapy with Hispanic clients: Results of a survey study. *Art Therapy*, 23(4), 165–171.

Betancourt, J. R., Green, A. R., Carrillo, J. E., & Owusu Ananeh-Firempong, I. I. (2016). Defining cultural competence: a practical framework for addressing racial/ethnic disparities in health and health care. *Public Health Reports*, 118, 293–302.

Betts, D. (2016). Art therapy assessments: An overview. In D. Gussak & M. Rosal (Eds.), *The Wiley handbook of art therapy* (pp. 501–513). Wiley-Blackwell.

Bogan, B. (2019). *Exploring the usage of found objects in art therapy for bereavement: A literature review.* Expressive Therapies Capstone Theses: Lesley University. 209. https://digitalcommons.lesley.edu/expressive_theses/209.

Boston, C. (2016). Art therapy and multiculturalism. In D. Gussak & M. Rosal (Eds.), *The Wiley handbook of art therapy* (pp. 822–827). Wiley-Blackwell.

Courtney, J. A. (2020). *Healing child and family trauma through expressive and play therapies: Art, nature, storytelling, body & mindfulness.* WW Norton & Company.

De Souza, R. D. A. (2015). *Project nature connect: Eco-art therapy creative activities that let earth teach.* www.researchgate.net/profile/Raquel_Souza15/publication/321084607_Development_Senses_in_Chidren_-_Eco-Art_Therapy_and_Art_Therapy/links/5a0c7f670f7e9b9e33a9c3e3/Development-Senses-in-Chidren-Eco-Art-Therapy-and-Art-Therapy.

Easley, T., & Horne, S. (2016). *The modern herbal dispensatory: A medicine-making guide.* North Atlantic Books.

Eisler, R. (2019, February). Sacred pleasure. (Interviewer: Bowie, S.) *Autre Magazine.* https://autre.love/new-products/pre-order-autre-volume-2-issue-9-maurizio-cattelan-banan-art-basel.

Fehr, K. K., Boog, K. E., & Leraas, B. C. (2019). Play behaviors: Definition and typology. In S. Hupp & J. Jewell (Eds.), *The encyclopedia of child and adolescent development* (pp. 1–10). doi:10.1002/9781119171492.wecad272.

Figueroa, L. (2020). *Nature, art, and identity: A heuristic arts-based study in multiethnicity and belonging.* Unpublished master's thesis: Pratt Institute, School of Art. https://cat.pratt.edu/record=b1250593.

Fish, B. J. (2019). Response art in art therapy: Historical and contemporary overview. *Art Therapy*, 36(3), 122–132.

Flowers, M., Lipsett, L., & Barrett, M. J. (2014). Animism, creativity, and a tree: Shifting into nature connection through attention to subtle energies and contemplative art practice. *Canadian Journal of Environmental Education (CJEE)*, 19, 111–126.

Gatfield, E. (2017). Augmenting Bowen family of origin work: Using the geno-gram and therapeutic art-based activity. *Australian and New Zealand Journal of Family Therapy*, 38(2), 272–282.

Geha, J. (2019). *Nature as an impermanent canvas: An intergenerational nature-based art community engagement project*. Expressive Therapies Capstone Theses: Lesley University. 113. https://digitalcommons.lesley.edu/expressive_theses/113.

Horovitz, E. G. (2017). *Spiritual art therapy: An alternate path*. Charles C Thomas Publisher.

Kaimal, G., & Arslanbek, A. (2020). Indigenous and traditional visual artistic practices: Implications for art therapy clinical practice and research. *Frontiers in Psychology*, 11, 1320. www.frontiersin.org/articles/10.3389/fpsyg.2020.01320/full=.

Kleinschroth, F., & Kowarik, I. (2020). Covid-19 crisis demonstrates the urgent need for urban greenspaces. *Frontiers in Ecology and the Environment*, 18(6), 318–319. www.ncbi.nlm.nih.gov/pmc/articles/PMC7436739.

Kopytin, A., & Rugh, M. (Eds.). (2017). *Environmental expressive therapies: Nature-assisted theory and practice*. Taylor & Francis.

Lloyd, B., Press, N., & Usiskin, M. (2018). The Calais Winds took our plans away: Art therapy as shelter. *Journal of Applied Arts & Health*, 9(2), 171–184.

Masterton, W., Carver, H., & Parkes, T. (2020). *Parks and green spaces are important for our mental health–but we need to make sure that everyone can benefit*. https://dspace.stir.ac.uk/retrieve/af8d1ac4-b4d3-48b7-9060-d8143fb8e29b/Masterton-Carver-Parkes-Conversation-2020.pdf.

McMaster, M. (2013). *Integrating nature into group art therapy interventions for clients with Dementia*. Unpublished research paper for the degree of Master of Arts: Concordia University. https://spectrum.library.concordia.ca/978027/1/McMaster_MA_F2013.pdf.

Moon, B. L., & Nolan, E. G. (2019). *Ethical issues in art therapy*. Charles C Thomas Publisher.

Morris, F. J., & Willis-Rauch, M. (2014). Join the art club: Exploring social empowerment in art therapy. *Art Therapy*, 31(1), 28–36.

Moula, Z. (2020). A systematic review of the effectiveness of art therapy delivered in school-based settings to children aged 5–12 years. *International Journal of Art Therapy*, 25(2), 88–99.

Neenan, M. (2009). Using Socratic questioning in coaching. *Journal of Rational-Emotive & Cognitive-Behavior Therapy*, 27(4), 249–264.

Pike, A. A. (2013). The effect of art therapy on cognitive performance among ethnically diverse older adults. *Art Therapy*, 30(4), 159–168.

Reis, A. J. (2019). *The metaphor of protected space in therapy with survivors of trauma: Development of an art therapy method*. Expressive Therapies Capstone Theses: Lesley University. 154. https://digitalcommons.lesley.edu/expressive_theses/154.

Shattuck, E. C., & Muehlenbein, M. P. (2020). Religiosity/spirituality and physiological markers of health. *Journal of Religion and Health*, 59(2), 1035–1054.

Speert, E. (2016). *Eco-art therapy: Deepening connections with the natural world*. www.artretreats.com/artretreats.com/wp-content/uploads/2016/11/artile-ecoAT.pdf.

Strongwater, P. (2018). *Planning for spontaneity: Music Therapy session prepara-tion, structure and procedures*. Expressive Therapies Capstone Theses: Lesley University. 49. https://digitalcommons.lesley.edu/expressive_theses/49.

Suchostawski, K. J. (2018). *Autism and mental health support: A closed art therapy group within a community art studio.* Unpublished master's thesis: Concordia University. https://spectrum.library.concordia.ca/984331/1/Suchostawski_MA_F2018.pdf.

Talwar, S. (2017). Ethics, law, and cultural competence in art therapy. *Art Therapy*, 34(3), 102–105.

Ter Maat, M. B. (2011). Developing and assessing multicultural competence with a focus on culture and ethnicity. *Art Therapy*, 28(1), 4–10.

Ugolini, F., Massetti, L., Calaza-Martínez, P., Cariñanos, P., Dobbs, C., Ostoic, S. K., Marin, A. M., Pearlmutter, D., Saaroni, H., Šaulienⵉ, I., Simoneti, M., Verlič, A., Vuletić, D., & Sanesi, G. (2020). Effects of the covid-19 pandemic on the use and perceptions of urban green space: An international exploratory study. *Urban Forestry & Urban Greening, 56*, 126888. www.ncbi.nlm.nih.gov/pmc/articles/PMC7566824.

Whitehead, T. (2020). *Plants of the garden – The Bible garden.* www.csu.edu.au/special/accc/biblegarden/plants-of-the-garden.

Wood, M., Jacobson, B., & Cridford, H. (Eds.). (2019). *The international handbook of art therapy in palliative and bereavement care.* Routledge.

Wycks, B. (2016). *Making contact: A neuro eco ed art inquiry into collective healing using the culture of bees as a lens to look at home.* Unpublished master's thesis: York University. https://yorkspace.library.yorku.ca/xmlui/bitstream/handle/10315/34775/MESMP02460.pdf?sequence=2&isAllowed=y.

Zagonari, F. (2020). Comparing religious environmental ethics to support efforts to achieve local and global sustainability: Empirical insights based on a theoretical framework. *Sustainability*, 12(7), 2590. www.mdpi.com/2071-1050/12/7/2590.

5 Methods and Materials

Session Protocols

Through eco-art therapy sessions, nature becomes both a metaphor and a means to explore coping. However, coping is a complex process. My hope is that you will take the protocols in Appendix A and adapt or revise them to meet individual client needs. For that reason, I have based each protocol on structured processes and three or more resources so the concepts apply to a variety of populations, including those who may have difficulty processing sensory input and are non-verbal (e.g., those with autism, dementia, PTSD; Ullmann, 2012). By adapting directives collaboratively with clients as appropriate, you will empower clients to take control of their health and foster their internal locus of control.

Each session protocol included within this book encourages the use of a variety of natural materials. Natural materials correspond to metaphors of human life; offer symbols of growth, impermanence, and loss; and reflect seasonal conditions of human experience (Whitaker, 2017). Materials found in the local environment are not only rich and varied sensorily and symbolically; they provide free media, therefore removing cost barriers to creativity (Speert, 2016). Art materials, like seedpods, feathers, and driftwood can turn up wherever clients may be and may encourage clients to independently collect materials in preparation for future sessions (Nicholson, 2018; Speert, 2016). By encouraging clients to look around in nature for art materials, the message we convey is that purchasing expensive materials is not a requirement for creating personally relevant and sensory-rich art (Speert, 2016). Nature itself is a living work of art (Whitaker, 2017).

All clients need is curiosity about the materials, where they came from, and what may be done with them to express culture, ideas, and emotions (Nicholson, 2018; Speert, 2016). Eco-art therapy incorporates mindfulness tenets to help clients notice details within nature so they increasingly appreciate its variety and novelty (Speert, 2016). The imagination is the only barrier to practicing eco-art therapy as a rich array of media is provided and relationships among aesthetics and ecology inspire therapeutic emotional connections (Neperaud, 1997, p. 19 as cited in Nicholson, 2018; Speert, 2016). Yet, when preparing to offer eco-art therapy sessions, keeping some basic art-making resources on hand can be helpful and can include: materials for drawing, painting, collage, and sculpture.

Materials for drawing traditionally include pencils, pastels, pens, and paper. These drawing materials allow for control and detail and are an important tool in art making (Hinz, 2019). In eco-art therapy, paper can be made from any plant material. Drawing utensil alternatives can include branch pencils, charcoal, and wood ash. Pens can be made by whittling the end of a stick until it is pointed and then soaking that end in water for 30 minutes to help it absorb ink. Inks can be derived from foraged leaves, beans, roots, flowers, and berries. Ink can also be created such as through an infusion of tea like rooibos, spinach, beets, tumeric, goldenrod, elderberry, onion skins, and more. Ink pens can be as simple as a pine needle or hollow stem like papaya dipped in the ink. Sanitized feathers such as from turkeys or hawks can serve as pens as well. These pens can be made by snipping the end of the feather to reveal the hollow interior. For oil pastels, beeswax melted into plant-dye-infused oil works well.

Materials for painting typically include watercolor sets and tempera paints in therapy settings given their non-toxic qualities. Painting materials can encourage the expression of feelings through color and brushstroke (Hinz, 2019). For eco-art therapy sessions, natural dye can be mixed with water, linseed oil, or cornstarch to yield a full-bodied paint. Cardstock can be created from the pulp of "weeds" using a blender. Paintbrushes can be constructed from natural materials such as pine needles, fennel fronts, and flower heads.

Materials for collage traditionally include pre-cut magazine images, construction paper, tissue paper, string, yarn, and glue. Collage is easy to control, provides structure, and stimulates the imagination (Hinz, 2019). During eco-art therapy, collage materials can include dried leaves, specimens including butterfly wings (ethically obtained), flowers, seeds, pods, sticks, feathers, sand, and more. Glue can be plant latex, root excretions, sap, or beeswax. Quartz sand glitters and vining plants work well as a string or yarn once dried and stripped of leaves.

Materials for sculpture typically include Model Magic, PlayDoh, cardboard, plasticine, wood, and water-based clay. Modeling with clay provides the opportunity to work in 3D and clients are able rework and reconstruct the vessels according to thoughts and feelings. Processing soil into clay is a great eco-art therapy process. As an alternative sculptural material, many fruits and vegetables can be dehydrated after carving to create engaging textures and effects. Apples, potatoes, pears, apricots, coconuts, and more work well for this purpose. Sculptural materials found in nature can include palmetto or lemongrass fronds for weaving and bamboo which can be formed into boxes, shapes, free-forms, and more. Gourds and luffa plant pods also serve as excellent sculptural bases.

Therapists depend on a variety of materials to engage clients at all stages and levels. Keeping materials on hand which are simple and unstructured enhances opportunities for creativity. Many of the materials art therapists have on hand are easily substituted with eco-friendly alternatives. Collaborating with clients to create the art materials in addition to using them for expression adds a dimension of exploration to the session. When clients create the materials they will use for self-expression, it slows the process down and imbues a higher level of intrinsic value to the resulting artwork. For example, consider collecting or obtaining flowers with a client, painting a canvas using dye obtained from half of those flowers, and then collaging with the other half of the flowers. The client may have a much higher level of investment and attachment to the final product than if they were to simply cut out images of flowers from a magazine. Additionally, when a client makes their own art materials, there is a corresponding feeling of self-sufficiency and self-efficacy which often emerges.

Establishing Priorities and Action Plans

The ultimate goal of this book is to help you incorporate eco-art therapy practices in ways which are feasible yet enriching for you and clients. With a clear goal, everything becomes easier and you will know where to best place your efforts to obtain eco-art therapy materials. The protocols offer a starting point for session planning while the content throughout this book has referenced many other methods meant to be adapted to your clients' needs. However, to begin planning eco-art therapy, your interests are, in many ways, as important as your clients'. That said, a clinical interest in practicing eco-art therapy is often rooted in: 1) values of sustainability, 2) a desire for healthier experiences and environments, 3) need for a range of methods to engage clients, and/ or 4) prioritizing high-quality therapy without the exponential costs of commercial art materials.

For example, if your goal is to align your clinical practice with values of sustainability, you may want to consider ways to use foraged, non-native, invasive plants as an eco-art therapy material since using these resources helps restore a sustainable balance to eco-systems. You may also want to follow the one-in-ten rule when wildcrafting native plants or plants which have wildlife value: pick one flower or plant for every ten plants growing in a particular location. If you want to cultivate healthier environments, you may want to consider ways to bring nature into a clinical setting as an art material on demand; this would mean bringing live plants into a client's home or your office or facility. If your goal is to have alternative methods to engage clients, going out in nature to collect or grow eco-art therapy materials is ripe with opportunity. Before you plan to take clients outdoors, scout new areas and assess them for appropriateness by taking casual walks to start. Exploring local areas will help you form an idea of what grows best in your area and which resources will serve as an on-going art material. You may also want to look around and identify what is thriving, especially perennials.

To accomplish all four goals, a step-by-step perspective may be necessary. The action plan shown in Figure 5.1 outlines a one-year implementation timeline with all four priorities balanced over four quarters.

As mentioned, therapists and educators may have many reasons for wanting to incorporate eco-art therapy practices. One goal may be driven by the desire to align therapeutic practices with values of sustainability. In this case, sustainability does not just apply to resources but also to the ability to practice eco-art therapy over the long term with diverse clients. By assessing clients and seeking feedback formally, you can ensure eco-art therapy practices align with client treatment goals and their individual interests and strengths. Although clients may be assessed at intake and during pre/post-tests prior to directives, formally assessing all clients on caseload as a cohort may yield insights into your practice impact as a whole. As an aside, informal assessments should be an on-going practice to maintain therapeutic insight and meaningful treatment planning.

Another goal is to cultivate healthier experiences and environments. By incorporating the six elements of an eco-art therapy space (e.g., aroma, light, color, space, texture, and sound) within the first month of deciding to integrate eco-art therapy practices, the therapy setting immediately becomes an enriched environment. Along these same lines, a third goal may be to have alternative methods to engage clients. Once an indoor

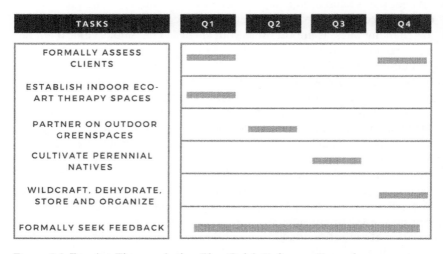

Figure 5.1 Eco-Art Therapy Action Plan Quick Reference Example
Note. In this figure, an action plan is itemized according to four primary goals to facilitate a quick reference.

eco-art therapy space is established, seeking outdoor locations can help you branch out in approaches with client. This requires establishing relationships with administrators at onsite locations such as native plant societies, nurseries, facilities, and natural parks. This may translate to free or reduced-cost plants, seeds, cuttings, permission to forage for onsite, invasive plants, or even budgetary assistance with creating an onsite garden. Additionally, through partnerships, you are naturally empowered to begin cultivating, wildcrafting, and storing art-making resources.

A fourth goal may be to provide high-quality therapy without the exponential costs of commercial art materials. By wildcrafting materials outdoors soon after ensuring an enriched indoor setting, resources can become well stocked within an organized therapeutic location. Additionally, high-quality therapy requires client engagement. By continuously seeking feedback such as through *Task Enjoyment Questionnaires*, you will ensure tailored, culturally sensitive approaches.

Methods of Eco-Art Therapy During Virtual Sessions

Modern technology has afforded clients and therapists with the opportunity for virtual sessions. In this case, clients need to have materials on hand. I have handled virtual art therapy sessions in several ways in terms of making sure clients have the necessary materials. Directing clients to forage independently may come with liability, resistance, and testimonies of inequalities related to access. Instead, I include a per-session material fee along with my hourly service fee and I have materials shipped or dropped off directly to the client. Apps like *Instacart* or *Amazon* make this easy. I find this especially relevant if the client is economically disadvantaged since the materials can serve both a physical and mental health need. For instance, consider a directive of creating a mandala. Rather than using markers, or colored pencil, the creative process can include creating a spice mandala where the client combines dried fruit, seeds, leaves, bark, and pods found in the kitchen to make a design (e.g., black pepper, clove, cardamom, cinnamon, anise). To explore new methods with clients, modeling what each material can do can be helpful. For example, teach basic skills about how to hold an eco-art therapy brush, how to mix flower dye into paint, and how to apply it to a surface. Show these techniques using the video camera if the session is virtual.

Creating hydroponic systems with clients works well in virtual sessions because it is so simple; the methods are easy to demonstrate on camera. The hydroponic *Kratky Method* essentially consists of simply growing plants in water such as in a water bottle; it has no moving parts and needs no electricity (Baras, 2018). This bottle can then be hung from the ceiling or placed on a wall shelf. Clients can engage in the process by painting the bottle, leaving only a strip unpainted to observe water levels. Painting the bottle black prevents algae from forming and competing for nutrients with your plant. Next, by using a bit of sponge, clients create a plug in the mouth of the bottle, and insert a cotton twine down through the sponge into the bottle of water to wick up water. Finally, they add seeds like lettuce, basil, mint, kale, Swiss chard, dill, cilantro, or even nasturtium flowers. To boost the growth of the plant, clients may want to add a few drops of plant nutrient like *FloraNova Grow* but that is not a requirement. A $10 bottle of plant nutrient will last around a year, maybe longer—a little goes a really long way. So for around $10, clients can have numerous bottle hydroponic systems in their home or office as a result of sessions. These systems can produce art-making resources in addition to transforming their environment into a green space.

Methods of Creating an Onsite Garden

For many therapists and educators, having an art-material garden would make eco-art therapy approaches much more practical. To cultivate this garden, use nature as your ally, harness its tendencies so you are tasked with considerably less work. For instance, insects are hardworking allies if you allow them to be present in the garden. Ants and wasps don't spring to mind as pollinators but they are important ones (Normandeau, 2020). There are safe ways to allow their presence such as marking their nests with flags so clients know to avoid those areas.

Effective pollinator habitat gardening means more materials for art making while also ensuring that gardens aren't just short-term endeavors. Instead, pollinator habitat gardening yields more resources in a shorter time period by permitting important creatures to mate, raise young, and increase their populations (Yarger, 2020). For example, critical pollinators, like groups of male butterflies, gather salts and "puddle" on mud to wait for female butterflies to flutter by—"a butterfly singles bar" (Yarger, 2020)! Similarly, two-thirds of native bee species will raise their young in underground burrows (Yarger, 2020). Given this, if we keep a few patches of bare ground in the garden, we're really just "wallpapering the baby's room—making it hospitable for needs and butterflies to rear young" (Yarger, 2020, p. 16). Having these pollinators onsite will quickly amplify the garden's productivity. To create a true butterfly oasis, keep a few wet areas for puddling and place flat stones in sunny areas so pollinators can sun themselves when temperatures drop (Lanza, 2020). Also, minimize or eliminate fungacides and insecticide use in your garden (Lanza, 2020). However, with pollinators come some compromises. Consider this vignette and words of wisdom from a knowledgeable gardener and researcher (Lanza, 2020, p. 33):

> 'You're happy that your parsley is being eaten?' My neighbor was incredulous. Yes, I was happy. The eaters munching away were the caterpillars of the black swallowtail butterfly…

In a garden, we will be sharing our resources with wildlife which will ultimately yield more art materials in the long run. Having a garden requires a long-term perspective.

Beyond growing materials, when incorporating art making in the garden during eco-art therapy interventions, choose materials which will hold up to the elements such as ceramic mosaics (Craig, 2012 as cited in McMaster, 2013). Concrete planters can be decorated and even formed as a work of art, and stones or flagstones can also become mosaics (Craig, 2012 as cited in McMaster, 2013). In addition to a pollinator garden, creating themed mini spaces, like a remembrance garden for a deceased loved one, can be therapeutic for clients.

If you have an administrator supporting eco-art therapy practices at your work location, you may be starting out with a blank slate of sod or turf grass and trying to figure out how to convert the space into an art-making resource. Modern technology, especially apps, can help you understand weather patterns, terrain shapes, water movement across the land, and sunlight distribution. However, there are low-tech options to this exploration as well and may be easier to do with clients.

For example, when I first bought my farm, the acreage was mostly covered with sod. To jump-start a transformation, I did a sun, rainfall, and native plant study simply by waiting to mow for one month. After one month, I went out with an aerial print-out from *Zillow*, the online real-estate website, and colored yellow where it was really hot and bright at 10am. That was my sun study. Those areas would easily get eight hours of sun. Then, after a heavy rainfall, I took the same print-out and used a blue colored pencil to indicate where puddles formed. This indicated "wet" areas with poor drainage. Plants that prefer lots of water and can tolerate wet roots could grow there. That was my water study. I then took a can of spray paint outdoors and drew a line border around these light and water zones which had large clusters of plants other than sod. The sod could not compete in these areas.

By doing a water and sun study, I ended up with more than two-dozen circles, ovals, and oblong-shaped "no-mow zones." Out of the two acres, 1.36 acres are "no-mow" zones—in other words, garden beds. To begin cultivating, I mulched borders around these zones, on top of the spray-paint lines, and started planting native pollinator plants in the mulch. Meanwhile, I let the area inside the zone grow wild for a few extra months to see what would emerge. Wildlife flocked to these zones, bringing with them additional seeds. I obtained a lot of interesting plants gifted by nature this way. These "no-mow" zones represented a variety of micro-ecosystems, and in many of these areas, marigolds, petunias, periwinkles, tassel flowers, day flowers, wild orchids, elephant ears, daisies, clovers, and even edibles like cassava grew without any help from me. They grew naturally and are excellent, on-going free art materials.

I paid $2 for the can of spray paint to mark zones, and in return, I saved countless hours since "no-mow" zones require very little maintenance. I do not irrigate my property and yet things are growing successfully. This is because I studied the area and used poor drainage areas as my on-going source of water. By mulching around areas that form puddles in the rain, neighboring garden beds absorb the water via the mulch and distribute it to other areas.

I kept mowed areas between the "no-mow" zones, so the property would quickly transform into a tranquil wilderness with meandering "trails." These trails are simply the mowed sod areas. This approach is known as permaculture since I did not displace what was thriving; instead, I simply added to it and managed it. The plants I added in my first round of planting inside the zone/beds included those which are easy to maintain and provide a gardener with a sense of immediate success. These plants included: fennel, calendula, sunflower, lemongrass, aloe, sweet potato, turmeric, and ginger. When I saw a desirable plant growing like marigolds, I collected its seeds and distributed those seeds to more areas to promote its spread. Within one year, all zones exploded with color and growth, providing plenty of art-making resources.

Methods of Cultivating Art Materials

By making art with objects found in nature, we set the context for emotional and psychological health (Speert, 2016). Our health, happiness, and vitality are all affected by naturalistic environments and even if you have never gardened before, you can easily and successfully cultivate art materials to promote your own and client health. The benefits of this choice to cultivate plants extends to the environment. Climate change is an ongoing topic among the scientific community, and many scientists report that things are changing faster than virtually all the models predicted (Ball, 2020). Luckily, you don't need to be a formally trained restoration ecologist to have a positive impact. Just a patch of soil, some patience, and a willingness to care about plants and animals; it doesn't matter if you have hundreds of acres or live in an apartment with just a window box or a planter on the porch (Burroughs, 2020). Plants can grow anywhere and with vertical towers, hydroponics, aquaponics, and other innovations, space is not an issue.

By cultivating your own art resources, you make a positive impact on the environment while modeling sustainability practices and decreasing the costs of materials. Personally, I enjoy prioritizing native plants so that the farm is full of butterflies and wildlife such as birds and bunnies, which create an enriching experience. Enjoying the experience of being outdoors is critical to ensuring an eco-art therapy session's therapeutic potential.

The *North American Native Plant Society* (NANPS) is an excellent resource when deciding which seeds to buy and plant in your particular area and you may be gifted free plants to help you get started. My local Native Plant Society has regular plant give-aways, providing me with free potted plants which I have transplanted throughout the farm. Native plants are hardy because they have adapted to local conditions and so they require less maintenance, including watering. Also, planting native specimens helps ensure a successful garden and on-going resources for art making as native plants may self-seed and spread.

Along these same lines, I've been given dozens of plants for free from local nurseries who needed to make space for one reason or another. For instance, one nursery gifted me two, 25-gallon live oak trees, which are butterfly host plants and the acorns can be used for dye (as well as eaten without processing!). Another nursery gave me 30 papaya plants since those plants were not likely female and would probably not grow fruit (papaya has three genders: male, female, hermaphrodite). Papaya leaves and flowers make excellent art-making materials, along with the stalk. Additionally, a plant with three genders has served as a metaphor and symbol in sessions when discussing the range in which sexuality can present. One of my clients, who was 16 and from a conservative family with devote religious beliefs, was born with ambiguous genitalia; the family rejected the child emotionally from birth and this rejection piqued once the child hit puberty and began to explore bi-sexuality. In this case, the papaya provided a symbol of diversity in nature and non-binary genders. Ultimately, the family interpreted the plant to mean that "God" or "nature" designs diversely, which helped us explore themes of acceptance.

This same nursery gifted me 20 guava trees since the fruit produced would be white (more like an apple) rather than the soft, fleshy pink version often preferred. A hard flesh like an apple is great for art making! Even if a nursery can't gift you plants, to save costs you can speak with the owner or manager and ask to collect seeds, or get cuttings as they prune. Cuttings grow plants much more quickly than seeds (just plunk them in soil in many cases) and these cuttings will grow up to resemble the parent plant more closely than seedlings.

In addition to having relationships with local nurseries, joining social media permaculture groups can provide you with an abundance of free seeds and cuttings as members exchange what they have from the previous harvest. Many gardeners will tell you that they have "volunteers" they need to give away to prevent plants from becoming overcrowded. These volunteers are simply sprouted seeds from a parent plant.

Seeds for growing art materials can be easily found in bulk at your local grocery store. I consider these seeds very practical since they are familiar, multipurpose, and often aromatic. For instance, flax seeds are an excellent resource for art making as the flowers are beautiful and buying them from the grocery store in bulk is a more affordable option than buying them in smaller quantities for planting. Sometimes, buying seeds, rhizomes, and roots to plant is more expensive than buying them to eat. I find this true for plants including beans, peas, coriander, fennel, flax, chia, squash, turmeric, and ginger. Much of the spice and bean aisle has potential; just be sure to check the legality in your area before scattering poppy or hemp seeds. Also, you'll want to purchase seeds which are "raw" and "unprocessed" to ensure they sprout.

If you buy foods: a) which were grown in your area such as at a local farmer's market or speciality food store, b) you eat them and c) you then plant the seeds to use as both a recycled food source and art material, you maximize your purchase. In my case, I recently purchased butternut squash, scraped out the seeds, ate the squash, and threw the seeds into a pan I keep in my fridge. Beyond being a food source, squash flowers are beautiful and the leaves are good for stamping in art making. The vine itself can be dehydrated for weaving and the squash serves as a nice still-life object. To maximize a food source turned art resource, I place food scraps in a fridge pan to create a compost; by keeping it in the fridge, there are no smells or pests to worry about and sometimes the seeds sprout faster since the fridge replicates a winter. Next, I layer in junk mail as it comes in to create a "lasagna compost": food scraps, junk mail (nothing shiny), food scraps. When the pan is full, I dump it on unwanted growth in my garden bed and cover with a flattened cardboard box (e.g., Amazon Prime) and then cover everything with a mulch layer. This process attracts worms, which create rich soil encouraging the seeds to sprout/germinate. In a few weeks, something inevitably sprouts up! In my case, butternut squash! Compost volunteers are such a delight!

Although many seeds are conveniently available, some plants only grow in certain parts of the world. A plant's associated *USDA hardiness zone* will indicate where it will grow. Some apps let you sort by zone. When I purchase seeds, cuttings, or roots, I like to use *eBay* since I can sort by sellers who are closest to me, meaning the plant was grown in my zone or close to it. eBay is the only site that I know of where I can do this effortlessly. Similarly, if I am grocery shopping using the *Instacart* app, I like to buy from stores which indicate the produce was grown in my state. For instance, pineapples grow great in Florida and I prefer to eat the fruit and then plant the crowns and seeds in my yard. For art making, the rigid leaves of a pineapple crown are a nice paper substitute and the fruit can be pureed and dehydrated into a fruit leather, which then serves as a paper.

Considering a plant's growth rate is important since the faster a plant grows, the more likely it will outpace "weeds" to serve as an on-going art-material resource. Annuals typically grow faster than perennials but need to replanted each year. If a plant is an annual, USDA hardiness zones do not apply since you can find a local variety. Just consider tomatoes which create a nice dye; tomatoes grow everywhere but *when* they grow and *which type* of tomato will grow varies by location. That said, not all professionals have the time to replant annuals each year. For that reason, perennial plants, which come back year after year, may offer considerable time savings. Some examples of perennials which grow in most zones include flax, lupine, coreopsis, daisy, pine trees, oak trees, maple trees, mint, sunflowers, roses, berries, and fennel.

Permaculture-Layer Art Materials

When itemizing which nature-based art resources you have on demand in your garden, consider permaculture layers (Lawton, 2008). Namely, by keeping in mind that there are nine layers of a forest, you and clients can look all around for resources. If eco-art therapy materials are sourced from all nine layers, there are plenty of options for collecting art resources even in the smallest of gardens. Those nine layers are (Kitsteiner, 2013): 1) Canopy/Tall Trees, 2) Sub-Canopy/Large Shrubs, 3) Small Shrubs, 4) Herbaceous, 5) Groundcover/Creeper, 6) Underground, 7) Vertical/Climber, 8) Aquatic/Wetland, and the 9) Mycelial/Fungal Layer. Using each of these layers optimizes the opportunity to harvest art materials all year.

The Canopy or Tall Tree Layer includes trees typically over 30 feet such as large nut trees and larger fruiting trees. These trees provide larger limbs for art directives such as carving and creating frames. I also retrieve husk and bark from this layer as a paper substitute. Using materials from this layer, clients can create leaf prints, shadow drawings, and more. Table 5.1 itemizes some examples of how to use this layer for art making.

The Sub-Canopy/Large Shrub Layer includes those shrubs between 10 and 30 feet which may be the canopy layer in smaller gardens. Most fruit trees fall into this layer and offer resources for sculpting and creating paper such as fruit leather as a paper base. The nuts of

Table 5.1 Canopy Eco-Art Therapy Material Examples

Eco-Material	Source	Process to Use
Wreath	Pine cones, needle greenery	Cut off the bottom of the pine cones using shears, leaving two or three rows of scales, paint the pine cone bottoms to resemble flowers, arrange with greenery to form a wreath, hot-gluing in place
Cyanotype non-toxic alternative	Maple leaves	Spread water over paper, add blotches of watercolor, lay fresh leaves on wet watercolor pigment, add more paint to make leaves "stick" to paper, let dry in sunlight, and then remove leaves to reveal print
Shadow drawing	Any large tree	Spread paper on the ground in the shadow of a large tree, trace the shadow on the paper

Table 5.2 Sub-Canopy Eco-Art Therapy Material Examples

Example	Source	Process to Use
Basket making	Mulberry	Collect young branches, pre-soak for 6 hours, weave a form using repeated under/over movements also called "randing"
Ball sculpture	Willow	Collect branches, strip leaves, pre-soak for 6–12 hours, tie a knot and repeatedly thread vine into a knot, forming a progressively larger ball
Banana leaf origami	Banana tree leaves	Cut the fibrous string/stem off each banana leaf, fold according to origami steps, and place in a cool, dry place to dry

Table 5.3 Shrub Eco-Art Therapy Material Examples

Example	Source	Process to Use
Blue ink	Blueberries	Freeze for 24 hours and then thaw outside or at room temperature to release pigment, strain
Crimson dye	Elderberries	Pour boiling water over seeds, mash in a jar, strain, refrigerate to preserve
Paper	Fruit	Blend to puree fruit, dehydrate into leather/paper, carve out negative space designs or paint on it

Table 5.4 Herbaceous Layer Eco-Art Therapy Material Examples

Example	Source (1 cup)	Process to Use
Stamp	Marigold	Paint a canvas black, dip a flower into white paint, and stamp the flower across the canvas
Purple, pink, or blue dye	Red cabbage	Cover with water, simmer for 1 hour, and strain to reveal purple dye; add 1 tablespoon of vinegar for pink dye or a tablespoon of baking soda for blue dye
Coiled container	Tall grasses	Collect an armful of 2–3 ft tall grass strands, bundle, coil, and sew in place using needle and thread

these fruits, such as with avocado, can also be carved. The leaves may be larger and offer an opportunity for stamping or serve as a paper when dehydrated. Large leaves can also be folded in an origami directive. Using materials from this layer, clients can create baskets, sculptures, and more. Table 5.2 itemizes some examples of how to use this layer for art making.

The Shrub Layer includes plants under 10 feet tall, commonly referred to as bushes, which include many nut, flowering, medicinal, and other beneficial plants. This layer yields materials such as flowers, thin pliable stems, and dyes. Using materials from this layer, clients can create ink, dye, paper, and more. Table 5.3 itemizes some examples of how to use this layer for art making.

The Herbaceous Layer includes those plants which die back to the ground in cold winters and include culinary and medicinal herbs which easily lend themselves to stamping, dying, and dehydrating. For basket making, I enjoy using lemongrass, which grows up to 5 ft and provides a pleasant aroma. Using materials from this layer, clients can create containers, stamps, and more. Table 5.4 itemizes some examples of how to use this layer for art making.

The Groundcover/Creeper Layer includes shade-tolerant plants which grow much closer to the ground densely to fill bare patches of soil, tolerating some foot traffic. Using materials from this layer, clients can create silhouettes, pounded prints, vessels, flower crowns, and more. Table 5.5 itemizes some examples of how to use this layer for art making.

The Underground Layer includes root crops such as a variety of edibles which can be carved and used as a stamp or dehydrated to preserve the gnarled form. Using materials from this layer, clients can create wreaths,

Table 5.5 Groundcover Eco-Art Therapy Material Examples

Example	*Source (1 bunch)*	*Process to Use*
Mosaic	Moss	Collect a variety of different-colored moss and create a pattern to form an image
Pounded flower print	Flowering groundcover	Collect flowers and stems, lay face down on paper, cover with towel, use hammer to pound, let dry for 24 hours
Lantern	Gourd	Use a dried gourd, cut off base and clean out inside, draw a pattern, cut out design, and insert a light

Table 5.6 Underground Eco-Art Therapy Material Examples

Example	Source (1 cup)	Process to Use
Watercolor	Turmeric	Mix 1 tablespoon of ground turmeric spice with 1/2 tablespoon of water
Diorama	Fennel roots	Dehydrate roots and use as tiny trees in diorama models and scenes
Portrait	Potato	Use black ink to depict a detailed, expressive face on the potato

Table 5.7 Climber Eco-Art Therapy Material Examples

Example	Source (1 bunch)	Process to Use
"Resist"/rubbing	Mint	Lay leaf under paper, rub paper with white crayon/beeswax, move leaf under page/repeat rubbing, add watercolor to reveal rubbing images
Nature mobiles	Ivy, virginia creeper	Collect 5–6 ft of vine, strip leaves, leave tendrils, pre-soak for 6–12 hours, select four strong pieces to be spokes, make a cross with spokes, and dangle remaining vines from the spokes with artifacts attached to the end
Bracelet	Honeysuckle	Collect 3ft of vine, strip leaves, pre-soak for 6–12 hours, cut into three, 12" pieces and braid into a bracelet

leaf prints, diorama artifacts, and more. Table 5.6 itemizes some examples of how to use this layer for art making.

The Vertical/Climber Layer spans multiple layers, depending on how the plants are trained or what they climb on. These plants are a great way to add more productivity to a small space and I have had success using these resources as twine, rope, yarn substitute, and thread. Using materials from this layer, clients can create mobiles, jewelry, and more. Table 5.7 itemizes some examples of how to use this layer for art making.

The Aquatic/Wetland Layer includes plants which thrive in water or at the water's edge. One example is a cattail, which can serve as a painting tool such as with pointillism blotting. Using materials from this layer, clients can create paintbrushes, oil paint pigments, sand drawings, and more. Table 5.8 itemizes some examples of how to use this layer for art making.

The Mycelial/Fungal Layer includes plants living on trees such as lichens and can serve as fascinating texture and dye resources. However,

Table 5.8 Aquatic Eco-Art Therapy Material Examples

Example	Source (1 cup)	Process to Use
Sunk relief	Beach or river	Create an image by digging in sand, then pour plaster into the impression to create a cast
Paintbrush	Cattail	Gather wild cattails and hang upside down to dry; then, dip in paint and use to blot color
Oil paint	River rocks	While wearing googles, gloves, and a face mask, crush colored rocks using a hammer and then a mortar and pestle; mix the colored powder with linseed oil

Table 5.9 Mycelial Eco-Art Therapy Material Examples

Eco-Material	Source (1 cup)	Process to Use
Collage	Lichens	Collect brightly colored lichens and arrange in a collage to create an image
Print	Any mushroom	Cut stem/cap to expose gills, press gills against paper to make a spore print
Living wall art	Air plants	Use hot glue to adhere to a frame and mist weekly to keep alive

when addressing mushrooms, be very cautious as there are poisonous varieties. To err on the side of caution, I use only very common varieties such as portobellos to create spore prints or dye. Using materials from this layer, clients can create living art, collage, prints, and more. Table 5.9 itemizes some examples of how to use this layer for art making.

Directives: "What Do I Need to Get Started?"

Directives help reduce resistance in session by introducing activities which are sequenced and structured according to a set progression. When using each of the protocols within Appendix A or those you create, six elements ensure engagement and alignment with best practices: 1) defined goals, 2) education, 3) pre and post-tests, 4) social skill emphasis, 5) structure, and 6) family and community engagement. Table 5.10 outlines these elements.

By defining goals at the onset of therapy, you promote a focus on the process rather than the product, reducing client anxiety over their abilities and creativity. At the start of each protocol, read through the steps,

Table 5.10 Protocol Elements and Eco-Art Therapy Purpose

Protocol Element	Eco-Art therapy Purpose
Defined goals and directive purpose	Promotes a focus on process over product
Includes education and modifications	Keeps clients focused, success-oriented, and safe
Assessments to evaluate outcomes	Empowers clients to see their own progress
Social skill emphasis	Fosters feelings of trust and interconnection
Structured models and frameworks	Creates predictability and rhythm
Culmination with an exhibit	Enhances confidence and communication

demonstrate any tricky techniques, and then let the client attempt each step, offering positive encouragement, only assisting if needed or requested. Let the client lead and be mindful not to impose. Only if something is harmful or dangerous is intervention required but in an explanatory, empowering way (Houghton & Worroll, 2016). At the end of a therapy duration, ask the client to reflect on their experience as this helps them to consolidate learning, engage in deeper thinking, and play an active part in their own growth (Houghton & Worroll, 2016). Ask questions like (Houghton & Worroll, 2016):

• What did you learn?
• What did you like about the experience?
• What did you find challenging?
• How did you overcome those challenges?
• How can you incorporate the processes you learned into everyday life?

Including modifications ensures safety and empowers clients to make progress. When you measure this progress, clients are able to see their growth and the therapeutic relationship can become further grounded in trust and interconnection. Structure paired with modifications can create predictability and rhythm while a closing exhibit can enhance client confidence and social skills, keeping family and community involved.

Elevating Experiences During Eco-Art Therapy

When a client creates an artwork, they may feel attached to it and be proud to share it with others because of an aesthetic experience. To increase the likelihood of this aesthetic experience and pride, eco-art therapy practices may include education on art techniques to facilitate clients' creative process. Techniques such as coiling, randing, dehydrating, and preserving can enhance a client's confidence in using eco-art therapy materials for self-expression. Eco-art therapy practices easily integrate education on how to use the materials and Table 5.11 outlines some common methods.

In addition to applying techniques, to help clients create artwork which provokes an aesthetic experience, educate them on visual elements to promote engagement (i.e., line, shape, form, space, texture, value, color, composition, and perspective). For instance, through a focus on line, clients can concentrate on varied expressions. Lines are a cognitive construct as the human eye perceives the edges, or "lines," of objects (Rush, 1987). Exploring contour line drawings by using dried vines saturated in dye and stamping the line can provide a means of discussing perception and boundaries while engaging client concentration, planning, and organization strategies.

To amplify opportunities for emotional expression during collage-making, educate clients on incorporating *ground*—in other words, how close the object is supposed to be to the viewer. Through ground, an artwork becomes a narrative imbued with metaphor and symbolism. Additionally, when empowered by knowledge on how to convey background, foreground, and middle ground, clients exercise visuospatial skills. When working with ground in compositions, such as when layering glued artifacts onto a surface, clients can explore themes and symbolism like personal space and interpersonal cohesion.

When using plant-based watercolors, client focus can be on incorporating negative space—the vacant space behind and around an object such as a background as well as positive space—the figure in the composition. When this duality is embedded, the seven principles of art can then become an additional consideration (i.e., balance, rhythm, emphasis, movement, contrast, pattern, unity). These principles can help a client communicate thoughts and feelings. So, for example, balance can be a nice metaphor and is easily explored with a leaf rubbing, resist painting technique to explore multiple types of visual balance like symmetrical, asymmetrical, and radial. Clients can use this directive as a symbolic point of reference to discuss life-work balance, for example.

Colors can represent physiological, cultural, personal, and emotional concepts, but conversely, the limitation of color such as with monochromatic works can convey feelings and thoughts dramatically. In this case, using only one hue/color and playing with values, tints, and shades of that one hue can help clients explore unity and continuity effects. During monochromatic works, clients can play with shading techniques like stippling, blending, cross-hatching, and hatching such as by using berry and tea-based dyes. With these visual cues related to contrast, therapeutic themes like differentiation and identity may apply.

Table 5.11 Art-Making Category and Eco-Art Therapy Method Example

Category	Material Example	Method Example: Description
Drawing	Sand or semolina	Vanuatu-sandroing: Creating an image using a continuous line to draft layers of geometric patterns and compositions
Sculpture	Sand, plaster	Sunk relief: Dig a design into the sand and pour plaster to capture and preserve the work
Basket making	Lemongrass, sawgrass	Coiling: Bundle grass, coil, wrap, and sew into a basket shape
Weaving	Vines, willow limbs	Randing: Form a series of X's with rods, weave a vine over and under the rods to join and form a vessel
Textile dying	Barks, leaves, fruits of trees like walnut, sumac, eucalyptus, and oak	Substantive dying: Use plants rich in tannins (e.g. bark, leaves, or acorns) to create lasting color without a mordant/fixative
Ink making	Herbs, berries	Adjective dying: Use plants mixed in with vinegar (to hold color) and salt (to preserve)
Water-color paint making	Beetroot, turmeric	Fugitive dying: Use plants which are ephemeral in nature; often edible
Oil-paint making	Linseed oil	Foraging pigment: Crush rock and mix with linseed oil
Paper making	Pulp from any plants	Furnish and formation: Pulp plants in a blender with water, pour through a screen to strain, remove wet sheet from screen and lay flat to dry
Air-drying	Plants, string	Hanging: Bundle plants at the stem and tie together using cotton string, leaving a loop to hang the bungle upside down for 2 weeks
Dehydrating	Microwave press	Pressing: Layer plants between cotton and ceramic or other hard material and microwave for 10 second bursts until dry
Desiccating	Silica	Gel: Cover plants in silica for 3–5 days in a cool, dry place
Protecting artifacts	UV resistant, non-yellowing sealant	Sealant: Apply to prevent artifacts from absorbing moisture and decomposing. Examples include resin, pH-neutral glue, lacquer, acrylic spray, and florist preservative spray. Review toxicity prior to use.
Preserving hue	Essential oil: thyme or clove, salt, vinegar, iron-oxide, soy milk	Mordant: Mix oil, salt, vinegar, or another mordant onto surface to be dyed or into dye to prolong the color and vibrancy

Eco-Art Therapy Materials for Anthropomorphic Storytelling

When working with clients using eco-art therapy approaches, storytelling centered on a material such as through fables is a way to inspire meaning-making. For instance, all materials offer an opportunity to explore cultural traditions and even mythology. Materials may evoke anthropomorphic images and this storytelling process of giving human characteristics to nature helps to promote feelings of connection. With these stories, the question is not "Is this factual?" but "Does the story teach us something about perception and experience?"

Consider the modern honey bee, which is a relatively recent arrival to the North and South American continents—one of the many agricultural imports carried over with European settlers (Mast, 2020). For some, honey bees are like many of us and our ancestors—immigrants to this country. They are the hardworking immigrants doing the job no one else wants to do (Mast, 2020).

Alice Algae and Freddy Fungus (Yieng, 2020) is a more detailed example of an anthropomorphic story centered on lichens and describes the symbiosis between fungus and algae. The story describes how "Freddie" the fungus builds a home for "Alice," the algae who, in turn, provides both of them with food. As a result, the fungus and algae take a "lichen" (liking) to each other, living happily ever after (Yieng, 2020).

I have used this story to imbue metaphor in group sessions and to highlight themes of interdependency as opposed to co-dependency or dependency. In one group, this story afforded a thematic exploration on interdependency, and later, themes related to stereotyping, gender roles, and bias came up. Food insecurity themes were also referenced. After exploring the story and the phenomenological elements behind the eco-art therapy material, we then created a collage using a variety of colored lichens. The images were rich with symbolism given the dialogue the story prompted. Eco-art therapy practices can be a means to incorporate storytelling to promote emotional insights and foster an enriching therapeutic experience for clients.

Themes and Metaphors

One of the most important aspects of eco-art therapy is its use of symbolism and metaphor. Consider the Chinese proverb: *"The wind got up in the night and took our plans away."* Therapists referenced this quote in their work with refugee families, explaining (Lloyd, Press, & Usiskin, 2018, p. 1):

> The Calais Winds have become a metaphor... the rapid weather changes mirror other external factors beyond people's control... arbitrary new rules and recurring violence... fear and uncertainty...

Metaphor and storytelling are modes of communicating abstract thoughts and feelings, as opposed to more rational experiences (Geha, 2019). Existential perspectives during eco-art therapy can offer opportunities to embrace multiple possibilities and meanings in life to create with a sense of wonder and awe and establish more respectful relationships (Moon, 2009, pp. xix–xx as cited in Geha, 2019). The natural environment with its metaphors can enable people to express the inexpressible (Kopytin & Rugh, 2017). In an eco-art therapy session, metaphor may be thought of as a perceived pattern through which "ways of seeing become deepened into ways of knowing" (Sewall, 1999, pp. 144–145 as cited in Ankenman, 2010). Exploring therapeutic themes metaphorically may spark new perceptions, connections, actions, and images. Consequently, ecological metaphors, explored through imagery and artwork, may enhance a clients' sense of well-being, and deepen their sense of knowing through new experiences (Ankenman, 2010).

Consider the following metaphoric quote (Axline, 1964, p. 215): *"Perhaps there is more understanding and beauty in life when the glaring sunlight is softened by the patterns of shadows. Perhaps there is more depth in a relationship that has weathered a few storms."*

Exploring metaphors with clients such as this one can facilitate a process of reflecting during art making. Just consider using this metaphor in couples therapy. Therein lies an opportunity for looking an experience in a different way, which may offer relief from stress and self-judgement. This metaphor is particularly suitable for eco-art therapy because it has visual references which are environmentally situated.

Signs and Symbols in Psycho-Education

Therapy and diagnosis have become stigmatized throughout history, in part because of the fear that an identified illness may lead to a loss of personal freedom. Because of this distrust, folk-healing approaches are still preferred by many cultural groups. Through incorporating explicit signs and symbols into the eco-art therapy process, clients don't worry about being psychoanalyzed. When the client chooses a symbol and meaning as an explicit, exploratory process which is known and discussed from the onset, engagement may increase and trust may become more apparent. Consider Table 5.12, for example, which draws from research on signs and symbols (Bradway, 2001; Burns & Kaufman, 2013; Ronnberg & Martin, 2010). I like to present this table as a print-out or email and request the following:

- What signs and symbols would you/the client enjoy exploring? Place an x beside the most appealing.

Symbols are an effective means of enhancing the therapeutic communication process (Kopytin & Rugh, 2017). However, symbols are personal and

Table 5.12 Signs, Symbols, and Eco-Art Therapy Material Examples

Symbol	Description	Eco-Art Therapy Material Example
Stars	Unmet needs and wishes	Star-shaped seed pods, sand dollar
Butterflies	Hunger for love; the soul; transformation	Specimens, empty cocoons
Plants	Reflections of growth; progress	Dehydrated plants
Bee	Creativity; diligence; nourishment	Honeycomb, deceased specimens, wax
Flowers	Beauty; femininity: Anima	Pressed flowers
Logs	Masculinity: Animus	Branches
Snakes	Sexuality; virility	Snake-shedding artifact
Fire	Death; anger; love/hate duality; power; wrath	Firebush buds, charred wood
Sun	Need for acceptance; prosperity; heroism	Sunflower
Rain	Sadness; purification	Plaster left in rain to capture droplet patterns
Bird	Spirit; freedom	Feathers
Spider/web	Persona; persistence; connection; unity	Spider specimens
Tree	Wisdom; the self	Bark
Clouds	The unknown; heaven	Drawing from observation
Crab	Moral and physical regeneration	Dried claw
Shadow	The unconscious/dark side	Shadow tracing
Ocean	Relationships	Shells
Moon	Fertility; mother	Photo-documentation
Cave	Womb; re/birth	Concave rocks
Egg/seed	Potential	Emptied shell

often cultural and so this table is *not* a comprehensive or definitive guide. Instead, resources like this are a starting point for dialogue and exploration with clients. For instance, in art therapy, the star symbol has been associated with unmet wants and needs, such as with a "wish upon a star" but can have astrological significance as well (Burns & Kaufman, 2013). Jung (1976) regarded the signs and planets of astrology as symbols for discussing basic psychological drives with clients (Datu, Valdez, & King, 2016).

Continuing with this example: to facilitate a symbolic process for clients, I have collected a variety of natural objects which have a star symbol either embedded or are shaped as a star. These include sea biscuit fossils, sand dollars, seed pods, and dried leaves and flowers. I also have a list of specific plants growing on my farm and the symbolic and cultural significance of each. Because each flower and plant has a unique meaning, I like to explore those metaphors with clients as they decide which to pick for the session. However, clients may want to explore meaning less overtly and that is welcome and encouraged as well. Having a signs and symbols resource can simply fuel creativity and serve as a starting point for open dialogue about goals and interests while preventing any feelings of insecurity based on fears of being judged or analyzed.

To empower clients, I keep a variety of flower dictionaries on hand which list historical meanings and symbolisms of flowers across cultures. For example, rosemary can represent remembrance, marigold may represent grief as well as celebration of life lived, and moss could stand for maternal love (Kirkby, 2011). Consider a mother mourning a miscarriage; creating a collage using these dried flowers and plants together may consciously allow her to express her grief while creating a work she could hang in a communal space without needing to explain herself or her grief.

Seasons, months, flowers, stones, and constellations all serve as a basis for symbology throughout cultures. For example, stones are sometimes referred to as bones of the earth (Murphy-Hiscock, 2017). Because these artifacts are rich with symbolism and folklore (e.g., quartz, amethyst, turquoise, jade), rituals abound and may include washing stones, leaving them in sunlight or moonlight, burying them in salt, or earth, or submerging them in water (Murphy-Hiscock, 2017). If culturally appropriate, these rituals can be included in the session. Table 5.13 shows a quick reference table of a variety of artifacts, their symbolism, and association with calendar months. However, symbolisms and artifacts vary by culture. Tables such as these merely provide a starting point for discussion and exploration with clients.

As therapists we have a duty to trust and inspire confidence in client self-knowledge. Even if clients select a sign or symbol from the chart or list as a means of initial engagement, all symbols and associations which originate with clients are unique to them and influenced by their history, culture, personal circumstances, and stage in therapy. The client is the expert on a symbol's meaning. Some therapists use symbols to begin a dialogue, trying to bring unconscious information into awareness. Others simply help the client explore their interests and preferences. In either case, visual imagery is the quintessential stuff of symbolism and symbols themselves are oversimplifications, helping clients to conserve mental energy; symbols are ready at-hand targets for projecting unfulfilled needs, feelings, and emotions (Kopytin & Rugh, 2017).

Table 5.13 Month and Eco-Art Therapy Metaphor

Month	Flower	Stone	Animal Constellation (Western/Eastern)
January	Carnation: bravery	Garnet: constancy	Mountain goat/ox: purpose
February	Violet: wisdom	Amethyst: health	Water-bearer/tiger: unity
March	Daffodil: rebirth	Aquamarine: serenity	Fish/rabbit: freedom
April	Daisy: innocence	Diamond: health	Ram/dragon: confidence
May	Lily of the valley: appreciation	Emerald: hope	Bull/snake: stability
June	Honeysuckle: gratitude	Pearl: love	Twins/horse: talent
July	Larkspur: bonds of love	Ruby: integrity	Crab/sheep: nurturing
August	Gladiolus: honor	Peridot: protection	Lion/monkey: willpower
September	Aster/morning glory: patience	Sapphire: calmness	Maiden/rooster: creativity
October	Marigold: passion	Opal: balance	Scales/dog: healing
November	Chrysanthemum: compassion	Topaz: friendship	Scorpion/boar: transformation
December	Poinsettia: success	Tanzanite: wisdom	(Centaur) Archer/rat: support

Some clients may ask for assistance in expressing an idea, feeling, or experience. In these cases, therapists can direct clients through referencing compositional aspects. Consistency, completeness, and geometry are ways clients can use natural materials to symbolize meaning (Hofstadter, 1979). By using materials and techniques in repetitious ways, rhythm is established and patterns revealed; intelligence loves patterns and engages both the viewer and creator (Hofstadter, 1979).

Enriched Environments as a Holding Space for Metaphor

With humanistic, existential, and transpersonal models, metaphor-related "sacred" spaces are relevant. A sacred space is an enriched environment which has an emotional meaning for the client. A blue or green space such as a converted therapy office, garden, beach, or wilderness can be both sacred and enriched if it increases somatic awareness and a sense of connection (Kopytin & Rugh, 2017). Not all clients have access to an outdoor space. Consider urban clients who may be receiving therapy virtually, logging into a session portal from their homes. These home environments may have health impediments which are beyond the therapist's or even client's control, yet metaphor can still transform the home into a sacred space.

Therapists can use humanistic, existential, and transpersonal models to turn any ordinary space into a sacred space. For instance, within a clinical office or a client's home, the coordinates, north, east, south, west can be mapped and indicated using a compass app on the phone or by referencing where the sun sets and rises. These cardinal directions can help imbue metaphor as long as they resonate with clients and hold meaning for them as individuals. Some of the metaphors associated with these directions were described beautifully in the book, *Nature and the Human Soul* and can correspond with seasonal themes as well (Plotkin, 2010). Presenting these associations to clients and asking them to visit various corners of their home to create using natural artifacts can enrich their experience. For instance, therapist and educators can guide the client to face a specific cardinal direction to process a therapeutic theme during art making. The therapist may also liken a seasonal theme to a client's point in life or therapeutic stage, such as throughout grief. Along these lines, consider the following metaphoric and symbolic associations (also see Figure 5.2):

- **East** is where the sun rises and is commonly associated with beginnings, origins, birth, enlightenment, renewal, spring, and the element wood and air (Plotkin, 2010). The associated therapeutic themes include trust, hope, gratitude, physiological needs, self-care, feelings of safety, and owning projections. The Expressive Therapies Continuum (ETC) component which relates is the kinesthetic/sensory level.
- **South** is the place of greatest summer warmth and light and is associated with fire, metal, and the midday zenith when plants are flowering, animals are growing, and humans are maturing (Plotkin, 2010). The south is matched with emotional connectedness and vulnerabilities, including physical and psychological healing. The associated therapeutic themes include identity, will, and sense of belonging. The ETC component which relates is the perceptual/affective level.
- **West** is where the conclusion of day brings darkness and is associated with autumn, the earth element, mystery, ambiguity, the subconscious and unconscious (Plotkin, 2010). West is the domain of storytelling, folklore, imagination, dreams, visions, introspection, and introversion. The associated therapeutic themes include intimacy, relationships, and esteem. The ETC component which relates is the cognitive/symbolic level.
- **North** is where the sun goes after it sets and is associated with the stillness of winter, water, and midnight (Plotkin, 2010). Northeast is said to represent death, facing the shadow. Therapeutic themes include integrity, wisdom, self-actualization, and transcendence. The ETC component which relates is the creative level, which integrates all other ETC levels.

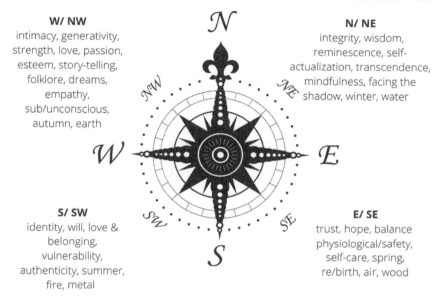

W/ NW
intimacy, generativity, strength, love, passion, esteem, story-telling, folklore, dreams, empathy, sub/unconscious, autumn, earth

N/ NE
integrity, wisdom, reminescence, self-actualization, transcendence, mindfulness, facing the shadow, winter, water

S/ SW
identity, will, love & belonging, vulnerability, authenticity, summer, fire, metal

E/ SE
trust, hope, balance physiological/safety, self-care, spring, re/birth, air, wood

Figure 5.2 Cardinal Direction Symbolism
Note. In this figure, the cardinal directions are associated with symbolism and metaphor as outlined in cross-cultural research and practice guides. However, client associations are the ultimate priority.

When clients create art using natural materials referencing cardinal directions as an inspirational starting metaphor, the art-making symbolism may be amplified for some clients. When symbolism and metaphor are amplified, the artwork is more likely to become a transitional object. In this case, the client may form an attachment to the art which gradually replaces the client's dependence on the therapist. Such a replacement can empower clients to create and engage in therapeutic activities autonomously.

To encourage an attachment to an eco-art therapy product, the therapist may want to encourage a slower pace throughout the creative process. Although some clients may not stay in therapy longer than one or two sessions such as those in a crisis shelter, other clients are in longer-term care. Associating ETC levels with the life-cycle of an artwork may also encourage attachment and the creation of transitional objects (e.g., see ETC levels within the Appendix A protocols). Table 5.14 outlines those life-cycles and the connection to ETC levels along with eco-art therapy examples.

The "birth" of an image relates to the moment when the image first emerges in session (Hinz, 2013, pp. 46–49). Taking on this initial process slowly helps the client address any feelings of anxiety or self-doubt at the onset so they can fully engage in the creative process. At this stage, focus

Table 5.14 ETC Level and Artwork Life-Cycle

Week	ETC	Life-Cycle	Example
1–2	K/S	Birth	Painting a single-color background
3–4	P/A	Infancy	Stamping designs for three layers of ground
5–6	C/Sy	Adolescence	Adding symbols to imbed meaning
7–8	P/A	Middle age	Enhancing color to clarify symbolism
9–10	K/S	Old age	Acknowledging impermanence by deciding whether to seal/varnish artwork

client attention on sensory and kinesthetic experiences so they naturally relax and experience a state of flow.

As "infant" art images emerge, it is best not to overwhelm the client with tremendous amounts of stimulation or interpretation so the images can be permitted to "just be" for a time without comment (Hinz, 2013, pp. 46–49). Allowing a slow start-up during the creative process limits the likelihood of *imagicide* whereas the client settles on a one fixed meaning of an image based on projections, eliminating opportunities for imagination and alternate views (Hinz, 2013, pp. 46–49). At this stage, focus client attention on perceptual and affective experiences so they explore multiple meanings and interpretations based on their culture. This exploration can open a dialogue which will promote later symbolism and metaphor.

The "maturation" of the image into adolescence may change the relationship between the artist and the art (Hinz, 2013, pp. 46–49). During this stage, the client may rebel against initial titles and meanings attributed to the artwork. At this stage, the artwork may take on new significance or may be influenced by input from the therapist (Hinz, 2013, pp. 46–49). At this stage, focus client attention on cognitive and symbolic experiences so they explore personal meanings which relate to culture within the artwork. This exploration can promote a client's ability to gain insight and motivation to make positive choices to enhance their life.

"Middle-age" images reach a point when clients clearly perceive an artwork to be portraying symbolic and metaphoric messages (Hinz, 2013, pp. 46–49). During this stage, the artwork can compel interpretations which help the client make life decisions (Hinz, 2013, pp. 46–49). At this stage, focus client attention on perceptual and affective experiences so they explore feelings of confidence related to decisions. This exploration can promote a client's ability to communicate clearly about their therapeutic progress.

The "old age" of an image is the point when the artwork is reincarnated into new creations or finalized and preserved for display to inspire a new generation of images, thoughts, or words (Hinz, 2013, pp. 46–49). At this stage, the "elderly" artwork may lend itself to the metaphor of death and dying, allowing the client and therapist to honor the significance of art images or using the creation in a new context or function (Hinz, 2013, pp. 46–49). Over time, eco-art therapy artifacts or resulting art products may fade in color or decompose. Some clients may choose not to preserve the work for symbolic reasons. At this stage, focus client attention on kinesthetic and sensory experiences so they have the emotional space to stay grounded in their attachment to the work. Explicitly empower the client to decide whether to preserve and protect the artwork and where or how to display the art. This process can promote a client's confidence in participating in community or family art shows, which helps to redefine the client from someone who may be isolated to someone who is admired and appreciated.

Applying Concepts: "How Can I Do This Today?"

You can get started with eco-art therapy practices today, if you'd like. Incorporating eco-art therapy practices can be as simple as including natural artifacts within your office and making them available to clients during creative processes. On your next walk to your car, look around and scan the environment for artifacts. To move beyond this initial step, you may want to introduce natural elements into your therapy space or mobile office. One example is a sand-play tray. Doing things indoors which can easily be transitioned outdoors is a way to build up to more immersive experiences and comfort with eco-art therapy for both you and the client.

As you gradually introduce eco-art therapy practices, regular check-ins can help guide you. By asking the client which materials they enjoy using, you'll empower them to fully engage. If a client enjoys modern technology, this does not necessarily rule out eco-art therapy as an approach. For instance, a client on the spectrum may be fascinated with technology. Going outdoors to photograph or film natural phenomena and discuss experiences during the digital art-making process can bridge therapeutic goals such as emotional and situational awareness. Film and video expands the lens of how therapists and educators relate to and connect with clients, and the qualities of film provide "distinct sensory and interactive experiences" (Carlton, 2014, p. 17 as cited in Duckrow, 2017). By understanding the client's initial interest, the eco-art therapy approach can be tailored to each client; for that reason, I include an interest query within my intake as an initial assessment (see *Intake* in Appendix B).

Intake Client Interest Assessment

What art materials would you/the client enjoy using? Place an x beside the most appealing. Circle favored examples within each category.

1   ___Nature-based materials like dried flowers, gnarled wood, leaves, shells, or insect specimens
2   ___Traditional art materials like acrylic paint, clay, or pastels
3   ___Scholastic instruments like watercolor paint, graphite pencil, or rulers
4   ___Modern technology like movie-making software, cameras, or video-game creation websites
5   ___Everyday found objects like magazine cut-outs, broken bits of watches, or old toys
6   ___Artisan tools like palms for weaving, body-casting plaster, or scraps for book-making
7   ___Home-life oriented resources like scrapbooks, embroidery, quilts, or bread sculpture
8   ___Textiles like crocheting, knitting, and sewing with yarns
9   ___Other (please explain):_____

Documenting Eco-Art Therapy Services

As with all mental health interventions, documentation serves to facilitate review and evaluation of client progress, maintain accountability, and provide safeguards regarding liability. The following template is one which has been helpful to me in both online and paper documentation as it serves as a starting point for quickly tracking session content:

ECO-ART THERAPY NOTE TEMPLATE (circle / fill-in as applicable)

Client:_____ **Date:**_____

Therapy content and goal of the directive was focused on: *(academic issues/ skills, anger management, daily living skills, decision making, assessment, boundaries, attention/ concentration, frustration tolerance, grief and bereavement, attachment, health issues, self-advocacy, self-esteem, self-determination, impulse control, social skills, symptom management, conflict management and resolution, coping skills, problem solving, parenting skills, organizational skills, other:_____).*

The format of session was (group, dyad individual, family, other:_____).

The location of the therapy was *(office, garden, public outdoor space, client's home, other:_____).*

The format was *(in-person, by phone, virtual/ online)* **and the duration was** *(45 minute, 1.5 hours, other:_____).*

The client presented with *(bright affect, dysthymic/ euthymic mood, poor/ appropriate hygiene).*

The directive used was *(psycho-educational, structured, centered on fine/ gross motor abilities, aimed at building rapport, informal assessment based, other:_____)* **and focused on** *(social, emotional, cognitive, self-care, communication, occupational, daily living, sensory/ motor, other:_____)* **skills.**

Client was *(compliant, resistant, passive, assertive, fully engaged, other: _____).*

Client insight into *(thoughts, feelings, behavior, symptoms) is (lacking, minimal, improving, affected by current stressors, other:_____).*

At the end of session, client affect was *(euthymic, bright, constricted, normal range, appropriate to context, flat, anxious, depressed, dysphoric, euphoric, angry, and irritable, other:_____).*

Plans for future sessions include *(a re-evaluation of clinical goals with this client; addressing and maintaining current progress with client; outside consultation for revised clinical strategies to better meet the needs of the client, other:_____).*

Overall, client is *(progressing, maintaining, regressing, inconsistent, other: _____)* **in using skills gained from session(s) targeting current goals.**

Important on-going considerations for this client include *(environmental stressors, substance abuse, medical/ health concerns, recent change in family dynamic, abuse history, other:_____).*

A copy of the research-based protocol/ directive with specific methods and materials used throughout session is *(attached, below, in file, other: _____).*

Intervention Categories: Approach, Goal, Format

How you employ eco-art therapy depends on each client's unique needs. Intervention categories help to differentiate and tailor session content. Selecting among categories of eco-art therapy approaches such as nature-as-material, setting, or subject helps to provide client–treatment fit. Likewise, pairing the approach with a goal category and outcome such as behavioral, cognitive, affective, or interpersonal enables the session to target client treatment-plan goals. Finally, deciding on format, be it individual, family, dyad, and group, personalizes the experience for clients. One client may benefit from: nature-as-material + cognitive goal + family format, while another may benefit from: nature-as-setting + emotional goal + group format.

A combined nature-as-material and subject approach can be a non-threatening approach and lends itself to addressing interpersonal symptoms during group and family sessions. Using dried flowers and plants as a collage material yields an aesthetically pleasing product and can reduce resistance because it requires no technical skill or age-specific ability. I have found this approach especially effective in family sessions when tensions are high and power struggles are apparent. The collaborative process of gluing dried artifacts onto a stretched canvas can help families bond, contribute, and feel cohesively involved. The members can cooperatively decide placement or work at a more associative of engagement, contributing to a part or section of the artwork. With the nature-as-material and subject approach, the therapist can more easily focus on observing and assessing dynamics while redirecting, and providing alternative interactions when maladaptive dynamics surface. With this approach, clients will not be preoccupied with learning an artistic technique and the therapist will not be distracted by external factors like weather. Additionally, with this approach, when the finished product is hung it serves to remind members they can support each other's contributions to achieve a shared goal.

Vignette: Nature-as-Material

Using a nature-as-material approach works well in individual sessions as well since it helps to target behaviors and the process of creating the artwork is primarily kinesthetic and sensory. To illustrate this, consider working with children. I once served an eight-year-old boy who presented with compulsivity and selective mutism. Intake paperwork explained that the mother's boyfriend had been incarcerated for drug possession and the little boy was exhibiting cruelty to animals. He had been repeatedly caught trying to drown the family's tiny poodle. In initial sessions, the client chose to only engage with the sandbox where he spent the hour "burying" a figurine to "drown" it. After weeks of this behavior, he suddenly began speaking in full sentences, telling me that his mother's boyfriend had drowned him in the family pool and then put him in the trunk of a car where the boy regained consciousness.

In sessions, redirecting the compulsion "to drown" proved therapeutic. We "buried" seeds in soil and "drowned" them in water. The metaphoric speech appealed to the child. Instead of experiencing shame and punishment for the compulsion, the child was able to witness beauty as a plant sprouted and flowered. The behavior was placed into a different context so that it could be constructive. The little boy needed an outlet which was contextually relevant to his trauma. Thanks to his engagement in therapy, we were able to grow some art-making materials, create narrative artwork, process trauma, and target coping skills.

Vignette: Nature-as-Setting and Subject

Using a combined nature-as-setting and subject approach offers many affective benefits, especially in one-on-one or even family sessions. A prime example is when I was serving a ten-year-old girl who presented for an office session with symptoms of depression. Her intake described a suicide attempt. During sessions in my office, she was reluctant to engage for fear of "making a mess." When I arrived for a home visit, the girl ran excitedly out of her home to greet me. The home sat on several acres of undeveloped land. She led me inside the home where a woman stood in the kitchen slowly rubbing a dirty counter with a soiled rag, staring out a window. The woman did not look up when I entered even though I greeted her. Three other children under the age of six were watching a graphic horror film on the sofa. My client tried to change the channel but the children called her stupid, screamed at her, told her to shut up, and pushed her. The home was unclean and cluttered; cigarette butts had been put out on surfaces everywhere—hundreds of cigarette butts.

My ten-year-old client told me that the outdoors was her favorite place and that she spent hours outside everyday alone. The scenery was beautiful outdoors but, when alone, the girl experienced troubling memories of being bullied. Although home-based family sessions aimed to address this bullying, most of our sessions were one-on-one and we routinely walked along identifying plants to pick for art making. By helping to develop this skill of identifying specific plants, she had a positive purpose outside rather than just waiting for the sun to set to avoid bullying. Also, we worked together to construct a safe place outdoors where she could create art independently and draw nature from observation to externalize her focus during solitary play. As she learned to externalize her focus and remain centered on here-and-now experiences, her symptoms of depression decreased. Additionally, as she developed skills (e.g., artistic, plant identification), her sense of self-worth increased and her resilience to bullying improved.

Vignette: Nature-as-Material and Setting

Using a combined nature-as-material and setting approach can help address cognitive distortions. I learned this while serving a mother and daughter dyad; the pre-teen daughter refused to maintain her hygiene. At intake, the mother did most of the talking, explaining how difficult and obstinate the girl was. In one-on-one sessions, the young girl was personable and engaging and we created a hygiene chart with a reward system. However, at one point, the mom rejoined sessions, started crying, and explained that her daughter had "rejected her" since "day one" when her daughter refused to breastfeed shortly after birth. As the mother explained, she started motherhood believing she was a failure and resented her daughter for that.

This cognitive distortion was at the root of many of the power struggles regarding hygiene and more. The mom believed love hinged on perfection and when mothering this child, she was incapable of perfection. Her daughter's imperfection was her own failure. These themes of rejection, perfectionism, and anger came up often and related to the mother's childhood and relationship with her own mother. Outdoor sessions in nature helped to exemplify how imperfection is not just acceptable—it can be beautiful. In subsequent sessions, we focused on the technical but forgiving process of weaving. We collected materials outdoors together as a means of positive and novel mother–daughter experiences. At a parallel interaction level, the mother and daughter each individually weaved a container to metaphorically symbolize interconnected, yet separate lives as well as the intention to create new, and heal previously severed, connections.

We filled the container with river rocks and explored the quote: *"There is nothing more receptive and flowing than water, yet there is nothing better for polishing stone—A mother's nature is paradox. Strength in gentleness; authority through consistency"* (McClure, 2011, p. 139). We created images on the river rocks to represent strategies for addressing power struggles as they arose and I provided psycho-education on conflict management and resolution strategies. Through exploring metaphors inherent in the nature-as-setting and material approach paired with psycho-education, the mother–daughter dyad engaged in a higher level of authenticity and honesty.

Beginning Your Eco-Art Therapy Practice

When tailored to client needs, eco-art therapy sessions are sure to benefit clients. Your choice to incorporate the methods and materials described in this book will help equalize disparities in access to nature and its health benefit. As you go forward to incorporate eco-art therapy practices, your own strengths and interests will help you decide how and when to utilize the resources within this book. Some may decide to incorporate eco-art therapy practices little-by-little beginning with nature-as-subject, progressing to nature-as-material, and then finally nature-as-setting. If this is your choice as well, you'll familiarize yourself and your clients with a range of possibilities while affording yourself time to maximize feelings of comfort and confidence in your ecological knowledge.

By utilizing the rich and diverse materials which nature offers, client engagement is sure to increase. Your own unique approach to practicing eco-art therapy will evolve and through referencing models and frameworks, you'll provide a safe and effective means to explore with clients. Although your own directives will be client specific, I hope that the resources in the Appendix will help you get started with exploring!

References

Ankenman, N. (2010). *An ecology of the imagination an ecology of the imagination: A theoretical and practical exploration of the imagination for holistic healing in the context of art therapy.* Eco Art Land: Landing in the Space Between Art and Ecology. https://ecoartland.wordpress.com/an-ecology-of-the-imagination/.

Axline, V. M. (1964). *Dibs in search of self.* Mansion.

Ball, J. (2020, April). Eyes on the sky. *2 Million Blossoms*, 1(2), 28–30.

Baras, T. (2018). *DIY hydroponic gardens: How to design and build an inexpensive system for growing plants in water.* Quatro Publishing Group, USA Inc.

Bradway, K. (2001). Symbol dictionary: Symbolic meanings of sandplay images. *Journal of Sandplay Therapy*, 10(1), 9–105. www.sandplay.org/wp-content/uploads/Symbol_Dictionary-English.pdf.

Burns, R. C., & Kaufman, S. H. (2013). *Action, styles, and symbols in kinetic family drawings KFD.* Routledge.

Burroughs, G. (2020, January). Plant it and they will come. *2 Million Blossoms*, 1(2), 49–56.

Datu, J. A. D., Valdez, J. P. M., & King, R. B. (2016). Perseverance counts but consistency does not! Validating the short grit scale in a collectivist setting. *Current Psychology*, 35(1), 121–130.

Duckrow, S. (2017). *Filmmaking as artistic inquiry: An examination of ceramic art therapy in a maximum-security forensic psychiatric facility.* Expressive Therapies Dissertations. 30. https://digitalcommons.lesley.edu/expressive_dissertations/30.

Geha, J. (2019). *Nature as an impermanent canvas: An intergenerational nature-based art community engagement project.* Expressive Therapies Capstone Theses: Lesley University. 113. https://digitalcommons.lesley.edu/expressive_theses/113.

Hinz, L. D. (2013). The life cycle of images: Revisiting the ethical treatment of the art therapy image. *Art Therapy*, 30(1), 46–49.

Hinz, L. D. (2019). *Expressive therapies continuum: A framework for using art in therapy.* Routledge.

Hofstadter, D. R. (1979). *Gödel, Escher, Bach: An eternal golden braid* (Vol. 13). Basic Books.

Houghton, P., & Worroll, J. (2016). *Play the forest school way: Woodland games, crafts and skills for adventurous kids.* Watkins Media Limited.

Jung, C. G. (1976). *The symbolic life* (Vol. 20). Pantheon Books.

Kirkby, M. (2011). *A Victorian flower dictionary: The language of flowers companion.* Random House Digital, Inc.

Kitsteiner, D. (2013). Nine layers of the edible forest garden (food forest). *Temperate Climate Permaculture.* https://tcpermaculture.com/site/2013/05/27/nine-layers-of-the-edible-forest-garden/.

Kopytin, A., & Rugh, M. (Eds.). (2017). *Environmental expressive therapies: Nature-assisted theory and practice.* Taylor & Francis.

Lanza, J. (2020, January). The parsley plant and the swallowtail. *2 Million Blossoms*, 1(2), 33–38.

Lawton, G. (2008). *Establishing a food forest the permaculture way.* Eco Films Australia.

Lloyd, B., Press, N., & Usiskin, M. (2018). The Calais Winds took our plans away: art therapy as shelter. *Journal of Applied Arts & Health*, 9(2), 171–184.

Mast, K. (2020, April). Bees as seeds. *2 Million Blossoms*, 1(2), 95–98.

McClure, V. (2011). *The Tao of motherhood.* New World Library.

McMaster, M. (2013). *Integrating nature into group art therapy interventions for clients with dementia.* Unpublished research paper for the degree of Master of Arts. Concordia University. https://spectrum.library.concordia.ca/978027/1/McMaster_MA_F2013.pdf.

Murphy-Hiscock, A. (2017). *The green witch: Your complete guide to the natural magic of herbs, flowers, essential oils, and more.* Simon & Schuster.

Nicholson, S. P. (2018). *Nature inspired art education for adults with Autism Spectrum Disorder.* A master's degree proposal submitted to Moore College of Art & Design, Philadelphia, PA. https://files.eric.ed.gov/fulltext/ED585197.pdf

Normandeau, S. (2020, April). Opossums as pollinators in Brazil. *2 Million Blossoms*, 1(2), 35–39.

Plotkin, B. (2010). *Nature and the human soul: Cultivating wholeness and community in a fragmented world.* New World Library.

Ronnberg, A., & Martin, K. (Eds.). (2010). *The book of symbols.* Taschen.

Rush, J. C. (1987). Interlocking images: The conceptual core of a discipline-based art lesson. *Studies in Art Education*, 28(4), 206–220.

Speert, E. (2016). Eco-art therapy: Deepening connections with the natural world. *ATR-BC, REAT.* www.artretreats.com/artretreats.com/wp-content/uploads/2016/11/artile-ecoAT.pdf.

Ullmann, P. (2012). Art therapy and children with autism: Gaining access to their world through creativity. *Fusion.* www.scribd.com/document/249760438/Art-Theraphy-Autism.

Whitaker, P. (2017). Art therapy and environment (Art-thérapie et environnement). *Canadian Art Therapy Association Journal*, 30(1), 1–3. doi:doi:10.1080/08322473.2017.1338915.

Yarger, A. (2020, January). Beyond blooms. *2 Million Blossoms*, 1(2), 15–21.

Yieng, J. (2020). *Alice Algae and Freddy Fungus.* www.scribd.com/document/435738237/Alice-Algae-and-Freddy-Fungus.

Appendix A: 25 Eco-Art Therapy Protocols

YOU ARE SAFE HERE

DIRECTIVE OVERVIEW

Eco-Art Therapy Approach: Subject, material
Therapeutic Themes: Safety, self-care, settings
Goal Category: Cognitive
Psychoeducation: Impact of setting on mental health
Recommended GAF: 50+
Relevant Resources: Lee et al., 2015; Rasmussen et al., 2014; Struckman, 2020

METHODS & MATERIALS

Setting: Client home
Duration/Frequency: 10 weekly, 1.5 hour sessions
Format: Individual
Assessment: Home Environment Index (HEI)

- **K/S (week 1 & 2 - goal review, pretest):** Fill rubber gloves with plaster, shaping gloves around a plant container. Once the plaster sets, remove the gloves from the plaster revealing casted hands.

- **P/A (week 3 & 4 - psychoeducation):** Paint hands a color associated with health, protection, and safety. Secure a plant container within the hands using glue or plaster.

- **C/Sy (week 5 & 6 - therapeutic themes):** Place an air plant or succulent within the container. Discuss plant's environmental needs. Use plant as a symbolic bridge to create a client home-environment enhancement plan.

- **P/A (week 7 & 8 - psychoeducation):** Foster a healthy environment where the plant will live. Discuss methods of maintaining and improving health through an organized home environment.

- **K/S (week 9 & 10 - progress review, post-test):** Photograph the plant in its healthy environment. Create a frame to enable exhibit.

COMPONENTS

Art Education: "Living sculptures," form
Social Skill Level: Cooperative; therapist assists with filling gloves and gluing
Signs, Symbols, & Metaphors: Holding environments
Budget: $9 - Plant containers, plaster, latex gloves, air plants (free outdoors)
Tools: Pliers to pull glove off plaster, hot glue gun; use recycled gloves if possible

SAFETY/ ETHICS MODIFICATIONS

Material Toxicity or Allergens: Ensure air circulation when pouring plaster powder
Client Resources & Skills: Episodic memory: remembering to water plant(s). Choose low-maintenance indoor plants or those suitable for Kratky hydroponics
Client History Considerations: Poorly organized/cluttered environment may reflect past trauma and may need processing to address

ORGANIC COLLAGE

DIRECTIVE OVERVIEW

Eco-Art Therapy Approach: Material, setting
Therapeutic Themes: Relationships, decision making, responsibility
Goal Category: Interpersonal
Psychoeducation: Interdependency, life satisfaction
Recommended GAF: 50+
Relevant Resources: Carpendale, 2010; Esnaola et al., 2017; Lun et al., 2008

METHODS & MATERIALS

Setting: Office, garden
Duration/Frequency: 10 weekly, 1.5 hour sessions
Format: Group
Assessment: Satisfaction with Life Scale (SwLS)

- **K/S (week 1 & 2 - goal review, pretest):** Collect moss, lichens or air plants. Sort by size, texture, and color.

- **P/A (week 3 & 4 - psychoeducation):** Discuss the concept of interdependency and symbiosis; refer to the life cycles of moss, lichens, and air plants. *How does interdependence contribute to survival? How are humans interdependent?* Draw a series of shapes on a masonite board to plan collage composition.

- **C/Sy (week 5 & 6 - therapeutic themes):** Use the concept of interdependency as a metaphor for relationships. Glue the plants within and around the shapes to symbolize healthy boundaries.

- **P/A (week 7 & 8 - psychoeducation):** Fill in all areas with the organic matter so that no masonite board shows through. Use color and texture to create a composition which exudes "calm confidence."

- **K/S (week 9 & 10 - progress review, post-test):** Attach a hanging apparatus on the back of the masonite board and hang in a shared space.

COMPONENTS

Art Education: Fractals, *Lichens for Skyscrapers Project*, texture, composition
Social Skill Level: Cooperative; therapist assists with collecting and adhering
Signs, Symbols, & Metaphors: Interdependence, symbiosis; negative/positive space
Budget: $5 - Masonite boards and sawtooth backs for hanging
Tools: Hot glue gun, nails, hammer

SAFETY & ETHICS: MODIFICATIONS

Material Toxicity or Allergens: Confirm safety of all plant materials; only use lichens attached to bark found on ground
Client Resources & Skills: Category formation
Client History Considerations: Frustration tolerance may be an issue if materials are brittle

DREAM CATCHER

DIRECTIVE OVERVIEW

Eco-Art Therapy Approach: Material
Therapeutic Themes: Self-care, impulse control
Goal Category: Behavioral
Psychoeducation: Methods to improve sleep
Recommended GAF: 40+
Relevant Resources: Daughtry, 2018; Knutson et al., 2017; Irish et al., 2015

METHODS & MATERIALS

Setting: Office or client home
Duration/Frequency: 10 weekly, 1.5 hour sessions
Format: Individual or family
Assessment: National Sleep Foundation Sleep Health Index

- **K/S (week 1 & 2 - goal review, pretest):** Select a thick vine (e.g., 2mm+) 18"+ long and a thin vine (e.g., .5mm+) 48"+ length. Cut thin vine into one long piece and three short pieces. Soak for malleability.

- **P/A (week 3 & 4 - psychoeducation):** Select artifacts associated with peace and tranquility (e.g. amethyst, arolla pine). Attach to thin vine short pieces.

- **C/Sy (week 5 & 6 - therapeutic themes):** Bend thick vine into circular shape and secure with thin, long vine woven into a dreamcatcher. Symbolize sleep as critical to goals. Dangle artifacts from dreamcatcher with vines.

- **P/A (week 7 & 8 - psychoeducation):** Paint feathers with symbols of sleep aid methods (e.g., exercise, nutrition, mindfulness, progressive muscle relaxation, guided imagery, sleep logging, decreasing technology in bed). Practice methods. Attach feathers.

- **K/S (week 9 & 10 - progress review, post-test):** Create a hanging apparatus. Mist a calming aroma onto the feathers (e.g., lavender essential oil)

COMPONENTS

Art Education: Metaphysics (e.g., crystals, stones, minerals, wood); shape
Social Skill Level: Spectator; therapist models methods of weaving
Signs, Symbols, & Metaphors: Hope, protection
Budget: $10 - Beads, crystals, twine, oil
Tools: Scissors to cut twine or vines, glue

SAFETY & ETHICS: MODIFICATIONS

Material Toxicity or Allergens: Avoid vines with sap
Client Resources & Skills: Fine motor skills
Client History Considerations: Those struggling with technology addiction may resist decreasing technology use in bed

SUNLIGHT PORTRAIT

DIRECTIVE OVERVIEW

Eco-Art Therapy Approach: Subject
Therapeutic Themes: Self-care, physiological needs
Goal Category: Behavioral
Psychoeducation: Sunlight & mental health
Recommended GAF: 20+
Relevant Resources: An et al., 2016; Bolek-Berquist et al., 2009; Thong, 2007

METHODS & MATERIALS

Setting: Office, client home, onsite garden
Duration/Frequency: 10 weekly, 1.5 hour sessions
Format: Individual, dyad
Assessment: Sun Exposure Questionnaire

- **K/S (week 1 & 2 - goal review, pretest):** Walk outdoors and observe different types of sunlight: direct, indirect, filtered, dappled, and partial.

- **P/A (week 3 & 4 - psychoeducation):** Learn about how sunlight helps release serotonin and enhance mood, sleep, and the immune system. Step into a variety of sunlight and document thoughts/feelings which arise.

- **C/Sy (week 5 & 6 - therapeutic themes):** Take a series of front-facing self-portraits. Focus the image on the face with eyes closed. Discuss symbolic impact of the photos. *What does the photo remind you of? How does the sunlight influence this perception?*

- **P/A (week 7 & 8 - psychoeducation):** Edit the photos to convey the emotional experience and the symbolic impact. Discuss ways to safely integrate sun exposure into a daily routine.

- **K/S (week 9 & 10 - progress review, post-test):** Print photos. Create a frame using natural materials such as sticks, bamboo, or twine to enable exhibit. Write out a sun exposure plan.

COMPONENTS

Art Education: Aperture; painting with light, value
Social Skill Level: Spectator; therapist models app during photography or editing
Signs, Symbols, & Metaphors: Recharging, "facing" feelings, aura
Budget: $5 - Aperture app
Tools: Smart phone, camera, or computer

SAFETY & ETHICS: MODIFICATIONS

Material Toxicity or Allergens: Avoid mid-day direct sunlight. Limit sun exposure to 15-minute increments. Plan for early morning/late afternoon sun
Client Resources & Skills: Ensure client is dressed to avoid overheating. Dappled sunlight may be most gentle
Client History Considerations: Those struggling with agoraphobia may prefer indoor/filtered light

APPLE DOLL

DIRECTIVE OVERVIEW

Eco-Art Therapy Approach: Material
Therapeutic Themes: Nutrition, problem solving
Goal Category: Behavioral
Psychoeducation: Nutrition and lifelong health
Recommended GAF: 40+
Relevant Resources: Gantt & Tabone, 1998;
Kritchevsky, 2016; Krystyniak, 2020

METHODS & MATERIALS

Setting: Office, client home or garden
Duration/Frequency: 10 weekly, 1.5 hour sessions
Format: Individual, group, or family
Assessment: Person Picking an Apple for Tree
(PPAT/ FEATS Scales: Logic, Realism, Problem-
solving)

- **K/S (week 1 & 2 - goal review, pretest):** Collect found objects such as sticks, vine, large flowers, leaves, and coconut husk to serve as doll body and clothing.

- **P/A (week 3 & 4 - psychoeducation):** Carve eyes, ears, nose, and mouth into an apple. Soak carved apple in 1 tbsp. salt dissolved in one cup of lemon juice. Dehydrate in sun or oven/ dehydrator. Process feelings associated with multigenerational relationships/ aging.

- **C/Sy (week 5 & 6 - therapeutic themes):** Assemble the "aged" doll using found objects body parts and clothing. Discuss gender features and explore problem solving. *Is healthy aging a life achievement? In what ways does lifestyle promote a long, healthy life?*

- **P/A (week 7 & 8 - psychoeducation):** Paint details onto the face using diluted food coloring and toothpicks; add details to clothing and body parts.

- **K/S (week 9 & 10 - progress review, post-test):** Create a display stand using sticks to enable exhibit.

COMPONENTS

Art Education: Apple dolls in folk art, form
Social Skill Level: Parallel; therapist models comfort with carving and dehydrating
Signs, Symbols, & Metaphors: Dignity, transitional objects
Budget: $5 - Apple, lemon juice, food coloring, salt, toothpicks
Tools: Spoon to carve apple and hammer to assemble stand

SAFETY & ETHICS: MODIFICATIONS

Material Toxicity or Allergens: Food coloring may dye skin
Client Resources & Skills: Praxis
Client History Considerations: Food insecurity will impact a client's interaction with materials

SENSORY STILL LIFE

DIRECTIVE OVERVIEW

Eco-Art Therapy Approach: Subject
Therapeutic Themes: Sublimation, transition, perception
Goal Category: Cognitive, Affective
Psychoeducation: Externalizing focus/positive distraction
Recommended GAF: 20+
Relevant Resources: Drake, Hastedt, & James, 2016; McMaster, 2013; Schotanus-Dijkstra et al., 2016

METHODS & MATERIALS

Setting: Office or client home
Duration/Frequency: 10 weekly, 1.5 hour sessions
Format: Individual or group
Assessment: A Favorite Kind of Day/The Flourishing Scale (FS)

- **K/S (week 1 & 2 - goal review, pretest):** Position colorful, aromatic, textured nature artifacts and edibles into a pleasing arrangement to represent *A Favorite Kind of Day*; note sensory responses to artifacts.

- **P/A (week 3 & 4 - psychoeducation):** Prioritize playful abstraction. *How can you abstract your image to show the objects are favored?* Draft shapes on canvas to map out still-life object placement in graphite.

- **C/Sy (week 5 & 6 - therapeutic themes):** Add painted tonal values to convey joy, contentment, or happiness.

- **P/A (week 7 & 8 - psychoeducation):** Discuss moments of self-acceptance. *How does self-acceptance impact a person's ability to flourish?* Add pen and ink design elements to convey personal style.

- **K/S (week 9 & 10 - progress review, post-test):** Write an expressive artist statement. Include title, medium, year in addition to the expressive description.

COMPONENTS

Art Education: MIT's "empathetic aesthetics" program, perspective
Social Skill Level: Associative; therapist contributes technical guidance on request
Signs, Symbols, & Metaphors: Choices
Budget: $0-$7 - Still-life objects
Tools: Table and light(s)

SAFETY & ETHICS: MODIFICATIONS

Material Toxicity or Allergens: Pumpkins and dried artifacts help to avoid insects
Client Resources & Skills: Sustained attention
Client History Considerations: Those with food insecurity, eating disorders or nutritional deficiencies may be triggered by edibles - address; avoid stimulants/alcohol in still life

BREAD SCULPTURE

DIRECTIVE OVERVIEW

Eco-Art Therapy Approach: Material
Therapeutic Themes: Internalization, growth-mindset
Goal Category: Cognitive
Psychoeducation: Self-actualization
Recommended GAF: 20+
Relevant Resources: D'Souza, Adams, & Fuss, 2015; Dhaese, 2011; Kaufman, 2018

METHODS & MATERIALS

Setting: Office or client home
Duration/Frequency: 10 weekly, 1.5 hour sessions
Format: Individual
Assessment: Self-Actualization Activity Inventory

- **K/S (week 1 & 2 - goal review, pretest):** Discuss facets of self-actualization. Mix clumps of whole-wheat bread dough with food dyes to create a color palette.

- **P/A (week 3 & 4 - psychoeducation):** Mold dough into balls - each representing talents or potentials. Add herbs symbolizing goals (e.g., chives for harmony, balance). Assemble to show the interconnection of talent and potential (e.g., caterpillar body segments). Bake.

- **C/Sy (week 5 & 6 - therapeutic themes):** Form dough to symbolize metamorphosis towards self-actualization (e.g., cocoon). Bake. *How are you growing as a person? How does intraspection aid this process?*

- **P/A (week 7 & 8 - psychoeducation):** Symbolize the process of self-actualizing as requiring action, goals, and strategy (e.g., butterfly in flight). Bake. Paint details with food-based dyes. *What goals do you have?*

- **K/S (week 9 & 10 - progress review, post-test):** Take home a portion of dough or ingredients to repeat bread-sculpture process with a family member. Teaching others is part of self-actualization.

COMPONENTS

Art Education: Marc Quinn bread sculptures, shape
Social Skill Level: Parallel; therapist models shaping techniques
Signs, Symbols, & Metaphors: Metamorphosis, stability, and plasticity
Budget: $5 - Flour, yeast/baking soda, water, salt
Tools: Convection oven

SAFETY & ETHICS: MODIFICATIONS

Material Toxicity or Allergens: Assess food allergies. Refrigerate bread in between sessions
Client Resources & Skills: Cognitive flexibility and control
Client History Considerations: Baker's clay is an inedible alternative. Address sensory aversions

SPORE PRINT

DIRECTIVE OVERVIEW

Eco-Art Therapy Approach: Material
Therapeutic Themes: Transformation, authenticity, vulnerability
Goal Category: Cognitive
Psychoeducation: Leadership and existentialism
Recommended GAF: 20+
Relevant Resources: Agbude et al., 2017; Allan & Shearer, 2012; Kennedy & Villaverde, 2014

METHODS & MATERIALS

Setting: Office or client home
Duration/Frequency: 10 weekly, 1.5 hour sessions
Format: Individual
Assessment: Scale for Existential Thinking

- **K/S (week 1 & 2 - goal review, pretest):** Touch mushroom gills and discuss fungi's symbolism (e.g., growth, networking and transformation). Place fungi gill-side down on white, acid-free paper; cover. Wait two days for spore drop. Secure with fixative.

- **P/A (week 3 & 4 - psychoeducation):** Analyze spore patterns. Associate forms with existential themes. Freely associate. *What could the print be transformed into?* Draft ideas in pencil over print.

- **C/Sy (week 5 & 6 - therapeutic themes):** Use pen and ink to define ideas and explore social, cultural and political symbolic connections.

- **P/A (week 7 & 8 - psychoeducation):** Reflect on experiences during free association. *How does meaning-making relate to personal growth?* Add color to represent growth and ability.

- **K/S (week 9 & 10 - progress review, post-test):** Create a frame using natural materials to enable exhibit.

COMPONENTS

Art Education: A/r/tography, line, pattern
Social Skill Level: Solitary; therapist may wish to encourage autonomy
Signs, Symbols, & Metaphors: Mutualistic and parasitic relationships, identity, embraced ideologies, escape into the unconscious
Budget: $3 - Mushrooms, paper
Tools: paper, glass bowl, colored pens

SAFETY & ETHICS: MODIFICATIONS

Material Toxicity or Allergens: Use edible mushrooms only
Client Resources & Skills: Cognitive flexibility and control
Client History Considerations: Those with a history of substance abuse may associate mushrooms with psychedelic use/abuse; themes of death/decomposition can trigger anxiety

FOUR EMOTIONS

DIRECTIVE OVERVIEW

Eco-Art Therapy Approach: Material
Therapeutic Themes: Self-monitoring, gratitude
Goal Category: Affective, Behavioral
Psychoeducation: Emotions and well-being
Recommended GAF: 60+
Relevant Resources: Hinz, 2009; Sansone & Sansone, 2010; Valikhani et al., 2019

METHODS & MATERIALS

Setting: Beach (waterfront) or office
Duration/Frequency: 10 weekly, 1.5 hour sessions
Format: Individual
Assessment: Gratitude Questionnaire (GQ-6)

- **K/S (week 1 & 2 - goal review, pretest):** Find a stick. Manually remove branches and bark. Collect sand. Make paint and a paint brush out of natural artifacts.

- **P/A (week 3 & 4 - psychoeducation):** Paint the stick with colors representing four emotions: gratitude, optimism, hope, spirituality/religiousness. Add geometric symbols in white or black to represent coping skills. Use the stick to draw four quadrants in the sand.

- **C/Sy (week 5 & 6 - therapeutic themes):** Depict emotions in quadrants. Symbolize: *What triggers the emotion? What are healthy ways to express the emotion? How do emotions impact productivity?*

- **P/A (week 7 & 8 - psychoeducation):** Represent a time and place when each of the emotions was experienced.

- **K/S (week 9 & 10 - progress review, post-test):** Photograph sand drawing to preserve and enable exhibit; clear the sand using methodical hand strokes and mindful breathing. Discuss impermanence of feelings and implications for well-being.

COMPONENTS

Art Education: Sand drawing, ni-Vanuatu, line
Social Skill Level: Solitary; therapist encourages autonomy
Signs, Symbols, & Metaphors: Coping, containment, and compartmentalization; impermanence
Budget: $0-5 - Stick, sand
Tools: Large tupperware container with lid to store sand, phone camera

SAFETY & ETHICS: MODIFICATIONS

Material Toxicity or Allergens: Avoid sticks with sap, thorns, or fungus; avoid sand contaminated by animals
Client Resources & Skills: Increase size of sand area if client has visuospatial limitations
Client History Considerations: Avoid sharp-ended or brittle sticks

INSECT MOVIE

DIRECTIVE OVERVIEW

Eco-Art Therapy Approach: Subject, setting
Therapeutic Themes: Roles in society, diversity
Goal Category: Cognitive
Psychoeducation: Self-empowerment
Recommended GAF: 70+
Relevant Resources: Darviri et al., 2014; Duckrow, 2017; Li, Louis Kruger, & Krishnan, 2016

METHODS & MATERIALS

Setting: Garden or park
Duration/Frequency: 10 weekly, 1.5 hour sessions
Format: Individual
Assessment: The Healthy Lifestyle and Personal Control Questionnaire (HLPCQ)

- **K/S (week 1 & 2 - goal review, pretest):** Go for a walk outdoors. Observe the color and textures of nature, looking for pollinator insects.

- **P/A (week 3 & 4 - psychoeducation):** Film observations in a spontaneous documentary. *What role do the insects play? How does having a role in life provide purpose and empowerment?*

- **C/Sy (week 5 & 6 - therapeutic themes):** Edit and compose a visual storytelling video 2 minutes in length. Give symbolic value by freezing frames to extend their duration or using slow motion.

- **P/A (week 7 & 8 - psychoeducation):** Adjust hues and saturation using video-editing tools. Add a voiceover of a composed haiku poem.

- **K/S (week 9 & 10 - progress review, post-test):** Export the video to an auto-play DVD or .mov file. Discuss implications of social media upload to ensure caution when sharing therapeutic products.

COMPONENTS

Art Education: Anthropomorphism, haiku, movement
Social Skill Level: Spectator; therapist may wish to model app use during filming or editing
Signs, Symbols, & Metaphors: Honey bee as an immigrant
Budget: $0-$25 - Filming/editing apps; macro-lens for smartphone
Tools: Smartphone, iPad, or other video device

SAFETY & ETHICS: MODIFICATIONS

Material Toxicity or Allergens: Avoid getting too close to stinging insects; inquire about allergies prior to outing; ensure appropriate clothing
Client Resources & Skills: Episodic, declarative memory
Client History Considerations: Those with limited home technology may need an associative level of engagement

EMOTION GUEST HOUSE

DIRECTIVE OVERVIEW

Eco-Art Therapy Approach: Material
Therapeutic Themes: Detached mindfulness, stability, externalizing
Goal Category: Affective
Psychoeducation: Felt sense: Naming and describing emotions
Recommended GAF: 40+
Relevant Resources: Badenes, Prado-Gascó, & Barrón, 2016; Jaworski, 2020; Lloyd, Press, & Usiskin, 2018

METHODS & MATERIALS

Setting: Office, client home, or onsite garden
Duration/Frequency: 10 weekly, 1.5 hour sessions
Format: Family
Assessment: Emotion Awareness Questionnaire

- **K/S (week 1 & 2 - goal review, pretest):** Clear a space where the shelter will be built. Gather bamboo, sticks, vines, twine, concrete or other natural resources

- **P/A (week 3 & 4 - psychoeducation):** Read the poem, *The Guest House* by Rumi. Draw a design for an "emotion guest house." Discuss externalization.

- **C/Sy (week 5 & 6 - therapeutic themes):** Build the structure, defining the interior and exterior aspects. *How do we 'house' emotions in our body?*

- **P/A (week 7 & 8 - psychoeducation):** Write out a plan for how and when to use the shelter to house emotions (e.g., hanging an *Daily Emotion Diary Chart* inside).

- **K/S (week 9 & 10 - progress review, post-test):** Photograph the shelter, frame the image, and hang it. Plant perennial plants at the base of the shelter to create a welcoming presence.

COMPONENTS

Art Education: Rumi's *The Guest House* poem, brush shelters, chickee huts, teepees, proportion
Social Skill Level: Cooperative; therapist assists with construction
Signs, Symbols, & Metaphors: House as self
Budget: $0-10 bamboo/sticks, twine
Tools: Shovel to dig holes, scissors

SAFETY & ETHICS: MODIFICATIONS

Material Toxicity or Allergens: Offer gloves to avoid splinters
Client Resources & Skills: Multiple simultaneous attention
Client History Considerations: A table-top/mini-shelter can be created indoors to suit a wide range of clients

PLACE EMBROIDERED

DIRECTIVE OVERVIEW

Eco-Art Therapy Approach: Subject
Therapeutic Themes: Coping, adjustment, grounding, identity
Goal Category: Cognitive
Psychoeducation: Habits of mind and identity
Recommended GAF: 40+
Relevant Resources: Bäckström, 2020; Benartzy, 2020; Moldovan, 2018

METHODS & MATERIALS

Setting: Office or client home
Duration/Frequency: 10 weekly, 1.5 hour sessions
Format: Family
Assessment: Fordyce Emotion Questionnaire

- **K/S (week 1 & 2 - goal review, pretest):** Print a "selfie" photo showing genuine happiness on a fabric sheet.

- **P/A (week 3 & 4 - psychoeducation):** Research plant symbolism. Choose those which symbolize happiness and relate to identity (e.g. birth month, country of origin). Plan out flora placement on fabric sheet.

- **C/Sy (week 5 & 6 - therapeutic themes):** Convey place-based identity by embroidering the symbolic plants onto the sheet around the selfie image. *How are happiness and identity related?*

- **P/A (week 7 & 8 - psychoeducation):** Decide how this artwork will represent place-based, cultural and social identity. Sew it onto a pillow, shirt, canvas, stuffed animal, or other artifact based on decision.

- **K/S (week 9 & 10 - progress review, post-test):** Pass the artifact around the family and notice the stylistic choices which align with each member's identity. Share positive observations.

COMPONENTS

Art Education: St Paul's Cathedr
altar cloth, pattern, backstitch
Social Skill Level: Parallel; thera
may wish to model embroidery tec
Signs, Symbols, & Metaphors:
Anchoring to the present, develop
roots, piecing together
Budget: $14 - Fabric sheet, sewin
Tools: Needles and assortment of
threads, printer, embroidery hoops
(optional)

SAFETY & ETHICS: MODIFICATIONS

Material Toxicity or Allergens:
cotton thread and consider providi
protective finger thimbles
Client Resources & Skills: Susta
attention
Client History Considerations: 1
with history of self-harm/ violenc
need one-to-one attention given us
needle

INSPIRED

DIRECTIVE OVERVIEW

Eco-Art Therapy Approach: Material, subject
Therapeutic Themes: Stress reduction, catharsis, mindfulness, self-monitoring, positive distraction, breathing as coping
Goal Category: Affective, Behavioral
Psychoeducation: Diaphramic breathing
Recommended GAF: 60+
Relevant Resources: Abbott, Shanahan, & Neufeld, 2013; Cohen, Kessler, & Gordon, 1997; Ma et al., 2017

METHODS & MATERIALS

Setting: Office
Duration/Frequency: 10 weekly, 1.5 hour sessions
Format: Individual
Assessment: Perceived Stress Scale (PSS)

- **K/S (week 1 & 2 - goal review, pretest):** Using plant materials, make paper and paint brushes.

- **P/A (week 3 & 4 - psychoeducation):** Associate nature scenes used in stress reduction with calming life experiences: *Ile St. Martin* by Claude Monet, *After the Rains* by Allan Stephenson, and *A River Through the Woods* by Christian Zacho.

- **C/Sy (week 5 & 6 - therapeutic themes):** Explore: *Which colors used in the image do you associate with calmness?* Using plant materials, make natural watercolors for those colors. Create response art on the paper. *Let the nature scenes inspire you.*

- **P/A (week 7 & 8 - psychoeducation):** Paint background, foreground, and middle ground. Exercise diaphragmatic breathing as coping while painting.

- **K/S (week 9 & 10 - progress review, post-test):** Add a sealant. Sign. Create a frame to enable exhibit.

COMPONENTS

Art Education: Color, form
Social Skill Level: Cooperative; therapist facilitates the technical process
Signs, Symbols, & Metaphors: Emotional landscape
Budget: $10 - Paper-making kit, paint, hanging apparatus
Tools: Blender to puree plants, container, nylon to strain paper, and a shaped wire hanger to scoop paper pulp to dry

SAFETY & ETHICS: MODIFICATIONS

Material Toxicity or Allergens: Use non-toxic paint sources
Client Resources & Skills: Visual search and identification
Client History Considerations: Discuss associations to assess potential trauma history

FAMILY WIND CHIME

DIRECTIVE OVERVIEW

Eco-Art Therapy Approach: Material
Therapeutic Themes: Family dynamics, insight
Goal Category: Interpersonal, Cognitive
Psychoeducation: Improving attachment style
Recommended GAF: 40+
Relevant Resources: Fok et al., 2014; Hinz, 2009; Jones et al., 2018

METHODS & MATERIALS

Setting: Office, client home
Duration/Frequency: 10 weekly, 1.5 hour sessions
Format: Individual or family
Assessment: Brief Family Relationship Scale (BFRS)

- **K/S (week 1 & 2 - goal review, pretest):** Collect and organize artifacts which are aesthetically pleasing and strong enough to be used for a wind-chime mobile (e.g. wood, native metals like copper, silver, iron, rocks, shells).

- **P/A (week 3 & 4 - psychoeducation):** Research the symbolic history of each artifact type and assign an artifact to represent each family member and your relationship with them.

- **C/Sy (week 5 & 6 - therapeutic themes):** Organize artifacts to symbolize patterns or behaviors concerning family members such as through object placement and proximity to denote emotional closeness.

- **P/A (week 7 & 8 - psychoeducation):** Add color to artifacts to symbolize family dynamics.

- **K/S (week 9 & 10 - progress review, post-test):** Construct the wind chime mobile using wire. Add a protective varnish to enable exhibit.

COMPONENTS

Art Education: Feng shui/Calder mobiles, balance
Social Skill Level: Associative; therapist aids in assembly to ensure stability
Signs, Symbols, & Metaphors: Object-relations; proximity, birth order, hierarchy, attachment
Budget: $5 - Wire, paint
Tools: Wire cutters and pliers to shape wire

SAFETY & ETHICS: MODIFICATIONS

Material Toxicity or Allergens: Bend wire ends upon cutting to avoid puncture
Client Resources & Skills: Visual search and identification; abstract/inductive reasoning
Client History Considerations: Families may be elaborately "blended" and "family" need not be biological

BIRD'S NEST

DIRECTIVE OVERVIEW

Eco-Art Therapy Approach: Material, subject
Therapeutic Themes: Nurturance, security, protection
Goal Category: Interpersonal
Psychoeducation: Types of support
Recommended GAF: 50+
Relevant Resources: Cohen & Hoberman, 1983; Payne et al., 2012; Sheller, 2007

METHODS & MATERIALS

Setting: Office or client home
Duration/Frequency: 10 weekly, 1.5 hour sessions
Format: Individual or family
Assessment: Interpersonal Support Evaluation List (ISEL)

- **K/S (week 1 & 2 - goal review, pretest):** Collect materials to construct a 3-D bird's nest (i.e., feathers, vines, eggs).

- **P/A (week 3 & 4 - psychoeducation):** Paint a representation of self onto the eggshell. Paint quills of feathers to represent people who provide: emotional, social, spiritual, monetary, etc support.

- **C/Sy (week 5 & 6 - therapeutic themes):** Associate vines with: physical safety, shared values, caring relationships, and experiences which teach positive behaviors and skills. Discuss sources of these supports in life. Weave into nest for egg.

- **P/A (week 7 & 8 - psychoeducation):** Use ink to add design elements to the egg to represent self-care habits. Place the egg in the nest on feathers. Secure with glue.

- **K/S (week 9 & 10 - progress review, post-test):** Create a display using natural materials such as a block of wood to enable exhibit.

COMPONENTS

Art Education: *The Nest: An Exhibition of Art in Nature* at Katonah Museum of Art
Social Skill Level: Associative; therapist prepares materials (e.g., egg) on behalf of client
Signs, Symbols, & Metaphors: Native American legends of birds and nest meanings
Budget: $4 - Egg, glue, pen/ink
Tools: Hot glue and needle, tape, and soap to empty and clean eggshell

SAFETY & ETHICS: MODIFICATIONS

Material Toxicity or Allergens: Clean egg for client to ensure hygiene
Client Resources & Skills: Episodic, declarative memory
Client History Considerations: Attachment style and abuse histories may surface

FRIENDSHIP MURAL

DIRECTIVE OVERVIEW

Eco-Art Therapy Approach: Subject
Therapeutic Themes: Conflict resolution, respect, collaboration
Goal Category: Interpersonal, Behavioral
Psychoeducation: Interpersonal communication
Recommended GAF: 30+
Relevant Resources: Deveci, & Ayish, 2018; Ullmann, 2012; Yeo & Teng, 2015

METHODS & MATERIALS

Setting: Office or school
Duration/Frequency: 10 weekly, 1.5 hour sessions
Format: Dyad or group
Assessment: TRIAD Social Skills Assessment (TSSA)

- **K/S (week 1 & 2 - goal review, pretest):** Select a subject (e.g., flowers, birds, trees). Trace and cut out large cardboard silhouettes/ stamps of the subject.

- **P/A (week 3 & 4 - psychoeducation):** As a group, discuss color associations and pick a color for friendship. Paint the wall with this base color.

- **C/Sy (week 5 & 6 - therapeutic themes):** As a group, arrange the cardboard stamps to form a pattern. Decide on location and proximity of the stamps. *Will the subjects be close together? Are they facing the same direction?*

- **P/A (week 7 & 8 - psychoeducation):** Decide if stamps will be black, white, or another contrasting color. Paint the stamps this color and press the stamp onto the wall in the pattern decided in week 5 & 6.

- **K/S (week 9 & 10 - progress review, post-test):** Add a protective sealant. Write a group artist statement and post beside the mural.

COMPONENTS

Art Education: Suiboku-ga painting effect, shape
Social Skill Level: Cooperative; therapist may want to moderate individual participation levels
Signs, Symbols, & Metaphors: Proximity, "human nature," sharing space, direction-goals
Budget: $5 - Paint
Tools: Scissors, paint roller, large foam or cardboard for stamp

SAFETY & ETHICS: MODIFICATIONS

Material Toxicity or Allergens: Use non-toxic paint
Client Resources & Skills: Impulse control, communication skills
Client History Considerations: Those with sensory sensitivities may want to wear gloves to avoid getting paint on their hands

ESTEEM QUILT

DIRECTIVE OVERVIEW

Eco-Art Therapy Approach: Subject, material
Therapeutic Themes: Heritage, legacy
Goal Category: Interpersonal
Psychoeducation: Generativity and contribution
Recommended GAF: 50+
Relevant Resources: Gardner, 2016; McAdams & de St Aubin, 1992; Soucie, Jia, Zhu, & Pratt, 2018

METHODS & MATERIALS

Setting: Office, onsite garden
Duration/Frequency: 10 weekly, 1.5 hour sessions
Format: Group
Assessment: Loyola Generativity Scale (LGS)

- **K/S (week 1 & 2 - goal review, pretest):** Collect scraps of aged, dark-colored natural fabric linked with significant life experiences. Cut into 5"×5" squares.
- **P/A (week 3 & 4 - psychoeducation):** Discuss history of fabric scraps. Associate the life cycle of the fabric with experiences. *How does the fabric represent your role in contributing to the well-being of others?*
- **C/Sy (week 5 & 6 - therapeutic themes):** Collect meaningful flowers, leaves and seeds. Discuss their significance. Organize the plant parts onto the fabric to form a symbolic design related to "care for the sustainability of future generations." Brush white fabric paint onto the plant parts and press onto the fabric.
- **P/A (week 7 & 8 - psychoeducation):** Cooperatively arrange the fabric squares into a cohesive whole. Collaboratively stitch the quilt together. Discuss ways to pass on skills, values, and traditions to others.
- **K/S (week 9 & 10 - progress review, post-test):** Create a display frame for the quilt using natural materials.

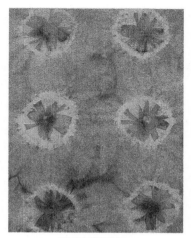

COMPONENTS

Art Education: Quilt-types, variety
Social Skill Level: Cooperative; therapist may wish to assist with collecting materials
Signs, Symbols, & Metaphors: Sustainability and community cohesion
Budget: $10 - Fabric paint
Tools: Needle and thread, paintbrushes, rulers

SAFETY & ETHICS: MODIFICATIONS

Material Toxicity or Allergens: Apply paint in well-ventilated area. Ensure plants are non-toxic
Client Resources & Skills: Episodic and procedural memory
Client History Considerations: Ensure an inclusive environment through structured group rules

SHELL MIRROR

DIRECTIVE OVERVIEW

Eco-Art Therapy Approach: Material
Therapeutic Themes: Body image, self-compassion, self-empathy
Goal Category: Behavioral
Psychoeducation: Compassionate self-talk
Recommended GAF: 60+
Relevant Resources: Bat Or & Megides, 2016; Neff, 2016; Petrocchi, Ottaviani, & Couyoumdjian, 2017

METHODS & MATERIALS

Setting: Office or beach
Duration/Frequency: 10 weekly, 1.5 hour sessions
Format: Individual
Assessment: Self-Compassion Scale (SCS)

- **K/S (week 1 & 2 - goal review, pretest):** Collect seashells. Listen to the sounds generated by the shells. Scrub shells with gentle cleanser (e.g., toothpaste) to preserve color. Select a mirror which has a thick frame.

- **P/A (week 3 & 4 - psychoeducation):** Think of phrases which soothe (e.g., *Take care of yourself. You deserve happiness*). Sort seashells by color, size, and texture.

- **C/Sy (week 5 & 6 - therapeutic themes):** Glue the larger shells onto the frame. Whenever your image becomes visible within the mirror, make eye contact and say one of the soothing statements.

- **P/A (week 7 & 8 - psychoeducation):** Continue the repetition of positive affirmations. Use small shells to fill in gaps between larger ones.

- **K/S (week 9 & 10 - progress review, post-test):** Clean the frame and mirror, removing the small strands of hot glue with a stiff paint brush. Coat the shells with a non-toxic, environmentally friendly varnish.

COMPONENTS

Art Education: Shell-type symbolism; unity
Social Skill Level: Solitary; therapist may wish to encourage autonomy
Signs, Symbols, & Metaphors: Body as shell, shells as a protective
Budget: $8 - 2nd-hand mirror, varnish
Tools: Hot glue gun, stiff paint brush

SAFETY & ETHICS: MODIFICATIONS

Material Toxicity or Allergens: Only collect empty shells; apply varnish in a well-ventilated area
Client Resources & Skills: Response inhibition
Client History Considerations: Those struggling with body dysmorphic disorder and eating disorders may need role playing prior to directive

PERSON IN THE RAIN

DIRECTIVE OVERVIEW

Eco-Art Therapy Approach: Material, subject
Therapeutic Themes: Self-care, adjustment
Goal Category: Behavioral, Affective
Psychoeducation: Fostering resilience
Recommended GAF: 20+
Relevant Resources: Gerber et al., 2018; Jue & Ha, 2019; Romero, 2019

METHODS & MATERIALS

Setting: Office or client home
Duration/Frequency: 10 weekly, 1.5 hour sessions
Format: individual or group
Assessment: Person-in-the-Rain Drawing/Self-Care Inventory - NAMI

- **K/S (week 1 & 2 - goal review, pretest):** Collect rainwater, add iron (e.g., bobby pins); allow to rust.
- **P/A (week 3 & 4 - psychoeducation):** Use the rusty, iron water as a watercolor paint. Paint a series of individuals in the rain, each having a different level of protection from the rain. *Which people show signs of self-care? How does self-care impact resiliency?*
- **C/Sy (week 5 & 6 - therapeutic themes):** Add a background and elaborate a baseline. *How can planning and preparation prevent feelings of being overwhelmed?* Depict the answers.
- **P/A (week 7 & 8 - psychoeducation):** Using ink, add design elements to show a range of emotional reactions to the rain among the people.
- **K/S (week 9 & 10 - progress review, post-test):** Create a frame using natural materials such as sticks, bamboo, or twine to enable exhibit.

COMPONENTS

Art Education: Rust dying, value
Social Skill Level: Solitary; therapist encourages autonomy
Signs, Symbols, & Metaphors: Resilience, unpredictability
Budget: $5 - Bobby pins, paper, brushes
Tools: Paintbrush, container for rain, watercolor paper

SAFETY & ETHICS: MODIFICATIONS

Material Toxicity or Allergens: Avoid sharp rusty objects (bobby pins have plastic end caps)
Client Resources & Skills: Cognitive flexibility and control
Client History Considerations: Those experiencing psychosis or depression may need a resource to recall varied emotion words and expressions

STRENGTHS MASK
DIRECTIVE OVERVIEW

Eco-Art Therapy Approach: Material, subject
Therapeutic Themes: Roles, defense mechanisms, boundaries
Goal Category: Cognitive, Interpersonal
Psychoeducation: Coping skills versus defense mechanisms
Recommended GAF: 60+
Relevant Resources: Diehl et al., 2014; Joseph et al., 2017; Wood et al., 2011

METHODS & MATERIALS

Setting: Office, garden
Duration/Frequency: 10 weekly, 1.5 hour sessions
Format: Individual or group
Assessment: Strengths Use Scale

- **K/S (week 1 & 2 - goal review, pretest):** Sort through found objects such as bark, broad leaf palms, hair, feathers, drift wood, native metals, etc. to select mask-making materials. Dehydrate the materials in silica or in the microwave. Arrange in the form of a mask.

- **P/A (week 3 & 4 - psychoeducation):** Select natural artifacts such as flowers, butterflies, star-shaped fossils, which have symbolic values representational of an animal or element totem. *How can this "totem" represent a type of outer strength you show to the world?*

- **C/Sy (week 5 & 6 - therapeutic themes):** Adhere the found objects and artifacts together. *How do you embody strength in times of difficulty?*

- **P/A (week 7 & 8 - psychoeducation):** Paint details onto the mask and incorporate suggestive patterns and lines.

- **K/S (week 9 & 10 - progress review, post-test):** Add a skin-safe sealant and twine to wear the mask. Add a hanging apparatus (e.g., key-hole tab).

COMPONENTS

Art Education: Zoomorphic and anthropomorphic masks, shape
Social Skill Level: Cooperative; therapist aids in the functionality of the mask
Signs, Symbols, & Metaphors: Totems, defenses
Budget: $5 - Sealant, silica
Tools: Scissors, microwave

SAFETY & ETHICS: MODIFICATIONS

Material Toxicity or Allergens: Varnish should be appropriate for contact with skin (e.g., resin). Apply in a highly ventilated area
Client Resources & Skills: Constructional praxis
Client History Considerations: Those with personality/identity disintegration may be triggered by this directive

AROMATIC MANDALA

DIRECTIVE OVERVIEW

Eco-Art Therapy Approach: Subject, material
Therapeutic Themes: Success-oriented tasks, meditation, self-soothing
Goal Category: Affective
Psychoeducation: Employing hope to foster resilience
Recommended GAF: 20+
Relevant Resources: Kim, Kim, Choe, & Kim, 2018; Pritchard, 2020; Snyder et al., 2007

METHODS & MATERIALS

Setting: Office, client home
Duration/Frequency: 10 weekly, 1.5 hour sessions
Format: Individual or group
Assessment: The Adult Hope Scale (AHS)

- **K/S (week 1 & 2 - goal review, pretest):** Make paper using plants. Sort through herbs, spices, and dried loose-leaf herbal tea materials to select pleasing smells and textures (e.g., star anise, bay leaf, cardamom).

- **P/A (week 3 & 4 - psychoeducation):** Associate the smells and textures with calming and positive life experiences. Rank materials by degree of positive association; choose top five for mandala.

- **C/Sy (week 5 & 6 - therapeutic themes):** Arrange natural artifacts on the paper starting the design in the center and radiating outward. Focus on feelings of hope. Symbolize structure, balance, and centering.

- **P/A (week 7 & 8 - psychoeducation):** Paint pH-neutral glue on the mandala design to secure placement; discuss experiences of how hope has positively impacted life; pair breath with movements.

- **K/S (week 9 & 10 - progress review, post-test):** Create a hanging apparatus such as a frame using natural materials such as sticks, bamboo, or twine.

COMPONENTS

Art Education: Flower fractals, pattern
Social Skill Level: Solitary; therapist encourages autonomy
Signs, Symbols, & Metaphors: Structure, centering (emotional)
Budget: $0-$10 - Spices, glue
Tools: Containers to organize artifacts, tweezers to select

SAFETY & ETHICS: MODIFICATIONS

Material Toxicity or Allergens: Avoid cinnamon powder/non-water-soluble spices in enclosed areas
Client Resources & Skills: Episodic, declarative memory
Client History Considerations: Those struggling with impulse control may try to consume materials

MOURNING BRACELET

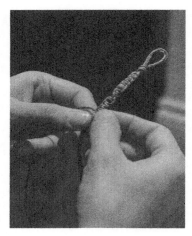

DIRECTIVE OVERVIEW

Eco-Art Therapy Approach: Material
Therapeutic Themes: Loss, rituals, social customs
Goal Category: Affective
Psychoeducation: Acceptance of pain meaning in life
Recommended GAF: 20+
Relevant Resources: Alonso-Llácer et al., 2020; Bogan, 2019; Chan, 2017

METHODS & MATERIALS

Setting: Office, garden, or client home
Duration/Frequency: 10 weekly, 1.5 hour sessions
Format: Individual
Assessment: Meaning of Life Questionnaire (MLQ)

- **K/S (week 1 & 2 - goal review, pretest):** Collect and prepare a natural fiber (e.g., vine) to use as cordage to knot a bracelet. Measure out the lengths for three or more strands.

- **P/A (week 3 & 4 - psychoeducation):** Associate the strands of the cordage to represent three or more positive memories of the deceased loved one. Order cordage by frequency of the memory and dye the cordage a color associated with each memory.

- **C/Sy (week 5 & 6 - therapeutic themes):** Use a single square knot pattern to create the bracelet. *How have these memories enriched your life? How do these memories give meaning to life?* Process the nature of grief experienced.

- **P/A (week 7 & 8 - psychoeducation):** Add found objects with symbolic value (e.g., pearls to represent tears) using jump rings; Process mixed emotions.

- **K/S (week 9 & 10 - progress review, post-test):** Add a clasp which is easy for the client to remove one-handed (e.g., toggle or S hook).

COMPONENTS

Art Education: Victorian-era bereavement jewelry, form
Social Skill Level: Parallel; therapist creates alongside to model techniques
Signs, Symbols, & Metaphors: Emotional knots
Budget: $5 - Hypoallergenic clasp, jump rings
Tools: Pliars and scissors

SAFETY & ETHICS: MODIFICATIONS

Material Toxicity or Allergens: Vine preparation may include dehydrating to eliminate sap and then soaking to make malleable.
Client Resources & Skills: Category formation
Client History Considerations: Grief may be for a loss - loved one, animal, or object; loss may not be related to death. Complicated grief symptoms may arise.

CENTERED COIL POT

DIRECTIVE OVERVIEW

Eco-Art Therapy Approach: Material, setting
Therapeutic Themes: Containment, meta-cognition
Goal Category: Cognitive
Psychoeducation: Values, mindfulness
Recommended GAF: 20+
Relevant Resources: Franquesa et al., 2017; Osman et al., 2016; Vespini, 2019

METHODS & MATERIALS

Setting: Office, client home, or onsite garden
Duration/Frequency: 10 weekly, 1.5 hour sessions
Format: Group
Assessment: The Mindful Attention Awareness Scale (MAAS)

- **K/S (week 1 & 2 - goal review, pretest):** Use wet extraction to get clay from soil. Fill bucket (1/3 soil, 2/3 water). Break up particles with hands. Allow sand/ rock to settle. Pour top slurry into a sheet-lined bucket. Gather sheet corners and hang from a tree to drain.

- **P/A (week 3 & 4 - psychoeducation):** Knead clay. Roll clay into ten thin, 12" long coils each associated with a step of mindfulness practice. Use the coils to create a pot by rolling and stacking. Practice each mindful attention step.

- **C/Sy (week 5 & 6 - therapeutic themes):** Slowly smooth the coil sides and form the final shape of your pot: *How can mindfulness serve as a 'container' of emotions?*

- **P/A (week 7 & 8 - psychoeducation):** Cut out forms representing personal values from the leather-hard clay. Allow to become bone dry.

- **K/S (week 9 & 10 - progress review, post-test):** Fire clay in an outdoor hearth/pit kiln or commercial kiln.

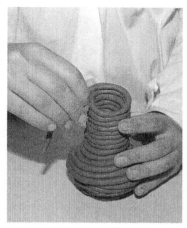

COMPONENTS

Art Education: Wet clay harvest; "mother clay"; Kintsukuroi/Kintsugi, balance
Social Skill Level: Parallel/cooperative; therapist assists with extraction
Signs, Symbols, & Metaphors: Molding and refining habitual thoughts
Budget: $0-$5 - Basic clay carving tools
Tools: Two 5-gallon buckets, sheet, shovel

SAFETY & ETHICS: MODIFICATIONS

Material Toxicity or Allergens: Ensure adequate ventilation due to clay dust
Client Resources & Skills: Sustained attention
Client History Considerations: Clients with high achievement may need to be slowed down to associate coils with mindfulness

BURNING INTEREST

DIRECTIVE OVERVIEW

Eco-Art Therapy Approach: Material, subject
Therapeutic Themes: Perseverance, consistency, grit
Goal Category: Cognition
Psychoeducation: Autonomy, growth mindset
Recommended GAF: 70+
Relevant Resources: Cauley, 2019; Datu, Valdez, & King, 2016; Perry, 2016

METHODS & MATERIALS

Setting: Office or client home (well-ventilated)
Duration/Frequency: 10 weekly, 1.5 hour sessions
Format: Individual
Assessment: The Grit Scale

- **K/S (week 1 & 2 - goal review, pretest):** Sand a piece of wood (220 grit sandpaper). Use water and rag to wipe wood. Let it dry. Sand again. Discuss interests, purposeful frustration and goal-making as key to grit.

- **P/A (week 3 & 4 - psychoeducation):** Draft a nature-based image related to an interest (e.g., astronomical constellation, stars, planets). Burn marks in wood to map out placement. Associate process with short-term versus long-term goals and locus of control.

- **C/Sy (week 5 & 6 - therapeutic themes):** Burn image into the wood through a series of tiny marks. Symbolize taking conscious steps each day to move closer to long-term goals which align with interests.

- **P/A (week 7 & 8 - psychoeducation):** Use natural dyes to add pigment to image.

- **K/S (week 9 & 10 - progress review, post-test):** Seal to preserve the colored elements. Add a hanging apparatus. Write a goal statement based on the work.

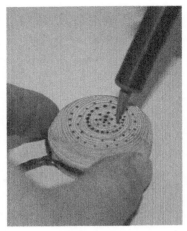

COMPONENTS

Art Education: Victorian-era pyrography; cross-cultural meanings in constellations (e.g., Orion)
Social Skill Level: Parallel; therapist models safety techniques
Signs, Symbols, & Metaphors: "Burning desire", "written in the stars"
Budget: $13 - Sealant, sawtooth backs for hanging
Tools: Pyrography kit

SAFETY & ETHICS: MODIFICATIONS

Material Toxicity or Allergens: Positively identify the wood; use resin-free wood; tie back hair; avoid dangling jewelry/clothing; offer gloves/mask
Client Resources & Skills: Multiple simultaneous attention
Client History Considerations: Discuss risk of burns and fires to ensure safety procedures

MEMORY ORB

DIRECTIVE OVERVIEW

Eco-Art Therapy Approach: Material
Therapeutic Themes: Personal/ cultural narratives
Goal Category: Interpersonal
Psychoeducation: Belonging; non-linear memories
Recommended GAF: 20+
Relevant Resources: Allen, 2019; Stace, 2016; Wastler, Lucksted, Phalen, & Drapalski, 2020

METHODS & MATERIALS

Setting: Office, client home, or onsite garden
Duration/Frequency: 10 weekly, 1.5 hour sessions
Format: Group
Assessment: Sense of Belonging Instrument (SOBI)

- **K/S (week 1 & 2 - goal review, pretest):** Collect two to eight 36" vines to represent *Erikson's Stages of Psychosocial Development* (e.g., number of vines correspond with age/stage). Dry and then soak vines.

- **P/A (week 3 & 4 - psychoeducation):** Use vine(s) as an autobiographical timeline; add color, symbols, and dates to mark milestones for each stage: hope, will, purpose, competency, fidelity, love, care, and/or wisdom.

- **C/Sy (week 5 & 6 - therapeutic themes):** Symbolize memory as non-linear. Weave vines into a knot to incorporate symbolism of early life, adolescence, adulthood and late-life as applicable.

- **P/A (week 7 & 8 - psychoeducation):** Tie twine to orb so it sways and dangles. Write a haiku on life experiences. *How have these experiences enabled you to contribute to others' well-being?*

- **K/S (week 9 & 10 - progress review, post-test):** Create a mobile frame using natural materials like bamboo and twine to enable exhibit. Dangle all orbs.

COMPONENTS

Art Education: Rattan balls, shape, movement
Social Skill Level: Parallel; therapist models technique
Signs, Symbols, & Metaphors: Tangled thoughts, life narrative
Budget: $0-$2 - Twine to hang
Tools: Shears to cut vines

SAFETY & ETHICS: MODIFICATIONS

Material Toxicity or Allergens: Positively identify vines
Client Resources & Skills: Episodic, declarative memory
Client History Considerations: Those with a trauma history may not want to vocalize all life events represented

References

Abbott, K., Shanahan, M., & Neufeld, R. (2013). Artistic tasks outperform nonartistic tasks for stress reduction. *Art Therapy*, 30, 71–78.

Agbude, G. A., Obayan, A., Ademola, L. L., & Abasilim, U. D. (2017). Leadership on trial: An existentialist assessment. *Covenant International Journal of Psychology*, 2(1).

Allan, B. A., & Shearer, C. B. (2012). The scale for existential thinking. *International Journal of Transpersonal Studies*, 31(1), 21–37.

Allen, K. A. (2019). Making sense of belonging. *InPsych*, 41(3). www.psychology.org.au/for-members/publications/inpsych/2019/june/Making-sense-of-belonging.

Alonso-Llácer, L., Martín, P. B., Ramos-Campos, M., Mesa-Gresa, P., Lacomba-Trejo, L., & Pérez-Marín, M. (2020). Mindfulness and grief: The MADED program mindfulness for the acceptance of pain and emotions in grief. *Psicooncologia*, 17(1), 105–116.

An, M., Colarelli, S. M., O'Brien, K., & Boyajian, M. E. (2016). Why we need more nature at work: Effects of natural elements and sunlight on employee mental health and work attitudes. *PLoS One*, 11(5). https://doi.org/10.1371/journal.pone.0155614.

Bäckström, M. (2020). *Hanging on by a thread: Confronting mental illness and manifesting love through embroidery.* www.diva-portal.org/smash/get/diva2:1432829/FULLTEXT01.pdf.

Badenes, L. V., Prado-Gascó, V., & Barrón, R. G. (2016). Emotion awareness, mood and personality as predictors of somatic complaints in children and adults. *Psicothema*, 28(4), 383–388.

Bat Or, M., & Megides, O. (2016). Found object/readymade art in the treatment of trauma and loss. *Journal of Clinical Art Therapy*, 3(1), 3.

Benartzy, A. (2020). *Place-based intercultural liminality and the potential of art therapy in cultural identity negotiations.* Expressive Therapies Capstone Theses: Lesley University. 345. https://digitalcommons.lesley.edu/expressive_theses/345.

Bogan, B. (2019). *Exploring the usage of found objects in art therapy for bereavement: A literature review.* Expressive Therapies Capstone Theses: Lesley University. 209. https://digitalcommons.lesley.edu/expressive_theses/209.

Bolek-Berquist J., Elliott M. E., & Gangnon R. E. (2009). Use of a questionnaire to assess vitamin D status in young adults. *Public Health Nutrition*, 12(2), 236–243. doi:10.1017/S136898000800356X.

Carpendale, M. (2010). Ecological identity & art therapy. *Canadian Art Therapy Association Journal*, 23(2), 53–57.

Cauley, N. (2019). *Trauma worlds: More-than-human stages of recovery.* Unpublished portfolio: York University. https://yorkspace.library.yorku.ca/xmlui/bitstream/handle/10315/36978/MESMP03274.pdf?sequence=1.

Chan, W. C. H. (2017). Assessing meaning in life in social work practice: Validation of the Meaning in Life Questionnaire among clinical samples. *British Journal of Social Work*, 47(1), 9–27.

Cohen, S., & Hoberman, H. M. (1983). Positive events and social supports as buffers of life change stress. *Journal of Applied Social Psychology*, 13(2), 99–125.

Cohen, S., Kessler, R. C., & Gordon, L. U. (Eds.). (1997). *Measuring stress: A guide for health and social scientists.* Oxford University Press.

D'Souza, J. F., Adams, C. K., & Fuss, B. (2015). A pilot study of self-actualization activity measurement. *Journal of the Indian Academy of Applied Psychology*, 41(3), 28–33.

Darviri, C., Alexopoulos, E. C., Artemiadis, A. K., Tigani, X., Kraniotou, C., Darvyri, P., & Chrousos, G. P. (2014). The Healthy Lifestyle and Personal Control Questionnaire (HLPCQ): A novel tool for assessing self-empowerment through a constellation of daily activities. *BMC Public Health*, 14(1), 995. http s://doi.org/10.1186/1471-2458-14-995.

Datu, J. A. D., Valdez, J. P. M., & King, R. B. (2016). Perseverance counts but consistency does not! Validating the short grit scale in a collectivist setting. *Current Psychology*, 35(1), 121–130.

Daughtry, K. M. (2018). *The effects of art therapy on the well-being of medical students in eastern North Carolina.* http://thescholarship.ecu.edu/handle/10342/6848.

Deveci, T., & Ayish, N. (2018). Personal responsibility and interpersonal communication in a project-based learning environment. *International Journal of Social Sciences and Education Research*, 4(1), 1–17.

Dhaese, M. J. (2011). Holistic Expressive Play Therapy. *Integrative Play Therapy*, 75–94. https://centreforexpressivetherapy.com/wp-content/uploads/2019/07/C05.pdf.

Diehl, M., Chui, H., Hay, E. L., Lumley, M. A., Grühn, D., & Labouvie-Vief, G. (2014). Change in coping and defense mechanisms across adulthood: Longitudinal findings in a European American sample. *Developmental Psychology*, 50(2), 634–648. doi:10.1037/a0033619.

Drake, J. E., Hastedt, I., & James, C. (2016). Drawing to distract: Examining the psychological benefits of drawing over time. *Psychology of Aesthetics, Creativity, and the Arts*, 10(3), 325–331. http://dx.doi.org/10.1037/aca0000064.

Duckrow, S. (2017). *Filmmaking as artistic inquiry: An examination of ceramic art therapy in a maximum-security forensic psychiatric facility.* Expressive Therapies Dissertations: Lesley University. 30. https://digitalcommons.lesley.edu/expres sive_dissertations/30.

Esnaola, I., Benito, M., Agirre, I. A., Freeman, J., & Sarasa, M. (2017). Measurement invariance of the Satisfaction with Life Scale (SWLS) by country, gender and age. *Psicothema*, 29(4), 596–601.

Fok, C. C. T., Allen, J., Henry, D., & Team, P. A. (2014). The Brief Family Relationship Scale: A brief measure of the relationship dimension in family functioning. *Assessment*, 21(1), 67–72.

Franquesa, A., Cebolla, A., García-Campayo, J., Demarzo, M., Elices, M., Pascual, J. C., & Soler, J. (2017). Meditation practice is associated with a values-oriented life: The mediating role of decentering and mindfulness. *Mindfulness*, 8(5), 1259–1268.

Gantt, L., & Tabone, C. (1998). *Formal elements art therapy scale: The rating manual.* Gargoyle Press. https://helpfortrauma.com/wp-content/uploads/2018/11/FEATS-Manual.pdf.

Gardner, J. (2016). *Quilting a connection: The use of quilting in group art therapy to promote well-being for older women.* Unpublished research paper for the degree of Masters of Arts: Concordia University. https://spectrum.library.con cordia.ca/981561/1/Gardner_F2016.pdf.

Gerber, M. M., Frankfurt, S. B., Contractor, A. A., Oudshoorn, K., Dranger, P., & Brown, L. A. (2018). Influence of multiple traumatic event types on mental health outcomes: Does count matter? *Journal of Psychopathology and Behavioral Assessment*, 40(4), 645–654.

Hinz, L. (2009). *Expressive therapies continuum: A framework for using art in therapy.* Routledge.

Irish, L. A., Kline, C. E., Gunn, H. E., Buysse, D. J., & Hall, M. H. (2015). The role of sleep hygiene in promoting public health: A review of empirical evidence. *Sleep Medicine Reviews*, 22, 23–36.

Jaworski, E. (2020). *Creating a space to externalize: Mindfulness based art therapy for childhood trauma, a literature review.* Expressive Therapies Capstone Theses: Lesley University. 328. https://digitalcommons.lesley.edu/expres sive_theses/328.

Jones, J. D., Fraley, R. C., Ehrlich, K. B., Stern, J. A., Lejuez, C. W., Shaver, P. R., & Cassidy, J. (2018). Stability of attachment style in adolescence: An empirical test of alternative developmental processes. *Child Development*, 89(3), 871–880.

Joseph, K., Bader, K., Wilson, S., Walker, M., Stephens, M., & Varpio, L. (2017). Unmasking identity dissonance: Exploring medical students' professional identity formation through mask making. *Perspectives on Medical Education*, 6(2), 99–107.

Jue, J., & Ha, J. H. (2019). The Person-in-the-Rain drawing test as an assessment of soldiers' army life adjustment and resilience. *Psychology*, 10(11), 1418–1434. doi:10.4236/psych.2019.1011093.

Kaufman, S. B. (2018). Self-actualizing people in the 21st century: Integration with contemporary theory and research on personality and well-being. *Journal of Humanistic Psychology.* doi:10.1177/0022167818809187.

Kennedy, C. L., & Villaverde, L. (2014). *Mycological provisions: An A/r/tographic portraiture of four contemporary teaching artists.* Doctoral dissertation: University of North Carolina at Greensboro. https://libres.uncg.edu/ir/uncg/f/Ken nedy_uncg_0154D_11412.pdf.

Kim, H., Kim, S., Choe, K., & Kim, J. S. (2018). Archives of psychiatric nursing effects of mandala art therapy on subjective well-being, resilience, and hope in psychiatric inpatients. *Archives of Psychiatric Nursing* 32, 167–173.

Knutson, K. L., Phelan, J., Paskow, M. J., Roach, A., Whiton, K., Langer, G., & Lichstein, K. L. (2017). The National Sleep Foundation's sleep health index. *Sleep Health*, 3(4), 234–240.

Kritchevsky, S. B. (2016). Nutrition and healthy aging. *The Journals of Gerontology*, 71(10), 1303–1305.

Krystyniak, J. (2020). *The use of dolls and figures in therapy: A literature review.* Expressive Therapies Capstone Theses: Lesley University. 321. https://digita lcommons.lesley.edu/expressive_theses/321.

Lee, M. S., Lee, J., Park, B. J., & Miyazaki, Y. (2015). Interaction with indoor plants may reduce psychological and physiological stress by suppressing autonomic nervous system activity in young adults: a randomized crossover study. *Journal of Physiological Anthropology*, 34(1), 21. https://doi.org/10.1186/ s40101-015-0060-8.

Li, C., Louis Kruger, P., & Krishnan, K. (2016). Empowering immigrant patients with disabilities: Advocating and self-advocating. *North American Journal of Medicine and Science*, 9(3), 116–122. doi:10.7156/najms.2016.0903116.

Lloyd, B., Press, N., & Usiskin, M. (2018). The Calais Winds took our plans away: art therapy as shelter. *Journal of Applied Arts & Health*, 9(2), 171–184.

Lun, J., Kesebir, S., & Oishi, S. (2008). On feeling understood and feeling well: The role of interdependence. *Journal of Research in Personality*, 42(6), 1623–1628.

Ma, X., Yue, Z. Q., Gong, Z. Q., Zhang, H., Duan, N. Y., Shi, Y. T., & Li, Y. F. (2017). The effect of diaphragmatic breathing on attention, negative affect and stress in healthy adults. *Frontiers in Psychology*, 8, 874. https://doi.org/10.3389/fpsyg.2017.00874.

McAdams, D. P., & de St. Aubin, E. D. (1992). A theory of generativity and its assessment through self-report, behavioral acts, and narrative themes in autobiography. *Journal of Personality and Social Psychology*, 62(6), 1003–1015.

McMaster, M. (2013). *Integrating nature into group art therapy interventions for clients with dementia.* Unpublished research paper for the degree of Masters of Arts: Concordia University. https://spectrum.library.concordia.ca/978027/1/McMaster_MA_F2013.pdf.

Moldovan, C. P. (2018). *AM Happy Scale: Reliability and validity of a single-item measure of happiness.* Loma Linda University Electronic Theses, Dissertations & Projects. 438. http://scholarsrepository.llu.edu/etd/438.

Neff, K. D. (2016). The self-compassion scale is a valid and theoretically coherent measure of self-compassion. *Mindfulness*, 7(1), 264–274.

Osman, A., Lamis, D. A., Bagge, C. L., Freedenthal, S., & Barnes, S. M. (2016). The mindful attention awareness scale: Further examination of dimensionality, reliability, and concurrent validity estimates. *Journal of Personality Assessment*, 98(2), 189–199.

Payne, T. J., Andrew, M., Butler, K. R., Wyatt, S. B., Dubbert, P. M., & Mosley, T. H. (2012). Psychometric evaluation of the interpersonal support evaluation list–short form in the ARIC study cohort. *Sage Open*, 2(3). doi:10.1177/2158244012461923.

Perry, G. (2016). *The birth of psychological astrology.* http://citeseerx.ist.psu.edu/viewdoc/download?doi=10.1.1.505.7874&rep=rep1&type=pdf.

Petrocchi, N., Ottaviani, C., & Couyoumdjian, A. (2017). Compassion at the mirror: Exposure to a mirror increases the efficacy of a self-compassion manipulation in enhancing soothing positive affect and heart rate variability. *The Journal of Positive Psychology*, 12(6), 525–536.

Pritchard, C. (2020). *Fostering hope in adolescents via art therapy teen group.* Expressive Therapies Capstone Theses: Lesley University. 267. https://digitalcommons.lesley.edu/expressive_theses/267.

Rasmussen, J. L., Steketee, G., Frost, R. O., Tolin, D. F., & Brown, T. A. (2014). Assessing squalor in hoarding: the home environment index. *Community Mental Health Journal*, 50(5), 591–596.

Romero, G. (2019). *The practice of self-care strategies among master or social work students.* Electronic Theses, Projects, and Dissertations: California State University, San Bernardino. 950. https://scholarworks.lib.csusb.edu/etd/950.

Sansone, R. A., & Sansone, L. A. (2010). Gratitude and well being: The benefits of appreciation. *Psychiatry (Edgmont, PA: Township)*, 7(11), 18–22.

Schotanus-Dijkstra, M., Peter, M., Drossaert, C. H., Pieterse, M. E., Bolier, L., Walburg, J. A., & Bohlmeijer, E. T. (2016). Validation of the Flourishing Scale in a sample of people with suboptimal levels of mental well-being. *BMC Psychology*, 4(1), 12. https://doi.org/10.1186/s40359-016-0116-5.

Sheller, S. (2007). Understanding insecure attachment: A study using children's bird nest imagery. *Art Therapy*, 24(3), 119–127.

Snyder, C. R., Harris, C., Anderson, J. R., Holleran, S. A., Irving, L. M., & Sigmon, S. T. (2007). Adult Hope Scale (AHS). *Journal of Personality and Social Psychology*, 60, 570–585.

Soucie, K. M., Jia, F., Zhu, N., & Pratt, M. W. (2018). The codevelopment of community involvement and generative concern pathways in emerging and young adulthood. *Developmental Psychology*, 54(10), 1971–1976. http://dx.doi.org/10.1037/dev0000563.

Stace, S. (2016). The use of sculptural lifelines in art psychotherapy. *Canadian Art Therapy Association Journal*, 29(1), 21–29.

Struckman, J. (2020). *Nature as metaphor in school art therapy: Development of a group method*. Expressive Therapies Capstone Theses: Lesley University. 235. https://digitalcommons.lesley.edu/expressive_theses/235.

Thong, S. A. (2007). Redefining the tools of art therapy. *Art Therapy*, 24(2), 52–58.

Ullmann, P. (2012). Art therapy and children with autism: Gaining access to their world through creativity. *Fusion*. www.scribd.com/document/249760438/Art-Theraphy-Autism.

Valikhani, A., Ahmadnia, F., Karimi, A., & Mills, P. J. (2019). The relationship between dispositional gratitude and quality of life: The mediating role of perceived stress and mental health. *Personality and Individual Differences*, 141, 40–46.

Vespini, S. (2019). *Clay work as a mindfulness-based practice*. Unpublished master's thesis: Indiana University. https://scholarworks.iupui.edu/bitstream/handle/1805/21208/Clay%20Work%20as%20a%20Mindfulness-Based%20Practice.pdf?sequence=1&isAllowed=y.

Wastler, H., Lucksted, A., Phalen, P., & Drapalski, A. (2020). Internalized stigma, sense of belonging, and suicidal ideation among veterans with serious mental illness. *Psychiatric Rehabilitation Journal*, 43(2), 91–96.

Wood, A. M., Linley, P. A., Maltby, J., Kashdan, T. B., & Hurling, R. (2011). Using personal and psychological strengths leads to increases in well-being over time: A longitudinal study and the development of the strengths use questionnaire. *Personality and Individual Differences*, 50(1), 15–19.

Yeo, K. J., & Teng, K. Y. (2015). Social skills deficits in autism: A study among students with autism spectrum disorder in inclusive classrooms. *Universal Journal of Educational Research*, 3(12), 1001–1007.

Appendix B: Intake and Check-in Forms

[DATE]

Dear Client,

Thank you for reaching out to [THERAPY PRACTICE NAME]. Enclosed within this packet is intake paperwork for eco-art therapy sessions. Please complete this packet prior to coming to the first session. If this is not possible, we can complete it together prior to the start of the first session.

Sincerely,

Name
Role

DEFINITION OF ECO-ART THERAPY

Eco-art therapy is a mental health practice in which clients, facilitated by the therapist, use natural art materials and settings, the creative process, and the resulting artwork to explore their feelings, reconcile emotional conflicts, foster self-awareness, manage behavior and addictions, develop social skills, improve reality orientation, reduce anxiety, and increase self-esteem.

CREDENTIALS

I am credentialed through the [INSERT CREDENTIALING BODY], which oversees ethical practices and may be contacted with any concerns.

Credentialing Body
Location
Phone number
Email

CONTACT

[THERAPY PRACTICE] strives to provide the highest quality of care to our clients. If there is anything that we can do to better our services and to better serve you, please do not hesitate to contact administration [NAME] at [PHONE], [EMAIL].

Informed Consent Involving Policies

Fees and Payment: Sessions are [COST] per hour. Payment is due on or before the day of the session. PayPal/all credit cards are accepted.

Introductions: If a child (anyone under 18) will be receiving the therapy, [ADMINISTRATOR] requests for parents to be present during the introductory session so that the child can have the security of a parent when in a new place/meeting a new person.

Therapy Sessions: Each eco-art therapy session will draw from a variety of models, frameworks, theories, and techniques. You are entitled to information about the methods and techniques used. You may seek a second opinion from another therapist or may terminate therapy at any time.

Cancellations: All appointments must be cancelled with a minimum of 24 hours notice or a [FEE] will be applied to the next session. Exceptions may be made for emergencies and sudden illness.

Confidentiality: All communications between/regarding client and therapist are considered confidential except where legal demands take precedence or there is a risk of harm to self/others. There is a chance that you may run into [THERAPY PRACTICE] staff/therapists in public. Rest assured that no content from therapy will ever be referenced in public, and conversations will be kept brief and pleasant.

Artwork: All art created during eco-art therapy sessions is confidential and the property of the client/family. However, it is [THERAPY PRAC-TICE]'s policy to photograph artwork to meet documentation and record-keeping requirements.

Materials: [THERAPY PRACTICE] provides basic art materials for sessions. You are welcome to bring additional materials to the session if you wish. Also, [THERAPY PRACTICE] is happy to purchase specific materials for sessions; however, a purchase fee of $[x] plus the cost of the materials will apply. Those materials will then belong to you. That said, many eco-art therapy materials can be found outdoors for free or grown for a low cost.

Duration and Frequency: By signing this form, you are indicating that you understand the policies outlined within this document. Eco-art therapy sessions are planned as a 1.5 hour session, ten-week duration on a weekly basis to start with, and then we can check in from there to see what feels right, whether to continue, or if your needs were met by those sessions.

Client Signature:_____ Date: _____

Therapist Signature:_____ Date: _____

ECO-ART THERAPY PHOTO-DOCUMENTATION CONSENT FORM

The following form asks you to acknowledge that the therapist will be photographing your artwork for documentation/ record-keeping purposes. There are other consent areas which are not currently requested unless directly indicated by your therapist.

Participation Consent: I have read or have had read to me the contents of this consent form and have been encouraged to ask questions. I have received answers to my questions.

I give permission to: (Check all that apply.)

    1. _____ Have my artwork photographed for documentation/ record-keeping purposes.

OPTIONAL

Confidentiality of Records: If any of the following are indicated, your identity will be kept confidential. Your name will be kept private.

    2. _____ Have the information from sessions used in professional publications and presentations.
    3. _____ Have my artwork used in professional presentations and publications
    4. _____ Have photos/video content posted online on websites to promote sessions.

I understand that:

_____ Artwork and information that is posted online, even when visibly removed from a website, remain accessible indefinitely.

Date: ___/___/_____

_____
Participant name (printed)

_____
Participant signature

_____
Therapist name (printed)

_____
Therapist signature

Eco-Art Therapy Intake Form

Therapy is for (circle one):   Self   Family member (minor)

Contact person: _____ **Contact Number:** __(____)_____-_____

Name of therapy recipient: _____ **Age:** _____

Date of birth: _____-_____-_____   **Gender:**   Male   Female
                    (month - day - year)

Ethnicity:_____ **Predominate language spoken at home:** _____

Relevant cultural or religious practices: (optional) _____

Optional section: The following questions will help me provide meaningful directives centered around your life milestones. Completing this section is optional. Please indicate which holidays you celebrate:

Winter holidays (e.g., Christmas, Martin Luther King Day, Hanukah, Winter Solstice, Purim):

_____

Spring holidays (e.g., Ramanavami, Easter, Passover, Edi al-Fitr, Spring Equinox):

_____

Summer holidays (e.g., Lailat Ul Qadr, Independence Day, Summer Solstice):

_____

Fall holidays (e.g., Veteran's Day, Eid al-Adha, Rosh Hashanah, Diwali, Thanksgiving):

_____

Additional Holidays: (optional)

_____

Have you/ the client experienced any of the following? (Put a check by those which apply)

___Seasonal allergies. Explain:

_____

___Skin reactions to certain plants. Explain:

_____

___Reactions to insect bites or stings. Explain:

_____

___A past experience involving a strong emotional experience while in nature. Explain:

_____

___Childhood memories related to the outdoors. Explain:

_____

Please circle any of the following issues which apply to your current reason(s) for seeking therapy:

(1) Anxiety
(2) Depression
(3) Extreme mood swings
(4) Health concerns
(5) Bed wetting
(6) Learning disability
(7) Self-inflicted pain or injury
(8) Social isolation
(9) Eating problems
(10) Sleep concerns (insomnia/ fatigue)
(11) Restlessness
(12) Recurrent dreams
(13) Hallucinations
(14) Speech difficulties
(15) Fears and phobias
(16) Suicidal ideas
(17) Difficulty making friends
(18) Lying (compulsive/ habitual)
(19) Excessive worry
(20) Difficulty making decisions
(21) Chronic illness
(22) Job problems   / Career decisions
(23) Other _____

(24) Abuse
(25) Development/Personal growth concerns
(26) Criminal behavior/incarceration
(27) Aggression/violence
(28) Overwhelming panic
(29) Recurrent conflicts with others
(30) Sexual concerns
(31) Separation/ Diverse/ Custody issues
(32) Parent-child relationship problem
(33) Sibling relationship problem
(34) Non-family relationship problem
(35) Nightmares
(36) Inferiority feelings
(37) Difficulty communicating
(38) Obsessions
(39) Shyness with people
(40) Fear of people
(41) ADHD symptoms
(42) Dislike for weekends/vacations
(43) Over-ambitiousness
(44) Addictions (e.g. drugs, gambling)
(45) Change in family (e.g. childbirth)
(46) Motor skills (fine/gross)

Motivation for session: Please describe the reason(s)/goal(s) for requesting services (be specific, if possible. When did the issue start? How does it affect you/their life?):

_____

_____

_____

_____

_____

What goals do you have for therapy?

_____

_____

_____

Put a check beside specific goals:

1. ___Stress reduction
2. ___Increased expressivity (non-verbal and verbal)
3. ___Improved self-esteem and self-worth
4. ___Identity and relationship exploration
5. ___Frustration tolerance/Anger management
6. ___Heightened emotional intelligence
7. ___Memory training
8. ___Relaxation and anxiety reduction
9. ___Enhanced fine/ gross motor coordination & visuospatial skills
10. ___Behavior regulation/ self-control/ autonomy
11. ___Coping skills/ self-soothing techniques
12. ___Improved social skills/ interpersonal skills
13. ___On-task behavioral skills/ concentration/ focus
14. ___Decision-making skills
15. ___Communication skills
16. ___ Other: _____

Complete each sentence.

1. I find outdoor, natural areas like _____ very relaxing.

2. Being in the wilderness is _____.

3. One of my memories being outdoors alone is _____.

4. When I see landscape paintings in a museum or as a home decor, I think

_____.

5. Outdoors, people collect things such as _____ to

_____.

6. People who paint outdoors are probably _____.

7. Using nature as an art material is _____.

8. In my home, I have _____ from nature.

What art materials would you/the client enjoy using? Place an x beside the most appealing. Circle favored examples within each category.

1.___Nature-based materials like dried flowers, gnarled wood, leaves, shells, or insect specimens
2.___Traditional art materials like acrylic paint, clay, or pastels
3.___Scholastic instruments like watercolor paint, graphite pencil, or rulers
4.___Modern technology like movie-making software, cameras, video-game creation websites
5.___Everyday found objects like magazine cut outs, broken bits of watches, or old toys
6.___Artisan tools like palms for weaving, body casting plaster, scraps for book-making
7.___Home-life oriented resources like scrapbooks, embroidery, quilts, or bread sculpture
8.___Textiles like crocheting, knitting, and sewing with yarns
9.___Other (please explain):_____

What would you describe as your/ the therapy recipient's strengths?

_____

_____

_____

_____

_____

Index